A WALK WITH YOUR SHEPHERD

A WALK WITH YOUR SHEPHERD

DR. WILLIAM GAULTIERE

MOODY PRESS
CHICAGO

ISBN 0-8024-9480-3

1 3 5 7 9 10 8 6 4 2

Printed in the United States of America

To the shepherds who have shown me the way,
the sheep who have gone with me,
and, most of all,
the Good Shepherd
who is the way, the truth, and the life

Contents

The Twelve Step Journey
of Psalm 23

1. Humbly admit you need God to be the Shepherd of your life.

2. Rest in God's care for you in the green pastures of the home ranch.

3. Drink in the still waters of God's love to see yourself as He does.

4. Confess that you've fallen down and sinned so that God can restore your soul.

5. Choose to walk the difficult narrow path rather than the broad path.

6. Persevere in the valley of the shadow of death and trust that God will work out for your good all the difficulties you will encounter.

7. Yield to the rod of discipline and protection.

8. Pass under the staff of accountability.

9. Forgive the enemies who surround you on Table Mountain.

10. Allow the oil that comforts your wounds to anoint you for ministry to others. Learn to give out of an overflowing cup rather than out of an empty cup or out of obligation.

11. Listen responsibly to your new heart so that goodness follows you as you retrace your steps back down the mountain.

12. Have the faith to be at home with the Lord wherever you may be on your life's journey.

The Twelve Principles
of Recovery

1. Humility
2. Trust
3. Accurate Perceptions of God and Self
4. Confession of Sin
5. Delayed Gratification
6. Perseverance
7. Boundaries
8. Accountability
9. Forgiveness
10. Giving to Others
11. Responsible Adulthood
12. Faith

The Twelve Steps
of Alcoholics Anonymous

1. We admitted we were powerless over alcohol—that our lives had become unmanageable.

2. Came to believe that a Power greater than ourselves could restore us to sanity.

3. Made a decision to turn our will and our lives over to the care of God *as we understood Him.*

4. Made a searching and fearless moral inventory of ourselves.

5. Admitted to God, to ourselves, and to another human being the exact nature of our wrongs.

6. Were entirely ready to have God remove all these defects of character.

7. Humbly asked Him to remove our shortcomings.

8. Made a list of all persons we had harmed, and became willing to make amends to them all.

9. Made direct amends to such people wherever possible, except when to do so would injure them or others.

10. Continued to take personal inventory and when we were wrong promptly admitted it.

11. Sought through prayer and meditation to improve our conscious contact with God *as we understood Him,* praying only for knowledge of His will for us and the power to carry that out.

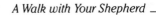

12. Having had a spiritual awakening as the result of these steps, we tried to carry this message to alcoholics, and to practice these principles in all our affairs.

Acknowledgments

I want to offer special thanks to those who helped make this project a reality.

To David, the shepherd boy turned king, who penned the psalm that I have recited to myself literally thousands of times.

To Phillip Keller, another shepherd, whose writing on Psalm 23 opened my eyes to the ways that I am like a sheep. His book *A Shepherd Looks at the Good Shepherd and His Sheep* remains a classic.

To Dave Stoop, once my supervisor, now my colleague, and always a mentor in shepherding, writing, and graciousness. Thanks for including me as a contributing editor in the *Life Recovery Bible*. Through working on that project with you I realized the Psalm 23 journey was one of recovery.

To Duncan Jaenicke, Jim Bell, and Jim Vincent at Moody Press. Thanks for shaping my thoughts, editing them when they weren't clear, and helping in their publication.

To Wayne Schroeder, whose personal caring has shepherded me in my own journey of recovery and whose mentoring has encouraged me in my shepherding of others.

To my colleagues and friends at the Minirth-Meier Clinic West in Orange, California, each of whom guides sheep in a special way: Linda, Katharine, Jim, Gerry, Ted, John, Karen, David, Joan, and Beckie.

To my sheep, the many men and women of great faith who have honored me by asking me to be their shepherd and taught me so much by sharing their struggles and triumphs with me. I hope you have seen the Good Shepherd in me.

To David, my little precious sheep. Someday you'll understand my sheep stories.

To Kristi, my wife and colleague. Thanks for always believing in me. Thanks for challenging me to grow by being you. Thanks for the extra time you put into our family, our home, and our lives so that I could put extra time into writing.

Introduction

For many years when I've needed help I've walked into the scenic drama and spiritual balm of Psalm 23 to meet my Shepherd. Maybe you too have found solace in this famous passage of the Bible. Whatever I need, my Shepherd seems able to provide. He gives rest to my anxious heart, He fills my empty soul, He heals my hurts, He forgives my sins, He guides me to the right path. He also encourages me to become all that I can be.

I have written *A Walk with Your Shepherd* so that you too can be led by your Shepherd on a journey of recovery. Perhaps you're seeking to be freed from compulsions like perfectionism, workaholism, sexual indiscretions, drug abuse, codependency, or overeating. You may need emotional healing from the effects of growing up in a dysfunctional family in which you were emotionally neglected, given conditional love, or abused verbally, physically, or sexually. Maybe you desire to be more helpful to a loved one who is addicted or hurting. Or maybe you've been feeling bored spiritually and you're looking for inspiration and challenge. If you're in one of these places of need then I believe this devotional on Psalm 23 and recovery will be helpful to you.

David wrote Psalm 23 about three thousand years ago. At the time he was just a shepherd boy who, while sitting in the grass and watching his sheep graze, liked to strum his harp and then take out his stylus and write down his feelings and insights. Of all the poems, songs, and meditations he wrote, none is more inspiring and well-known than Psalm 23. Over the centuries millions of people have found comfort and healing by entering into the setting and drama of this psalm, which describes a shepherd leading his sheep on a year-long journey. It's no wonder, because the Psalm 23 journey has an amazing parallel to the Twelve Step program of recovery from addictive behaviors and emotional traumas.

Today approximately 15 million people are actively involved in recovery groups. These include such groups as Alcoholics Anonymous, Overeaters Anonymous, Co-dependents Anonymous, Incest Survivors Anonymous, Adult Children of Alcoholics, Workaholics Anonymous, Sexaholics Anonymous, and Emotions Anonymous. Alcoholics Anonymous, the first Twelve Step program, was born in the mid-1930s. The recovering alcoholics in this group developed their program as an adaption of a Christian revival organization referred to as the Oxford Group. More recently, Overcomer's Outreach and other Christian recovery groups have recognized and expanded upon the biblical foundation of the Twelve Steps and applied them to Christians in recovery.

In my own journey of recovery and in my work as a psychologist with others who are in recovery the Bible has been an integral tool to the process of change and healing. In the pages of Scripture I find truths that provide inspiration, guidance, and comfort. The Bible speaks of the recovery process, and it introduces us to the God of recovery—the Shepherd of our souls. I hope that you also will find the Bible to aid in your recovery. Throughout this devotional I will refer to various stories, truths, and principles from the Bible. And at the end of each chapter I have footnoted the biblical references so that you can read them in your own Bible.

In *A Walk with Your Shepherd* you will start your own recovery as you join a flock of sheep on their one-year journey with Good Shepherd. This fun and instructive journey will begin in the winter at the home ranch, where we humbly admit our powerlessness over our dependencies and our need for a shepherd to guide us to sanity. In this allegorical story we, like the other sheep, learn to yield our wills and lives to His care by resting with Him in the green pastures. Soon you'll be drinking in His love for you at the still waters. And like all the other sheep, there will be times on your journey when you fall down and can't get back up unless you take a moral inventory and call out for your Shepherd to restore your soul.

This year-long Psalm 23 journey can be your year for recovery. That's because you will be following twelve biblical steps to recovery one month at a time. Each month's recovery step will be introduced by an allegorical sheep story that illustrates one aspect of the Psalm 23 journey. You'll find yourself caught up in the drama of the lives of sheep like wandering Wanda, wobbling Wobble, and timid Timi. With them and other sheep, you'll go on adventures in which you receive the Shepherd's blessings, learn from your mistakes, encounter various difficulties, and progress in your recovery and your spiritual growth.

This book is a devotional, written in a weekly format and containing fifty-two meditations. Thus busy people won't feel pressured to hurry the slow process of recovery. Recovery can be hard, painful, and long, so it's important to be patient with the process. You may not want to follow the weekly format exactly; but you'll find that once you meet your Shepherd at the still waters, you will want to take as much time as you need to work through your issues. This way you'll learn best what He is teaching you.

Each week's recovery meditation will expand upon the significance of the allegorical sheep story from the Psalm 23 journey. The meditations will help you look in depth at aspects of the recovery process; they combine biblical insights with recovery testimonials.

Following each meditation a series of personal reflection questions will invite you to probe into your own life to work through personal issues pertinent to recovery. Many of these questions are best answered in a personal journal or by sharing with a friend. Others will invite you to meditate on a passage from the Bible.

Along the way in this journey to recovery, you'll be reminded of the wisdom of Good Shepherd for our lives. When spring blossoms forth it will be time to follow your Shepherd and start on a new and right path in which He will help you begin the long and painful process of taking steps to remove your shortcomings and your defects of character. With His rod He will discipline you to help you grow and He'll protect you from bears, cougars, and other dangers. And with His staff He'll guide You and keep you accountable to doing what is right and good.

As the heat of summer approaches, you, the other sheep, and your Shepherd will all climb up the ridgeline path to the cool mountain plateau. There your Shepherd will have prepared a lush table of grass for you to graze on. On the tableland your Shepherd will help you to make peace with your enemies by seeking forgiveness for your sins, making amends to those you've wronged, and offering forgiveness to those who have sinned against you. He'll apply His oil to protect you and to soothe your wounds. This same oil will anoint you for ministry in which you share your message of recovery with others.

It's my prayer that you will join with other people who are in recovery and meet your Shepherd in a dynamic way. If you'd like to contact me, you may write to: Dr. William Gaultiere, Minirith-Meier Clinic West, 1028 Town & Country Rd., Orange, CA 92668.

As you learn the meaning of "The Lord is my Shepherd, I shall not be in want," you will open your heart to God's healing love and careful guidance. Join me as we begin that journey to wholeness.

"We admitted we were powerless over our dependencies—that our lives had become unmanageable. Came to believe that a Power greater than ourselves could restore us to sanity."

STEPS 1 and 2 adapted,
Alcoholics Anonymous' Twelve Steps

"The Lord is my shepherd, I shall not be in want."

Psalm 23:1

STEP 1

Humility

There was a sheep named Wanda. She was named after her tendency to wander from the flock. She was looking for something—she wasn't sure what—but she was certain that she must be missing something.

On the outside Wanda looked beautiful. She had the whitest coat of wool and cute little ears. And she almost always smiled. Her eyes, though, seemed to reflect some inner emptiness. They flitted about from here to there, hither and yon, looking for a greener pasture somewhere—anywhere.

One day Wanda was feeling hot and bored, so she meandered from the pasture where the others were grazing. Her curiosity led her back around some brush and into a shallow ravine, looking to see what was there. The ravine got deeper and deeper and narrower and narrower until it turned into a canyon. At the base of the canyon wall large rocks jutted out to form a cave. In front of the cave Wanda spotted water in a little gully. Wanda lapped up some of the water, not even noticing that it was dirty.

The temperature was very warm this winter afternoon, and the sun beat upon her back. Underneath her wool coat she was sweating. The cave's shade looked inviting, so Wanda stepped in. She walked way into the back where it felt very cool and sighed. "Ahhhh—now that feels nice. This is what I was looking for."

Wanda sat down on the ground. In only a few minutes, though, her pleasure was interrupted by a sick feeling in her stomach. She thought back on the dirty water she had foolishly drunk.

Late afternoon soon turned to evening, and the sun gradually dropped behind the other side of the canyon until it cast a dark shadow at the cave's opening. The shadow scared Wanda. She frantically jumped to her feet and looked for the sunlit path she had followed into the cave, but she couldn't find it. Trying to find her way out of the dark cave she kept bumping into the walls. A breeze started to swirl at the mouth of the cave and created a sudden rustling of a leaf, which sent her into a startled panic, causing her to hit her head on one of the rock walls. Her head throbbed in pain and her little heart began racing in fear. The breeze made the cave's dampness all the colder and sent chills down Wanda's back.

What am I going to do? she worried. *I'm trapped in this cave. I'll never find my way back to the sheepfold.* Standing there in the dark, chilled, confused, scared, and unable to help herself, Wanda cried out for help, "Ba-aa-aa-ah! Ba-aa-aa-ah!"

Wanda's shepherd hadn't forgotten about her. He knew about her tendency to wander. Even though he had been tending the needs of a little lamb, he had kept one eye and one ear in Wanda's direction. He saw her walk away and now he heard her cries for help. She hadn't drifted beyond his care.

Walking toward the rocky canyon the shepherd sang out his familiar sheep call, "Yee-dee-ohh-dee-dee-ollie!" "Yee-dee-ohh-dee-dee-ollie!"

As he approached the canyon wall he squinted to see through the shadows and noted the caves imbedded in the rock wall. Picking up a handful of stones, he threw them one by one in front of each cave. After throwing the third stone he heard a rustling in that cave. Smiling, he cheerfully sang out, "Yee-dee-ohh-dee-dee-ollie! Waaan-da! My precious lost ewe, I am here to find you!"

Wanda was still huddled in the corner of the dark cave. She had heard her shepherd's call even before he threw the stone. But the thoughts swirled around her head like a swarm of annoying gnats. _Is it him? It must be—It is! It's Good Shepherd! He's looking for me—Oh, but he'll be mad at me. I blew it. I wandered away again—What if he doesn't find me? It's so dark in here—Ohhhh! Ouch! I bumped my head again. What was that startling sound?_

Wanda felt overwhelmed. Then she heard the sound again. _Oh, it's him—I hear him coming closer. His call sounds happy. He's calling my name!_

Good Shepherd reached his strong hands into the cave and gently pulled Wanda out. Smiling from ear to ear, he looked into her eyes, pulled her up to his bearded face, and kissed her. He looked her over closely. Gently he rubbed his healing oil on the bruise on her head. Briskly but gracefully he swiped the dirt off her wool.

Then he picked up Wanda and put her atop his shoulders. Holding her forelegs in his right hand and her hind legs in his left, he carried her back up the canyon, through the short stretch of barren desert and back towards the green pasture, happily singing and whistling the whole way.

Wanda was bumbling around in the dark, bumping into the cave walls, until she accepted the fact that she was stuck in the cave. She couldn't get out. She was lost in the dark. She was helpless to do anything but stand there and cry for help. From the midst of her lost and powerless condition Wanda didn't lie down and give up nor did she endlessly grope around, striking the walls. Instead she acknowledged her feelings of embarrassment and took the humble initiative to cry out for help. It was only at this point that Good Shepherd went to help her. He didn't rescue her before she had learned from her mistake.

Recovery begins here. You won't begin the process of finding healing for your hurts nor will you start making movement toward positive change in your life until you take this first step of humility. It's most humbling to admit your powerlessness over your dependencies; to say to yourself, to another, to God, "I have made some mistakes. My attempts to cope by avoiding my pain aren't working. My life is unmanageable. I can't get out of this rut and move forward on my own. I need help. I need a shepherd."

However, that is what we must do. For instance, the alcoholic never sobers up until he gets out of denial and humbly admits that he is powerless over his dependency and he can't handle his struggles without using alcohol to cope. Many alcoholics never reach this point. Instead they keep minimizing their problem. They may deceive themselves into thinking that they have control over their drinking because they are able to stop or to cut back on their drinking for brief periods of time. Yet they deny the simple fact that they need to use drinking to deal with their depression, feelings of inadequacy, or life stress. And that makes alcohol a major focus in their lives.

Some people think an addict is someone who is lying in a gutter on skid row. Nothing could be farther from the truth. Your problem may not be abusing alcohol or drugs to cope with emotional pain. You may have other compulsive tendencies or emotional struggles. If so, you need to enter into a recovery process of your own.

Ask yourself if you struggle with any of the following compulsive tendencies: overeating, overworking, constant busyness, losing control of your temper, compulsive sex, thrill-seeking, or codependent tendencies to lose yourself in helping others. These kinds of behaviors—in fact, most any behavior taken to excess—become destructive when they begin to be ways of avoiding the need to express your feelings, to understand your issues and struggles, to accept your internal world as a part of the reality of your daily living. Even such behaviors as becoming lost in the "boob tube" or trying to become the perfect Christian can be destructive ways of handling personal struggles

True sobriety from any excessive or compulsive behavior includes not only abstinence (no longer using the substance or activity to cope with your problems) but also the developing of new coping mechanisms. You must replace the destructive coping mechanism with a healthy one. The apostle Paul said it this way: "Overcome evil with good."[1]

As long as you're focused on an unhealthy behavior it has power over you. Obsessions tend to generate compulsions. The more you think about not doing something the more likely you are to do it. So instead of determining to not do something bad it is better to determine to do something good.

The "something good" starts with humbly asking somebody for help. This might mean making a commitment to call a friend whenever you're tempted to engage in the destructive behavior. Or it might mean joining a twelve step support group or seeking the help of a counselor. This first step is actually one of personal responsibility. It's up to you to tell somebody of your struggle and to ask for help. Again and again Jesus told His followers to take responsibility for themselves and to ask and keep asking for what they needed; only then would they receive and find full joy.[2]

Many people entering recovery confuse this step of humbly asking for help with being ashamed. For instance, Joan, an overeater, uses food to numb her loneliness and depression. She doesn't want to admit that she's powerless to stop her pattern of using food to numb pain because "who wants to say she's a bad, awful, and hopelessly unsaveable person?" That kind of self-dislike and hopelessness actually inhibits recovery. It's part of what keeps Joan stuck in a vicious cycle: feeling so bad about herself, Joan believes she's incapable of taking the responsibility to make a change for herself.

People in recovery also sometimes conclude that asking for help means they are helpless, unable to be responsible for their needs and their lostness. Thus they seek to be magically rescued by someone else. *If someone gives me the "right" advice, that will fix the mess I'm in,* they reason. In other cases they're able to evoke pity from people and get from them all kinds of special favors, loans, second and third chances, and countless other things, as others take responsibility for their problems.

When it comes to getting started in our recovery some of us are like the invalid seeking a healing at a Jerusalem pool. Two thousand years ago he and many other disabled people sat at the edge of the pool of water waiting for the periodic stirring of the waters from the underground spring. The belief in those days was that an angel of the Lord stirred the waters and that the first one in the water would be healed.[3] This poor invalid had sat there for thirty-eight years trying to get into the waters first, but somebody else always beat him. He felt ashamed and saw himself as helpless.

Jesus knew this man's story because He'd walked past him many times. One day Jesus said to him, "Do you want to get well?"

"Well of course I do, but I—I can't. No one helps me into the water when it stirs."

According to the apostle John, Jesus replied, "Get up! Pick up your mat and walk"—which we might translate as, "You don't need to feel ashamed anymore. You're not helpless. You don't need to make excuses and wait for someone to rescue you. You have legs and feet that can strengthen with My help."

The man had faith that with God's help, he could walk. He stood up and began taking short steps. It takes "guts" to look in the mirror at yourself—your issues and your struggles —and look straight on and say, "My life is out of control. It isn't working and it won't work until I take responsibility to get help and to start in a new direction."

Personal Reflections

1. This week consider the concept that a behavior becomes addictive or compulsive when it is something that you "need" to do in order to deal with uncomfortable feelings whenever they come up. What do you think?

2. Wanda was named for her compulsive desire to wander. This week identify the name of your problem. Check off any of the following compulsive or destructive behaviors that

you struggle with or are tempted by. (You may find yourself trying to minimize your compulsive tendencies, but go ahead and be honest. This is your first step in the recovery process.)

☐ Alcohol or drug abuse
☐ Compulsive sex
☐ Perfectionism

☐ Overworking
☐ Getting too busy
☐ Losing yourself in the TV

☐ Religious perfectionism
☐ Shopping and shopping
☐ Losing control of your temper

☐ Repeated thrill-seeking
☐ Using a hobby to escape
☐ Overeating or other food compulsions

☐ Codependent needs to help others who are struggling

3. Can you see how you might use these behaviors as a shaded cave to hide out from the heat of uncomfortable feelings? The way to be "found" is to identify your feelings. Check off any of the following feelings or struggles that you might be hiding underneath compulsive behavior.

☐ Insecurity   ☐ Depression   ☐ Self-dislike
☐ Loneliness   ☐ Inadequacy   ☐ Confusion
☐ Anger   ☐ Lostness   ☐ Conflict
☐ Being out of control   ☐ Disorganization
☐ Performance anxiety   ☐ Fear of abandonment
☐ Fear of failure   ☐ Fear of rejection
☐ Another feeling: _____

4. Set aside some quiet, uninterrupted time today or another day this week to get in touch with your feelings. With pen and paper write out how you're feeling. Write whatever feelings or experiences come to your mind and try to describe what it is like to be you at this point in time.

5. Find a friend you are comfortable with and tell him or her some of the discoveries you made this week. Maybe this friend can be like a shepherd who helps you out of the dark cave you've been lost in. If so, he/she will rejoice with you as you begin your recovery.

My Needs and Wants

"The Lord is my shepherd,
I shall not be in want."
Psalm 23:1

Wanda was a typical sheep, for sheep without a shepherd will wander aimlessly. If they're not given direction sheep will drift from one field to another, searching for a tuft of grass here or there. They need a shepherd to guide them to food and water and safe shelter.

Wanda hadn't learned to depend upon her shepherd for her needs. She was prone to stray and get lost. She didn't know what she needed, but knew something was missing in her life. Even when she was in the sheepfold she felt lost. She didn't feel a part of the group. Oh, she mingled and said "Bahh-ahh-ahh" with the other sheep, but rarely did she rub up against others while eating or sit close with anyone else and share her heart. She acted happy and sociable on the outside, but inside she was empty and lonely, longing for something more in life. It wasn't until Good Shepherd found Wanda in the cave and carried her close to his heart that she realized what she really wanted was to be at the center of the sheepfold, right beside her shepherd.

Most of the people who seek my help as a psychologist are like Wanda. They are lost. Something is missing in their lives. They're stuck in a destructive pattern. They want direction. They need to be found.

A flight attendant named Cindi was feeling tired and run down. (In this and all other case examples real names and identifying information have been changed in order to keep confidentiality.) I asked her, "What do you want?" With a bewildered look she sighed. "I don't know—I guess I just want people to like me. I try so hard to please everyone—my husband and my daughter, the people on the airplane, my friends, my mother, the church, God. The list goes on and on."

Like many people I know Cindi did not know how to really answer the question of "What do you want?" She wasn't in touch with her inner needs. Instead she was preoccupied with pleasing other people, helping them feel better, doing what they wanted her to do and being who they wanted her to be. She was literally "waiting on" everyone in her life to be at their service. At most any given time she was more aware of what her husband, her mother, or someone else needed from her than she was aware of her own needs. Usually, the only feelings of her own that she was aware of were those that were in response to other people's feelings.

If she didn't please others she felt anxious and insecure, fearing they would be disappointed in her.

Cindi's pattern of needing to please and appease others in order to feel good about herself kept her distant from her own needs. Her life had become unmanageable and she was powerless over her dependency upon pleasing other people. As a result she was like a wandering and lost sheep without a shepherd. She had no sense of direction and was unable to recognize what was good and right to her. She didn't know what she wanted.

In time I became like a shepherd to Cindi because I knew she was lost, and I looked for her. Again and again I would look into her eyes and ask, "How do you feel? What do you want? What do you need?" Slowly, after being listened to and heard, over time she began to find her "self." She began to be more consistently in touch with and aware of her own inner feelings, needs, and values.

We discovered that she was very sad and lonely inside. Cindi longed to be understood and known. She realized that she hadn't been living consistent with her values and wanted to put more priority on relationships and enjoyment and less priority on work and accomplishing things.

Everybody who begins the recovery process—whatever pain or struggle he is recovering from—does so from a "lost" place. Because of this the first question I ask all my clients is, "What do you need?" And I ask it often and in many different ways. I find that most people have difficulty really answering that question from their hearts.

It may sound "selfish" to you to think about your own needs and wants. It is, but it's selfish in a healthy sense. When you know what you need you can ask for it instead of pretending you don't need anything or expecting other people to somehow know what you need. We all have basic needs for things like affirmation, caring, and respect. When we take responsibility for ourselves by asking for what we need, we give others a chance to show us their love. And the more our needs are being met the better we can care for others. When we do think of our "selves" this way, we will tend to love others as we love ourselves. Jesus stated this principle when He said, "Love your neighbor as yourself."[4]

A word of caution, however, when it comes to loving yourself. The way to love yourself is not to retreat to some remote island where each day you give yourself a hug and look in a mirror and say, "I love you!" Instead, it's a matter of becoming aware of your needs and humbly bringing them into relationship with caring people who provide you a sense of safety. Thus, healthy self-love is really better understood as self-loveableness, believing that you are valued and worthwhile to someone you respect.

Personal Reflections

1. What do you think? Is it inappropriate to think of your own needs? Why or why not? Ask a friend and see what he or she thinks.

2. Some time this week make a list of what you value most. What is most important to you? Don't list what "should" be most important to you. Instead, think in terms of what you find most fulfilling and enjoyable in your life.

  1. _____
  2. _____
  3. _____
  4. _____

3. Review the above list of values. Think back over the last month of your life. Based on your allotment of time and energy in recent weeks, how have you actually been prioritizing your values? Seeing the discrepancies between the most fulfilling/enjoyable values and where you actually are devoting your time will help you see the changes you need to start making this week in order to be more fulfilled.

4. Perhaps in some ways you're like a lost sheep. Over the next seven days try to check and recheck in with yourself each day by frequently pausing to ask yourself, "What do I need?" You might try asking yourself this in the context of a decision you're facing or some issue you're struggling with.

5. Create time in your schedule this week for your most enjoyable value.

What Do I Really Want?

"The Lord is my shepherd,
I shall not be in want."
Psalm 23:1

Wanda wandered from thing to thing. She believed the old saying "The grass is greener on the other side of the fence." So even when she was with other sheep in the fold she was looking for something else, something other than what she had access to. She was looking in the wrong place. She thought she would be happier if she found a better pasture or a different sheepfold. She was always looking for something new and different, which is how she got lost.

When Good Shepherd found her in the cave and carried her on his shoulders back to the home ranch she finally realized what she really wanted—to be loved and accepted by her shepherd and the rest of the fold. Until she was found and welcomed into the fold Wanda didn't know why she was so empty inside. She had been so busy following her momentary impulses and whims that she hadn't taken the time to get to know deep inside her heart what she really wanted and needed.

Some people don't have any trouble asking themselves, "What do I want?" Their problem is that they answer the question superficially and impulsively. They know that something is missing, and they want to fill that inner void right now with anything that seems to fit. They long for a greener pasture and are quick to hop fences in hopes of finding what they want. Yet once the newness of the other pasture wears off they realize that they are still empty inside.

Most people with compulsive behavior patterns want to feel good fast. They feel depressed or anxious and react impulsively out of this feeling to engage in the destructive behavior.

A young woman named Tammy told me that she had been molested twice by an older neighbor boy who babysat her and her younger sister when she was nine years old. Her adolescent and young adulthood years were dotted with sexual relationships in which she gave her body to men in order to feel wanted by them. As she recounted her story to me she said, "I hate myself for doing this! Why do I keep letting men use me and discard me?"

Like many other victims of abuse—whether sexual, physical, or emotional—Tammy was particularly vulnerable to being abused because she didn't feel loved and valued in her childhood home. She grew up in a single-parent home with a mother who provided well and "tried her best" but was for the most part too busy to give her the personal, caring attention she needed. Tammy felt desirable when she was in a sexual relationship, though. Even if the relationship was abusive, at least she was being noticed and was getting attention.

Tammy didn't like what her neighbor did to her, especially at first. It was painful, shameful, confusing, and disgusting to her. "I didn't want him to touch me, but I couldn't stop him. I was just a little girl. And I thought maybe it was OK. I wasn't sure, but I guess I did trust him; after all, my mother had asked him to babysit." Once she tried to tell her mother about it, feeling uncomfortable. Her mother said she must be exaggerating because her neighbor was "such a nice young man and a Christian, too."

The second time her neighbor touched her Tammy realized that it felt good and she felt important to him. He treated her so special, saying nice things about her and giving her ice cream. Beginning with these childhood experiences and continuing into her early adulthood years, sexual affection and caring had been blurred for this young woman. Tammy felt cared for in a sexual embrace—until the next morning when he was gone or until she was slapped in anger and told to "stop being so emotional." At times she felt guilty for violating her moral standards, but if anything her guilt perpetuated her destructive behavior because it confirmed her feelings that she didn't deserve to be valued anyway. She felt "eligible" to be abused.

What did Tammy really want? She thought she wanted the feeling of being sexually pursued by a man. She discovered that deep inside she wanted to be valued and affirmed for who she was. This was actually a nonsexual need. Only unconditional acceptance—no-strings-attached love—would even begin to fill the hole in her soul. As long as she felt she had to look or act a certain way, give sex, or please a man in order to feel accepted, the caring she received came with conditions, and she didn't feel loved for the person she really was inside.

When ministers and theologians talk about "grace" it is this unconditional acceptance they are referring to. Deep inside we all want and need to experience the grace that sees the real me inside, values me for me, forgives my shortcomings, and encourages me to live out my potential in a way that is genuinely me. God alone loves us with perfect grace. But apart from supernatural experiences, the way we can come to know and experience God's grace is through people who represent and express God's love to us.[5]

Inevitably these human ambassadors love us imperfectly. That's OK, though, as long as we receive a sufficient degree of this caring—enough to feel valued and affirmed as a person. Then we will be encouraged to believe "The Lord is my shepherd, I shall not be in want," and we will look to Him for a perfect love.

Personal Reflections

1. This week consider whether you're like Wanda the wandering sheep. Have you ever caught yourself living by the philosophy that the grass is greener on the other side? Do you emotionally escape from present discomforts or difficulties by hoping, dreaming, or fantasizing about a better and brighter future if only . . ?

2. Take some time this week to ask yourself, "What are the greener pastures on the other side of the fence that I long for?" Do you sometimes say to yourself, "If only I had _____ then I'd be happy"? Check any of the following that you use to fill in the blank:

☐ A new relationship   ☐ A different job
☐ Retirement   ☐ More money
☐ A new car   ☐ Having a family
☐ Finishing a project   ☐ A promotion
☐ An accomplishment   ☐ Getting married
☐ A certain vacation   ☐ Get a spouse or friend
                                to change
☐ Moving to a better home or a different location
☐ Another unfulfilled desire

3. What is the reality of the pasture you're in? What do you like about your current life situation? What don't you like?

_____

_____

4. This week try to graze in the pasture you are in. What can you do to make your pasture better for you? Your pasture may seem to be a barren wasteland that cannot be cultivated. Before you look for a greener pasture, however, see what you can do to learn from and improve your current situation.

5. Humility is not a cousin to humiliation. Humility might be defined as "seeing yourself rightly and accurately." It takes a courageous humility to express what you see in you—your true longings and your frustrations—to someone else. Make it a point to share some of this week's humble reflections with somebody who accepts you without conditions.

WEEK 4

Listening for Your Shepherd's Voice

"The Lord is my shepherd,
I shall not be in want."

Psalm 23:1

On those almost sleepless nights when you count sheep on your bedroom ceiling, they may all look alike. But to the alert shepherd, sheep are not identical. He knows each sheep of his flock by name. Every sheep is distinctive in appearance or personality, and the shepherd recognizes each one. And when he calls their names, the sheep respond.

Not only do they respond to their names, but also to their shepherd's voice. In fact, if two flocks of sheep were scattered and mixed together, the two shepherds could stand on opposite sides of the pasture and call their sheep, and the sheep would quickly recognize their own shepherd's voice. The two flocks would again become distinct. The unique sheep call of each shepherd assures that his sheep will gather to him.

Wanda had feared that her shepherd would be angry with her. After all, she had once again wandered from the flock and now he had to come after her. Contrary to her expectation, however, Good Shepherd was gentle, tender, patient, and merciful. He didn't need to punish her because he knew that she had learned from the consequences of her wandering. She didn't want to get lost in a dark, cold cave again.

Good Shepherd gave Wanda her name, knowing well her wandering character. Therefore he kept his eyes on her regularly. When she strayed he knew that she had strayed and he knew where to look. He called out, "Yee-dee-ohh-dee-dee-ollie!" and called her name, and she knew it was him.

Jesus once described the Good Shepherd as a father who looks for those who wander. When He finds them, He does not reject or even scold. He rejoices. Like the father of the wayward and rebellious prodigal son in Jesus' famous parable, God looks for you and waits for you. When you come home to Him He runs out to you and welcomes you into His family.[6]

As our shepherd, God can watch over us as Good Shepherd watches Wanda and the other sheep. Good Shepherd cares for his sheep twenty-four hours a day, is incredibly powerful and able to protect, save, and care for them, and guides them into the ways that are true and good. He knows all their shortcomings, pains, and susceptibilities as well as their character strengths, joys, and abilities; and he remains loving and gracious towards them.

No wonder David sang in Psalm 23: "The Lord is my Shepherd, I shall not be in want." David knew that we have a God who is always good to us and who seeks to restore our painful and unmanageable lives. Sadly, few of us sheep know His voice and experience Him in this intimate way.

It takes faith to believe in a God like this when we can't see Him with our eyes, touch Him with our hands, or hear Him with our physical ears.

It also takes humility to acknowledge the need for faith in God. Many of us would like to be our own "Higher Power" and live as we please. We would like to manage our own lives without help. However, if we're honest in assessing our lives, our needs, and our struggles, we will see our lostness and our need for a shepherd to guide us.

It is difficult to have humble faith in the Good Shepherd when the human shepherds in our lives have been far from good. If you haven't received a sufficient degree of love and respect from others, especially in your formative childhood years, feeling God's love will be very difficult. That is true until you enter a recovery process where you can experience emotional healing for past hurts and also learn to change your life patterns and develop healthy relationships in which you feel loved.

You need both healing for your past and new relationships for your present and future. If you work only at your healing, then you will be living hopelessly in the past without the love you need today to fill your empty places inside. If you only work at making new relationships, you will be living unrealistically in the future, trying to get other people to make up for your past hurts. You need to _work through your unresolved issues from the past_ in order to keep them from repeating in the present and future. And you need to _work at developing healthy relationships in the present_ and the future in order to fill in the empty places left behind from your past.

Wherever you are in your journey of faith I hope you're comforted by the possibility that there is a Good Shepherd who can restore you. He is looking for you. You don't have to find Him. Nor must you try to measure up to some set of expectations to earn His grace. His love seeks you out.[7] All you need to do is say, "Amen," or, "It is true. I'm lost and hurting. I need help! I need your grace. Save me, Lord."[8]

Personal Reflections

1. This week reflect on your relationship with God. Have you worked at finding God, being "devoted" to Him, or being "more committed"? Some people work too hard at trying to find God and don't know how to let Him find them. This week get in touch with your hunger for God and then ask Him to fill you with His love. For an example of encoun-

tering God read Psalm 63, in which David meets God and is satisfied by His love.

2. Good Shepherd found Wanda in her cave by throwing a stone at the mouth of the cave and listening for her startled shuffle of feet. In what ways has God gotten your attention recently by startling you?

☐ A sudden difficulty   ☐ A surprise blessing
☐ An unexpected mes-   ☐ A new insight
   sage
☐ A friend reaching out   ☐ A powerful
   to you   experience

3. Set aside some time this week to wait on God and let Him find you. See if you can in some way see, hear, touch, taste, or smell His goodness. Then write down what God shows you.

_____

_____

4. Think of the shepherds you have depended on. Which ones strengthened your faith in the Good Shepherd? Which ones hindered your faith and gave you the impression that maybe the Shepherd isn't good?

_____

_____

5. Probably the shepherding you've received is not so clear-cut; in most cases the same shepherds offered you some good things and some bad things. Try to begin the difficult task of differentiating between the good and the not so good that you have received. Make a list of the good and the bad in these people. (If you are early in your recovery process some key shepherds will feel "all bad." If you are idealistic and haven't really seen the need for personal recovery, then key shepherds will seem "all good.")

NOTES

1. Romans 12:21.
2. Matthew 7:7-8; 18:19; John 14:13-14; 16:24.
3. John 5:1-9.
4. Matthew 22:39.
5. 2 Corinthians 5:20.
6. Luke 15:20-24.
7. Romans 5:8.
8. Ephesians 2:8-9.

"Made a decision to turn our will and our lives over to the care of God as we understood Him."

STEP 3, Alcoholics Anonymous' Twelve Steps

"He makes me lie down in green pastures."

Psalm 23:2a

STEP 2

Trust

The next morning Wanda awoke with a smile. She was glad to be back at the home ranch under the care of Good Shepherd. She saw that most of the flock was already awake and grazing. She didn't want to wander around on the outside of the pasture. So she nudged her way through the flock until she found her shepherd standing amid all the sheep. She looked adoringly over at him, and he smiled back.

Wanda turned to an older ewe named Wobble, who was grazing next to her. "I'm so glad Good Shepherd found me in that terrible cave and carried me back home on his shoulders. He really is good to us, isn't he?"

Wobble nodded as she was munching on a mouthful of grass. Wanda herself began to enjoy the lush green grass.

While chewing she noticed for the first time the neighboring pasture.

"Wobble, look at that pasture! It's so pale and dry compared to ours! And it's full of thistles."

"Yeah, we're fortunate that Good Shepherd tends our pasture," Wanda answered. "I remember when he built the home ranch here. He took the dry desert ground and removed the rocks and weeds and he cultivated the soil. Then he made a watering system and planted this grass."

Suddenly, Wanda and Wobble heard Good Shepherd gasp. They turned with a start to see the shepherd's worried look. Following his gaze, they spotted a coyote slyly approaching their friend Lone, a ram who was grazing alone at the edge of the pasture. Wanda became quite scared. Fear gripped her heart. Yesterday, that was her! She had been grazing alone away from the flock.

Wanda noticed a stirring among some timid sheep on the outskirts of the flock, closest to the coyote. They had seen the coyote and in fear were trying to push their way into the flock to get away from the danger. Wanda too started to panic. She was about to bolt when her eyes again caught Good Shepherd. He calmly but swiftly reached into his pocket and pulled out a slingshot and a rock. In a split second he had loaded the rock into the slingshot and fired at the coyote, hitting him on the shoulder and knocking him to the ground. Dazed and stunned, the coyote slowly rose to its feet and whimpered before limping away.

Good Shepherd went to Lone, gathered him in his arms, and carried him back into the fold. The shepherd's alertness had clearly saved Lone's life. He also prevented the whole flock from stampeding in terror. Many sheep would have been injured and others killed in such a stampede.

It had all happened in a few short seconds, but it seemed to Wanda like many minutes before she finally swallowed the lump in her throat and took a breath again. Her little heart, though, was still rapidly thumping against her rib cage. As soon as Good Shepherd returned to the center of the fold Wanda ran up to him and clung to his leg. Good Shepherd stooped down in front of Wanda, looked into her eyes, and reassured her.

"That was scary for you, Wanda, wasn't it? Well, I'm here to protect you, so stay close to me."

Another of the large ewes in the flock named Jelly had been watching Wanda. Secretly she enjoyed seeing Wanda get scared. In fact, Jelly had even hoped that Wanda would scatter, start a stampede, and get hurt or get reprimanded by the shepherd! That's because Jelly had a problem with jealousy. She had been aflame with jealousy the last evening when she saw Wanda returning to the fold atop the shepherd's shoulders. All day she had been snickering at Wanda, wishing that she, in place of Wanda, were grazing at the shepherd's side. Now that Wanda was snuggling with the shepherd she was infuriated!

Jelly strutted toward Wanda with a stiff-legged gait and arched neck. Along the way she was shoving other sheep out of her way. Her glaring eyes turned Wanda's previously abounding joy into a paralyzing fear. Wanda froze as she watched Jelly strut closer, her hooves flicking up dirt with each step.

When she was only a few yards from Wanda, Jelly lowered her head, preparing to ram into Wanda and give her a head butt. Just then Good Shepherd stepped in front of Wanda. Jelly's icy stare ran into Good Shepherd's warm eyes and immediately melted into tears. Jelly dropped her head and slowly turned to walk away in shame. She was in mid-step when Good Shepherd interrupted her retreat with shocking words of compassion. "Jelly, there is room for you at my side also."

Jelly looked over her shoulder at the shepherd. _His eyes seem so tender. His voice sounds so compassionate. Could_ *he really mean it? How could he love me?* Jelly turned back around in disbelief and walked away from the shepherd and the rest of the flock.

Once again Wanda breathed a contented sigh of relief and looked admiringly at her shepherd. She trusted him more than ever. Good Shepherd fed her from the lush green pasture. He protected her from the sly coyote. He stopped Jelly from attacking her. Wanda's hunger was satisfied and her fears were relieved, so she lay down next to her shepherd in the soft green pastures under a cool shade tree. She rested her head in Good Shepherd's lap.

Lone was also lying down in the grass under the tree. There the sheep rested peacefully, trusting in their shepherd. As they sat they chewed their cuds as their food was being digested.

"He makes me lie down
in green pastures."
Psalm 23:2*a*

Like a typical sheep, Wanda didn't know what was good for her. She was dissatisfied and felt bad about herself inside. So she wandered through life looking for goodness "out there," somewhere, anywhere. This got her into trouble. She drank from dirty water and became sick. She ignored her fearful hesitations about wandering so far from the flock and ended up lost in a dark cave.

Wanda stepped out of her cave of fearfulness and lonely isolation when she recognized her shepherd's loving voice and felt his strong yet gentle hands on her side. She learned that there was "no place like home," where the grass was lush and green. She could lay down in the grass at her shepherd's side under the cool shade of a tree. She could trust her shepherd to protect her from coyotes and even head butts! Through her experiences with Good Shepherd Wanda learned to trust him.

People also learn to trust or not to trust through their experiences with others. Trust is an especially difficult step for people in recovery. When you have been wounded, abandoned, neglected, disappointed, or abused by people whom you had once trusted, your basic trust is damaged. As a result, you fear that to trust again means to be hurt again.

Some people override these natural fears. Rather than processing and understanding their fears and being careful, they unrealistically hope that things will turn out OK; yet they don't feel safe.

Wounded people long for someone to care for them. Yet they feel undeserving of the care they need. Thus, they tend to hope against hope that next time will be different and a situation that doesn't feel safe will somehow turn out OK and become safe. They may overlook signals of caution and invest themselves heavily in a relationship in which the other person is taking things lightly. With a naive optimism they may reassure themselves that an untrustworthy person really does have their best interests in mind.

Eventually, when they become disappointed or feel violated, they are not surprised because the role is familiar and they believe they don't deserve better treatment.

If you have trusted someone only to be disappointed, you will be tempted to retreat from others, to put up a wall and protect yourself. This is lonely and depressing, though, and soon your longings for acceptance and caring will motivate you to try again and hope against hope that someone will care for you. Yet until you recover from your negative experiences and regain your sense of trust so that you can better discern people's character, you're likely to be disappointed.

The result: you don't know when it's safe to be vulnerable, and you swing up and down on the teeter-totter of trust. You go from flying high in the air of hoping for intimacy and being too trusting to screeching down and banging on the ground of being overly cautious and withdrawn.

You may become so frightened on this wild teeter-totter ride that you close your eyes and are unaware of what comes your way.

If you're having trouble balancing your teeter-totter, first open your eyes wide. Look at your history of trusting and not trusting. And then in every new relational situation you enter remember that "a righteous man is cautious in friendship."[1] But it's also true that you will need to take risks if you want to find "a friend who sticks closer than a brother."[2]

No one balances needs for caution and risk in friendship perfectly, but the only way to even come close is by trial and error in which you monitor and trust your feelings about people and relationships and seek to learn from your experiences along the way.

Personal Reflections

1. Which end on the teeter-totter of trust do you usually lean toward? Are you more prone to trust too quickly or to isolate from others as protection? Maybe your teeter-totter swings from one extreme to the other. Check any of the following symptoms that apply to you.

Too Trusting	_Isolating_
☐ Get too vulnerable	☐ Stay closed off
☐ Am overly optimistic	☐ Am overly pessimistic
☐ Discount fears of hurt	☐ Live in fear of hurt
☐ Ignore disappoint-ments	☐ Don't recover from hurt
☐ Take blind risks	☐ Overly cautious
☐ Am impulsive	☐ Am compulsive
☐ Feel like a doormat	☐ Think I don't need help

2. Sometime this week think back on some past experiences in which you trusted someone and were hurt. Write these down. How have these experiences affected your ability to turn your will and your life over to the care of God?

3. Isolating from others and detaching from painful feelings are defense mechanisms that you may use to protect yourself from fears of being vulnerable with others. They don't work very well, especially when done unconsciously. What are your fears of trusting?

☐ rejection ☐ abandonment ☐ criticism
☐ abuse ☐ ridicule ☐ being judged
☐ not feeling understood ☐ being pitied
☐ being told that you're too sensitive
☐ having your friend overidentify with you

4. Do you struggle to believe you deserve understanding, caring, and respect? On a scale of 1 to 10, with 10 being the highest, rate the degree to which you feel deserving of loving care and respect.

1   2   3   4   5   6   7   8   9   10

During the week think about your personal patterns of trust or mistrust. If you have a tendency to trust quickly and feel violated, maybe you feel that it's OK for others to mistreat you. If you have a tendency to withdraw from people, maybe you feel as if others really don't care about your feelings.

5. This week find someone you are willing to risk with. At an appropriate time and place share your feelings and insights with this person. (Remember to be cautious.)

WEEK 6

Entering the Sheepfold

"He makes me lie down
in green pastures"
Psalm 23:2*a*

Lone had isolated himself in a world of suspicion and pessimistic mistrust. He withdrew from the rest of the sheep in the sheepfold because he didn't believe that the other sheep wanted him in their group. Besides, he thought he could manage on his own anyway. He was lonely inside, but he kept himself busy grazing and thinking in order to remain detached from his lonely feelings.

Through his coyote scare, Lone learned a dramatic lesson about trust. He was almost eaten alive because he drifted beyond the pasture. He discovered that no sheep is safe as a loner. He really did need other sheep. And he needed the protection of being in the sheepfold with Good Shepherd nearby.

Some people, like those we mentioned last week who felt abandoned, violated, or injured by those they trusted, become like lost sheep that detach from the flock. They try to protect themselves from being hurt again by isolating themselves. They're afraid to take the risk of trusting and being hurt or disappointed, so they hide from others. In the end they hurt themselves by avoiding the care they need. They fail to realize that there are some people who can offer safety and comfort.

They are members of the "Turtle Troop." Like the turtle who fearfully pulls his head under his shell, they hide their inner needs for caring from others under a shell of indifference and self-sufficiency. Secretly they feel lonely, insecure, unworthy, and desperate for love, but they try to hide these feelings even from themselves lest they give in to them and, in reaching for help, get their hand slapped again.

I have found another group of people who isolate in this way. They may not have been acutely or overtly damaged in their childhoods. They may not even be recovering from an addiction. I frequently meet people from this other group in our outpatient hospital program. They sit quietly in the corner during their first few meetings comparing themselves to those who have been molested, beaten, abandoned, or traumatized in some other way. Usually by their second or third day in the program they will speak up and say, "I don't belong here. I don't have any trauma in my background. There's no reason for my pain."

"Maybe you do belong here," I reply. "Even though you don't see acute trauma in your past and even though your pain seems so vague and unfounded, you need recovery too. Oh, you look fine on the outside, but inside you are secretly aching. You feel unnoticed, alone, forgotten in the corner of life. Your pain is tremendous because it's always there; yet you're sure it shouldn't be there."

The "No Trauma Troop" is huge in numbers. I meet these people not just in our hospital programs, but everywhere. They suffer with the silent pain of having received "hidden love" from people important to them. Because they often have been neglected emotionally, they naturally tend to neglect themselves. They're embarrassed because of their needs. They're ashamed of feeling depressed, lonely, or insignificant. Often they hide their struggles behind the facade of an ideal self; they pose as being happy, fulfilled, successful, or intelligent. They tend to live detached from their feelings and needs in a world of thoughts, activities, work, or other people's problems.

Typically in their first counseling session these emotionally detached people will give me a thirty-minute summary of their problem, sometimes even offering explanations for why they think they have this problem, and then they will ask me,

"How can I change this pattern? What can I do to fix this?" They want simple answers to complex problems. I could give them "wise" advice, but it would only perpetuate their real problem of detaching from their feelings and isolating from people. They are impatient with their usually lost and forgotten inner child; they neglect to consider their emotional needs because no one has ever seemed to care about their feelings before.

If you are a member of the No Trauma Troop, building relationships must become a priority. This means making time in your busy schedule for conversations, taking the initiative to pursue and develop friendships, and sharing your feelings and needs with others.

Being vulnerable with others _is_ a risk. You will be disappointed sometimes when you try to develop relationships. At times you may feel rejected or even betrayed. Yet it is only through experiences of trusting—trial and error—that you can learn to discern how safe it is to trust another person, and in what situations and times you feel safety.

Members of the Turtle and No Trauma troops need to work at risking while still acknowledging their fears of being hurt. If in assessing your recent history you see that you've been avoiding relational encounters, you need to admit that you're afraid inside. You're afraid for a reason. You know what it feels like to be in a relational accident, to be stranded at the side of the road of life, or to drive alone down an endless stretch of highway. Acknowledge those fears as a part of your reality, and then begin looking for relational intersections.

But proceed with caution. Approach every intersection as though it had a blinking yellow light and then look both ways; get to know the person and assess how you feel in the situation. "Résumés" and recommendations from others should mean little to you compared with your personal experience of this person. In time you will learn how to discern whether to continue with the relationship.

Personal Reflections

1. Describe a trustworthy friend. What personality characteristics make a person trustworthy? What relationship characteristics are important to you?

_____

_____

2. This week consider if you, like Lone, have strayed outside the sheepfold. We all need the comfort of other sheep who can share in our joys and in our trials. And we need a shepherd to care for us, guide us, and protect us. Ideally, family, church, and support groups are comforting sheepfolds, and parents, ministers, and friends are caring shepherds. What has your experience been?

_____

_____

3. Are you in need of recovery? Maybe you're part of the No Trauma Troop and you compare your struggles or your childhood with others and feel that your pain is "no big deal." Perhaps your issues emerged not out of a background with overt trauma but in one with emotional neglect: warm caring was lacking or was only indirectly expressed. Over the next few days reflect on the sheepfold of your childhood. Write down your insights or share them with a friend.

_____

_____

_____

4. Do you identify with Lone? Check any of the following characteristics that describe your tendencies:

☐ Lonely   ☐ Detached from feelings
☐ Self-sufficient   ☐ Overly analytical
☐ Introverted   ☐ Little time for social life
☐ Work, work, work   ☐ Unmet longings for caring
☐ Self-neglectful   ☐ Isolating as a defense
☐ Untrusting   ☐ Blindly trusting
☐ Indifferent   ☐ Pessimistic
☐ Lost in a crowd   ☐ Lack of affection as child

5. Sometimes the most tangible way to turn your will and your life over to the care of God regarding a specific issue is to trust a friend "as unto God." Do you have a friend whom you trust by sharing your feelings, needs, struggles, and dreams with? Sometime this week take the risk of approaching a friend (or someone you'd like to become a friend) and share some of your insights and feelings about what you've discovered this week.

Learning to Rest

"He makes me lie down
in green pastures."

Psalm 23:2*a*

Rest is very important to sheep. Constant grazing in the hot sun and moving from one pasture to another is tiring. And sheep need to lie down in the shade and chew their cud for their food to digest well. Yet, as much as sheep need rest, they will simply not lie down on their own. They need to be "made" to lie down in the green pastures by their shepherd.

Hungry sheep will wander about endlessly scrounging for a tuft of forage here or there, trying to relieve their gnawing hunger pains. They will literally graze to exhaustion if they are not properly fed. Sheep also must be free from fear of predators, frictions within the flock, and annoying insects if they are to rest. By caring for Wanda in these ways, Good Shepherd inspired Wanda to trust him and to lie down in the green pastures.

Like sheep, people will graze to exhaustion if not made to lie down. Many people fill restless lives with activity and business to occupy their time. The homemaker puts countless hours into cleaning and recleaning her home, the business person puts in long hours working day after day, the worker is obsessed with earning and saving more and more money; even the "couch potato" and the video junkie who lose themselves in the television screen fill their days with never ending activity. The shopper who shops and shops until she drops and the codependent Christian who spends all his time serving in the church and helping out people in need are no different, filling their lives with constant motion.

Recently I asked myself the hard question: "Why do I fill my life with an endless stream of activity?" I had allowed my commitments of work, parenting, marriage, church, and remodeling a new home to overcrowd my life with activities and pressures. Gone was time for me to relax, reflect, and process my feelings. I was out of touch with my feelings and my needs. I had used being busy to help me feel significant, yet inside I felt empty and unfulfilled. I needed to lie down and rest.

When we're busy we're focused on things outside of us, things other than how we feel. Often this busyness becomes a way of distracting ourselves from uncomfortable feelings.

We can't live life without encountering pain, disappointment, anxiety, conflict, and distress. For many of us, though, our families of origin did not provide us with healthy models for expressing and dealing with our feelings. We may have been taught to ignore uncomfortable feelings, punished for crying, judged as weak or silly for feeling, or shown by a parent's behavior that having strong feeling meant being out of control and destructive. If your family was like this and you haven't worked through those issues, then most likely you have trouble staying in touch with your feelings.

Listening to your feelings requires slowing down from activity and resting quietly; it means taking the time to "digest" your feelings by feeling or processing them in order to come to a better understanding of yourself. To stay in touch with how you feel and what you need you must take periodic "Sabbaths." You need time to be quiet and rest in order to hear what's going on inside you and to reflect on how you're living your life. This requires making a conscious decision and disciplining yourself to follow through.

At first it's uncomfortable to slow down. Endless striving and activity not only provide a superficial sense of purpose and direction to your life, but they also give you a physiological adrenaline high that feels good. When you slow down from a hectic pace you will experience an initial loss in meaning and will lack a sense of accomplishment; and physiologically you'll feel the depressing effects of an adrenaline comedown.

Furthermore, once your soul is quieted, the uncomfortable feelings that you've been repressing will begin to emerge into awareness from your unconscious. You won't feel good being reminded of those feelings and then having to risk sharing those same feelings with someone else.

In fact, I tell people in recovery that they will probably feel worse before they feel better. Yet, if they stick with the process of feeling their feelings and sharing them with people they trust, they discover that it feels good to be affirmed. By accepting their feelings, they can stand firmly on the ground of reality. By expressing those feelings to someone who understands and cares, they feel valued and encouraged. They feel freer to put aside the pretenses of their ideal self and genuinely be who they are.

We all long for the freedom to live out from our hearts the message "I am who I am. I am me. My feelings and my needs are important parts of me. I am valuable and likable." God said something like this to Moses when He spoke from the burning bush and said His name was "I AM."[3] God identified Himself as the "to be verb," the ground of existence, the very essence of what it means to be and to live. Everything that is genuine and real and true reflects the Being of God.[4]

We reflect the Being of God and become increasingly genuine when like God we are free to identify ourselves as "I am." This freedom comes when we slow down enough to hear and trust in our hearts God's words to David and to us: "Be still and know that I am God."[5] Augustine echoed this basic need in saying, "Our hearts are restless until they rest in Thee." The only way to rest in this life is to slow down and turn our wills and our lives over to the the care of the God who is "I AM" and who helps us to become "I ams."

Personal Reflections

1. This week consider if you need to be made to lie down under a shade tree in the green pastures. Perhaps you're having trouble turning your will and your life over to God's care because your life is overcrowded with busyness or anxious activity. Check off any of the following symptoms of restlessness that apply to you.

☐ Impatient waiting in lines
☐ Don't take much vacation
☐ Overcrowded schedule
☐ Little time to play
☐ Under time pressure
☐ Always in a hurry
☐ Feel like there isn't enough time in the day
☐ Use the TV or radio for background noise
☐ Try to get by on less than seven hours of sleep per night

2. Think about how your parents taught you to express feelings as a child. Your past experience has affected the way you deal with (or don't deal with) your feelings today. In order to live by the theme of "I am" you need to affirm the reality of your feelings. Put a check by any of the following statements that describe your childhood experience.

☐ Punished for crying
☐ Punished for expressing anger
☐ Ridiculed or teased for showing feelings
☐ Taught to ignore uncomfortable feelings
☐ Shown by a parent's behavior that having strong feelings meant being out of control or destructive
☐ I was rarely asked, "How do you feel?"

☐ My feelings weren't considered as important as others'.
☐ I had to be strong or calm for a needy, inadequate parent.
☐ My parents were responsive to my needs.

3. Have you experienced either the loss of apparent meaning or the adrenaline comedown that results from slowing down from a hectic lifestyle? Describe how that feels.

_____

_____

4. How often do you take Sabbath rests? Take the better part of a day this week as a Sabbath (it doesn't have to be Sunday) in which you don't do any "work." Instead take time for you, just for you. Go to a quiet place alone like a park, a beach, the woods, or your own back yard and try to "be" without "doing." Take a journal and write down what you feel and think.

5. Weekly Sabbath rests are a minimum. We really need more time than that, which is why some people have daily "quiet times." Without getting legalistic, you might try this. Over the next seven days or so set aside ten quiet minutes each day. You might read from the Bible and then apply to yourself what you read and pray about what you learn. Or you might try praying a psalm to God in which you share whatever you're feeling with God; then wait to listen to Him speak to your heart.

WEEK 8

The Secret of Contentment

"He makes me lie down
in green pastures."

Psalm 23:2*a*

To lie down and rest securely sheep need to trust in their shepherd's care for them. They need to be well fed, free from fear of predators, not pestered by insects, and without friction in the flock. In the green pasture Wanda was finding contentment. Her hungers were beginning to be satisfied as she grazed at Good Shepherd's side and took in his loving care.

On the other hand, Jelly was not content to lie down in the green pasture. Inside she felt insecure and ashamed; she didn't like herself. She compared herself to Wanda and others and felt inferior and jealous of what they had. She wasn't comfortable with who she was or with what she had. She lived in the physical presence of Good Shepherd but emotionally she was distant from him, unable to trust him and take his goodness into her hungry soul.

To be content we also need to be comfortable with the persons we are and to feel that our needs are being met. We all need to feel that our inner person is loved and respected by the people who are significant to us. When love and respect are lacking we become discontent and search for ways to feel accepted and valued in the eyes of others. But this puts conditions on our worth—we must do something additional, be someone we're not, or have something special in order to be valued as worthwhile.

Valerie seemed to be a woman with an active, fulfilling life. She entered our clinic dressed and made up like a model, which I later learned was her profession. She had married a wealthy real estate developer and thereby became an instant member in an elite social group. She seemed to get whatever she wanted in life and thought that it should be that way.

Each day Valerie arrived at our group meeting in her new blue convertible Corvette and parked it in the handicapped space closest to the entrance. When her "parking behavior" was brought to her attention, she became very angry that I made it an issue. But this became an inroad to her jealousy problem. She couldn't stand to see her husband talking with another woman. She constantly compared herself with other women and tried to be "better" than they. Even in the clinic Valerie was jealous when she thought that other patients were getting favorable attention.

Valerie discovered that underneath her perfect self-presentation was an insecure little girl, self-conscious and anxious about getting others' approval. She had been trying to achieve contentment in her life by looking good, succeeding, having money and nice things, or getting attention from men. But inside she felt ugly, inadequate, impoverished, and alone. She seemed to get everything she wanted but almost nothing that she really needed. She had very little idea of who her real self was. Out of embarrassment she had hidden this "unacceptable" inner self.

Valerie began to find contentment when she walked through the door of trust. She became increasingly honest with me and other clinic staff and patients about what she really felt inside, underneath her makeup. She began to value her inner self as she discovered that others actually accepted the "un-made-up" parts of her. She finally realized that she really hungered not for the latest fashion but relationships with people who cared for her, the real Valerie.

Taking a close look at your inner self is risky. It's even riskier to trust someone else enough to look with you. Yet you can't really look at yourself unless someone else is already looking, giving needed perspective. It takes tremendous courage to face your fears of being vulnerable and to get to know what's inside you. But it's the only path I know to contentment. You won't feel content and comfortable with who you are until you begin to feel God's faithful and secure love expressed to the real you inside through people you trust.[6] This kind of contentment is an undiscovered secret for most people. That's because contentment is not found in circumstances, money, or any "thing."[7] Even if you had things just the way you wanted them (highly unlikely, of course), you would remain discontent until you developed relationships that have mutual honesty and respect.

Personal Reflections

1. I define contentment as "a feeling of comfort with yourself that emerges in response to expressing the real you and feeling valued." Do you agree with with this definition?

2. During the next week, take some time to think about your own level of contentment. What are some of the dead-end paths you've taken to try and find contentment? Check any that apply.

☐ Being smart or intelli-   ☐ Climbing the job
   gent   ladder
☐ Looking a certain way   ☐ Buying things I want
☐ Going someplace spe-   ☐ Pleasing others and
   cial   God
☐ Giving to others   ☐ Earning money

3. Have you ever wanted to give somebody a "head butt"—to attack in anger—because you were jealous of him? You may have tighter controls on your angry fantasies than

Jelly, but you probably have felt at least a twinge of jealousy from time to time. Take some time this week to reflect on your level of jealousy. What kinds of people bring out jealous feelings in you? What do you find yourself jealously wanting to be, have, or do?

_____

_____

4. After you have identified any areas of jealousy, consider Good Shepherd's response to Jelly: "There is room for you at my side also." This week try to find security and contentment in your Shepherd's love for you by turning your will and your life over to His care. What do you need to turn over to God?

_____

_____

5. To what extent do you feel accepted and valued for the person you are inside? In the past, what have you had to be, do, or have in order to be accepted by those important to you?

WEEK 9

Surrender

"He makes me lie down
in green pastures."
Psalm 23:2*a*

In a way sheep are aimless, dumb, and defenseless creatures. They have such a poor sense of direction that they can't direct their own lives; if left to themselves they will wander about in circles unable even to find their own food and water. And if they don't "feel just right" they'll continue wandering endlessly, not even able to find shelter from the sun or from a storm. Furthermore, their squatty legs slowly move their soft, round bodies, so that sheep are easy prey for wild animals.

Sheep just can't care for themselves. They must depend on the shepherd to provide them with food, water, rest, shelter, protection, and guidance. For the shepherd to fully manage them, however, the sheep must be willing to entrust their lives to his care.

Jelly wasn't ready to take the step of trusting Good Shepherd's love for her. So she declined Good Shepherd's invitation to lie down at his side in the green pastures with Wanda. She turned and walked away, taking her familiar route of believing herself to be unlovable and believing the other sheep to have a better deal than she had. Not only did Jelly feel unworthy inside, but she was stubborn. She wanted to be top sheep. She didn't want anybody but herself to manage her life.

Like sheep, people need help managing their lives but have tremendous difficulty trusting anybody to do it. And "anybody" often includes God. Even Christians who believe God to be loving, faithful, and completely trustworthy sometimes have trouble surrendering their will and their emotions to His care.

Melinda, a mother of four young children, told me that that was the hardest step in her recovery journey. People in her church had no idea that she went to a Twelve Step support group. And she didn't dare tell them because, whenever she shared her struggles as a mother or her temptations to fill her sad, empty places with food, they told her simply to "let go and let God."

Melinda tried surrendering her struggles to God. She did what she was advised and tried going to church, praying more, studying the Bible better—going to church, praying more, studying the Bible better—going to church, praying more, studying the Bible better. And trying harder only got her more of the same—frustration, depression, and unending emptiness inside.

Indeed, Melinda had a trust problem, but it was not as simple as some of her zealous, but ignorant, friends made it sound.[8] She was actually too quick to trust others and often found herself "talking too much." Yet her trust in others was superficial. She shared her struggles while keeping herself distant from her actual feelings. She would not let people know her true fears. Meanwhile, she gladly elicited advice and "how to fix it" responses from other people to give herself simple reassurances that it wasn't as hopeless as it seemed.

Ironically, her path *was* hopeless. That's because the reassurance she kept seeking from others and from God was empty. There were no easy answers. When she became aware of her pattern and started being more honest with what she was feeling in the here and now, she discovered why she trusted superficially and held herself back from others. It was because inside she felt so ashamed and unworthy that she didn't think anyone really wanted to listen to how she felt. She didn't think anyone would be patient enough to stay with her as she worked through her struggles.

Melinda made progress in her recovery when she developed a trusting relationship with a sponsor in Overeaters Anonymous. Her sponsor was a mother and housewife who had worked through the Twelve Steps and had maintained abstinence from eating food to comfort herself and numb emotional pain. Melinda's sponsor was a peer who was farther along in her recovery.

Melinda told her friend about her struggles with food and her feelings of loneliness and shame. In time she learned to feel her feelings and to understand them so that her sharing wasn't just "dumping." She became patient with the slow process of recovery, and she accepted the fact that there were no easy answers.

In the course of her recovery, Melinda's trust in God increased too. "I guess as a Christian I can have struggles," she told me. She now understood that God Himself neither demands perfection nor is emotionally distant. "I know He forgives and has compassion." She saw new meaning to God's sacrifice of Himself in Christ at the cross. In response to that kind of love she felt free to be herself and to surrender her life fully to God.[9] She didn't have to do anything for Him or hide anything from Him.

Personal Reflections

1. David said that the way to enjoy safe pasture is to trust in the Lord.[10] This week consider your own needs to trust God. Meditate on Proverbs 3:5-6: "Trust in the Lord with all your heart and lean not on your own understanding; in all your ways acknowledge him, and he will make your paths straight."

2. Do you ever feel that you keep trying harder to do all that good people "should" do but it doesn't seem to work for you? This week rest from all the things you have been doing to please God. Instead surrender to Him by asking God for what you need from Him and then trusting Him to do that for you. Write down your need as a way of bringing it to the altar.

---

3. This week think about the degree to which you've "turned your will and your life over to the care of God." On a feeling level, how much do you trust God? Do you pray to Him about your personal issues and problems? Do you express your feelings and needs to Him? Are you comfortable confessing your sins to Him? Can you be a "struggling Christian" with Him, or do you feel as if you need to "get your act together" before you go to Him? Rate your degree of emotional trust in God on a scale of 1 to 10, with 10 being complete trust in God for whatever you need.

  1   2   3   4   5   6   7   8   9   10

4. To accurately assess the degree to which you trust God, consider how much you trust your closest friend. After all, your trust in your closest friend whom you can see, touch, and hear probably is deeper on an emotional level than your trust in a God who is physically invisible and inaudible. How much do you trust the person closest to you? What does this person not know about you? What shortcomings do you hide from your friend? What feelings are you hesitant to share with him or her? These questions are hard to answer because things that we hide from others may also be hidden from ourselves! Take some time this week to reflect on this and then write down your discoveries. You might ask

your friends how well they think they know you and how
close they feel to you.

_____

_____

    5. David, the Psalm 23 poet, knew the importance of
learning to trust God by trusting people. He said to God,
"You made me trust in you even at my mother's breast."[11] If
you think that this has been somewhat true for you, what
good things and what bad things did you learn about God
from your experience with your mother? On a feeling level,
how trustworthy was she?

_____

_____

NOTES

1. Proverbs 12:26*a*.
2. Proverbs 18:24*b*.
3. Exodus 3:13-14.
4. Acts 17:28
5. Psalm 46:10.
6. Hebrews 13:5.
7. Philippians 4:11-13, 19.
8. Proverbs 19:2*a*.
9. Romans 5:8; 12:1-2.
10. Psalm 37:3.
11. Psalm 22:9.

"Made a decision to turn our will and our lives over to the care of God as we understood Him."

STEP 3, Alcoholics Anonymous' Twelve Steps

"He leads me beside quiet waters."

Psalm 23:2b

STEP 3

Accurate Perceptions of God and Self

Wanda and Lone were lying under the shade tree in the soft grass during a lazy afternoon. They shared Good Shepherd's lap; each had his head resting on one of his thighs. From their spot they watched Jelly and some others in the flock grazing under the hot sun. Good Shepherd wiped a drop of sweat that was forming on his brow. Even under the shade tree it was hot.

Good Shepherd decided that it was time to find water. So he stood up and made the announcement: "Yee-dee-ohh-dee-dee-ollie! It's time for us to go to the watering hole!"

A wave of excitement rolled across the flock. Wanda and Lone rubbed noses and smiled with glee. Others were wiggling their ears, stretching their legs, bobbing their heads, bouncing up and down, or darting around in little circles. The sheep were familiar with the routine of grazing, resting, and then finding water. The steaming sun had awakened their thirst, and they were ready to go to the watering hole.

On this particular day Good Shepherd had planned a special treat. He would lead them to his favorite stream on the far side of the field at the base of Table Mountain. A familiar backdrop to the home ranch, Table Mountain was the tallest mountain in the range and an awesome sight. In the coming summer Good Shepherd and his sheep would climb to the top of Table Mountain, where a large plateau awaited. There the sheep would graze on a lush green tabletop of grass in cool air. At present the mountain wore its snowy winter mantle. As the snow melted, a cool, inviting stream flowed all the way down the mountain.

The sheep quickly gathered around Good Shepherd and walked toward the stream. As they were walking they approached a ditch that was full of stagnant water. This water was dirty from blowing dust; algae now grew on the sides, and little insects buzzed atop the water. It was probably also polluted with microscopic parasites.

A thirsty ram named Imp had been out in front of the flock, anxiously awaiting the promised watering hole. He was so anxious and so sure that he knew what he was doing that he was even out in front of the shepherd. When Imp saw the water he thought it was the promised watering hole and began sprinting toward it as fast as his legs would take him.

"Stop, Imp! No, don't drink that water!" Good Shepherd yelled out in a stern voice. Imp continued running as if he hadn't even heard. In seconds the excited sheep was gleefully and ignorantly lapping up the contaminated water. This kind of behavior was typical of Imp, who was named after his impulsive tendencies.

When Good Shepherd and the rest of the flock caught up with Imp, Good Shepherd pulled Imp by the ear—yanking his head enough to startle him. He looked into his eyes and with a firm voice said, "No!" This stopped Imp from drinking, but the damage was already done. For the young lambs especially, though, this served as a good learning experience.

During this incident, Wanda had stayed at Good Shepherd's side. She knew about the dirty water in the ditch because it was the same ditch that she got sick from the day she wandered away and got lost in the cave. She felt sad as she watched Imp drop his head and shuffle to the back of the flock.

As the sheep came closer to the base of Table Mountain they heard the rushing, splashing waterfall. The soothing sound signaled that they were close to the stream. Wanda was the first to see the stream. She looked up at Good Shepherd, and he smiled at her and nodded. In no time she was off and running. Naturally, Jelly became jealous. Not wanting to be left out she made it a race and chased after Wanda. The two looked like a comedy team bumping into each other and falling and getting up, as they stumbled and bumbled their way to the stream.

No wonder this was Good Shepherd's favorite spot to drink! The waterfall off to the side resounded, a soothing symphony from a confident orchestra. The water was a ceaseless, happy cascade, tumbling over the side of the cliff, splashing and spraying its mist, which cooled the hot air. Finally the waterfall poured into a wide and slowly moving stream.

Wanda and Jelly arrived at the narrow part of the stream where the waters churned and rushed passed them. They were both afraid and backed away from the dangerous waters. Wanda looked back at Good Shepherd and saw him pointing downstream. "Jelly, look over there! The quiet waters!"

The two sheep dashed downstream along the bank. There they found a section of the stream where a fallen tree had partly dammed the water into a quiet pond. Wanda and Jelly lapped the deliciously cold, pure water. The liquid runoff from the melting snows on the mountain's lower elevation was a true thirst-quencher; the two sheep took their time to enjoy it.

After drinking all she could, Wanda went over to the side where Good Shepherd sat watching on a rock. Wanda leaned against the rock and looked toward the stream. There she saw Imp plopped down flat on his belly at the stream's edge. *Poor Imp,* Wanda thought. *I know how it feels to be so sick that you can't even move. If only he would have waited he could have enjoyed that wonderful water!*

Imp was lying in a groggy lump feeling sorry for himself and blaming the shepherd for his own mistake. As he watched Jelly and Wanda and the other sheep drink he mumbled under his breath, "Why didn't Good Shepherd stop me before I drank the bad water? Why didn't he tell me not to drink it?"

Good Shepherd knew Imp's thoughts. With tenderness he said, "Imp, I did warn you, but you didn't listen. I'm sad for you that you're sick, but I do hope you've learned a lesson."

Jelly had just finished drinking and was standing at the edge of the still waters looking around when her gaze caught sight of her reflection in the water. At first she was startled, but then she looked closely at herself. The closer she looked the more she started to see herself. She became aware of the parts of herself she was ashamed of—her wool coat was dirty and sweaty, her eyes flitted about never satisfied with any one thing, and in her heart was her jealousy of Wanda, her uncontrolled temper, and her insecurities. She did not like what she saw.

She looked over at Good Shepherd. He was watching her and looking right at her with those same eyes of knowledge and compassion that looked into her soul earlier in the day after she had tried to head butt Wanda. Good Shepherd saw the bad in Jelly, and he still loved her.

This time Jelly didn't drop her head in shame. *I want a clean coat!* she thought, and, believing that she was lovable, she jumped into the water. After that initial leap of faith, she splashed freely in the shallow water, frolicking until she felt clean. Then she climbed out and shook herself dry. She looked over to see Good Shepherd smiling at her with pride and approval.

Jelly's gaze returned to the now-still water; all the ripples from her frolicking around had faded into the bank. This time when she looked into the still waters she saw herself through her loving shepherd's eyes. She saw a hurting little sheep who was thirsting for love. She drank some more and then went over to Good Shepherd, climbed up the rock he was sitting on, and nudged her way into his lap.

WEEK 10

Thirsting for the One Necessary Thing

"He leads me beside
quiet waters."

Psalm 23:2b

Hours of grazing in the hot sun and dry desert air leave sheep very thirsty, so thirsty that if left to themselves they could die from dehydration. They may drink from dirty potholes full of old, stagnant water or even from a ditch that has collected water runoff contaminated by sheep urine, feces, and all kinds of parasites. Sheep don't discriminate very well between clean and dirty water. They need a shepherd to find and "lead them beside quiet waters" to drink from. And as Imp learned, they also need a shepherd to help them learn to avoid drinking polluted water.

Imp's impulsiveness got him into trouble. He didn't wait for Good Shepherd to guide him to good water. Instead, he ran ahead of his shepherd and drank from the first water he found, which was contaminated. He impatiently reacted to his thirstiness and satisfied his longings with water that only made him sick. He failed to listen to his shepherd's warning, yet he blamed his shepherd for letting him drink the bad water. Because Imp drank the bad water he ended up nauseated and sluggish as he sat on the edge of a fresh, pure, cold mountain spring. Having tried to satisfy his need with the wrong water, he was now too sick to drink from the very water he thirsted for in the first place.

Imp needed to learn to follow the example of Wanda and Jelly. They were patient. They walked past the polluted water in the ditch, and they avoided the violent waters in the churning section of the stream. They waited for Good Shepherd to guide them to the quiet waters.

Thirsty people can be a lot like sheep. Like Imp we also need to slow our pace and wait to be "led beside quiet waters." Our souls are deathly thirsty for love, yet we tend to rush ourselves; we become so impatient that, if we're not led, we tend to drink impulsively from the first or easiest-to-reach thing that comes along and promises to make us feel good. Yet such things don't quench our soul's thirst. Instead, they make us sick and leave us unsatisfied. Amazingly, we go back for more, because it's easy and we're still thirsty.

Our world offers us many polluted potholes. Temptations to accumulate wealth, have what others have or do what others are doing, impress others, achieve something great, be more beautiful, or have power over others can all be polluted potholes. They are seemingly pleasurable things, yet they don't satisfy our thirst and can become destructive when they occupy our hearts.[1]

Most of us don't plan to drink form dirty, contaminated potholes. Instead, we pursue mirages that look like clean, thirst-quenching streams, and we mock the fools who drink from potholes. Therefore, accumulating wealth for noble reasons like being able to give to others who are in need is attractive, whereas becoming rich and stingy is repulsive. A little extra indulgence at dinner or dessert seems understandable, but we wonder why kids can't "just say no" to drugs. We'll invest all our money, time, and energies in a home for our family and friends to enjoy, but we shake our heads at the rich man who builds a mansion. We'll gossip with the pretense of passing on important information at work, yet we frown on those who purchase the gossipy grocery store tabloids.

These mirages around us entice our thirsty souls to drink, but they don't satisfy. The pleasure is momentary and fleeting; it leaves us going back for more again and again even though it makes us sick. It's hard to avoid indulging in temptations that our culture advertises everywhere around us. How do you not engage in behavior that everyone else seems to be doing anyway? The apostle Paul answers: "Overcome evil with good."[2] We need to understand what "the good" is that our thirsty souls long for and then monitor our pursuits accordingly.

What is it that we thirst for deep inside? The shepherd-poet David certainly knew the longings of a thirsty sheep in the desert when he cried, "O God . . . my soul thirsts for you . . . in a dry and weary land where there is no water."[3] A world without God at the center is like a dry desert that leaves us weary and thirsty.

The Creator made humankind with a God-shaped vacuum that only He can fill. His Spirit pleads, "Come, all you who are thirsty, come to the waters."[4] God offers a different kind of water: a spring of living water that wells up into eternal life. We drink of this water when we receive God's Spirit into our souls. This living water quenches our thirst because it's a spring in our souls that keeps flowing.[5]

But what does it mean to thirst for God? Many people think they are seeking for God, and yet they feel anything but satisfied. They've made a decision to turn their will and their lives over to the care of God as they understand Him, but it hasn't seemed to make a difference. The answer to our question depends upon two things: how you define "thirsting" and how you define or understand "God."

One day Jesus visited the house of two sisters named Mary and Martha. Mary gladly let Him in and invited Him to sit down. Then she sat at Jesus' feet and listened to Him talk. Meanwhile, Martha was working furiously, trying to finish cleaning the house and preparing the afternoon meal. She wanted things to be just right for her special guest. While she was working she became upset at Mary because Mary wasn't helping her. *She's just sitting down on the job,* Martha thought, so she asked Jesus to get Mary moving. Jesus replied, "Martha, Martha, you are worried and upset about many things, but *only one thing is needed.* Mary has chosen what is better, and it will not be taken away from her."[6]

Martha defined thirsting as doing things just right to please God, and she defined God as some distant and impersonal being who is demanding and very difficult to please. Mary defined thirsting as being who she was, a woman who needed to be loved and valued by God, and she defined God as being available, personal, and freely accepting of her.

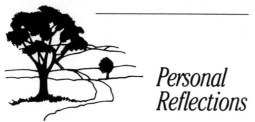

Personal Reflections

1. This week take time to slow down. Walk past the rushing and polluted waters in your life. What is the "one necessary thing" for which you are thirsting in your soul?

_____

_____

2. As you reflect on your soul's thirstings, you may realize that you've been pursuing some mirages. Which of the following mirages tempt you?

☐ More money   ☐ Impress others
☐ Have things that others ☐ Achieve more
   have   success
☐ Be desired by others   ☐ Go someplace special
☐ Indulge with food   ☐ Pleasure-seeking
☐ Have power over others ☐ Be more beautiful
☐ Another mirage _____

3. Do you identify with Imp? What dirty potholes have you impulsively drunk from in the past that made you sick?

What sinful choices have you made that hurt you? Did you blame God for giving you bad water to drink?

_____

_____

    4. Some time this week meditate on the story of Mary and Martha in Luke 10:38-42. Where are you in this story? Would you be like Martha and be so busy serving the Lord that you don't have time to enjoy Him and take His love into your thirsty soul? Maybe you wouldn't have even been home because it would have been so hard to believe that God would really come to visit you personally. Can you picture yourself following Mary's example of sitting at Jesus' feet?

    5. Sometime this week share with a friend what you've learned about yourself.

Seeing Yourself Through Your Shepherd's Eyes

"He leads me beside
quiet waters."

Psalm 23:2*b*

Jelly's jealousy problem was rooted in her low self-esteem. She compared herself unfavorably to Wanda and others. She was angry at all the love Wanda received from Good Shepherd because she didn't feel deserving of that same love. When Good Shepherd offered his forgiveness and compassion to Jelly the first time, she turned and walked sadly away.

Something happened, though, when Jelly walked past the churning, rapid waters down to the still, quiet part of the stream. At the quiet waters she slowed her pace and, for the first time, slowly drank in her shepherd's cool and refreshing love. This enabled her to really look at herself honestly. When she did she saw her sins and shortcomings, but she also saw herself as forgivable and lovable as she began to see herself as Good Shepherd saw her. This faith in his love for her prompted Jelly to jump into the water and have her dirty faults washed away in Good Shepherd's forgiving love. When she came out and looked into the still waters again she saw herself through Good Shepherd's eyes: her faults forgiven and her hurting heart thirsting to be freely loved.

When Jelly took the time to look into the quiet waters she found something very special, something that you and I need lots of: *mirroring.* She found that the still waters reflected an image back to herself. This mirror was no ordinary mirror, though. It reflected back to Jelly what Good Shepherd saw when he looked at her with his all-knowing, all-loving eyes. We also need a shepherd to "lead us beside quiet wa-

85

ters" so that we can see ourselves as God sees us.

Mirroring is one of our earliest developmental needs. When my son David was an infant I played the "mirror game" with him. I would reflect back to him what I heard and saw in him. To some I probably looked silly flapping my hands around, smiling so big, and then sticking out my tongue and babbling things like, "Eel-geek-al-ooh-aya!" But David just loved it! He would play this game with me without tiring for almost thirty minutes. (As an infant there weren't many things that could occupy him for more than ten minutes.)

I was doing more than just imitating my son. I was entering into his world, communicating in his language, being with him on his level and showing him his own emerging self as I saw it. As adults we too need this kind of mirroring. We need people to see us and to know us and then to reflect back to us in a loving way what they see. And it's all the better if they like us and enjoy doing this! I think that's what David enjoyed most—he knew I loved playing with him in that way. He felt affirmed and valued in the process.

Looking in the mirror is something we cannot do effectively by ourselves. We need a shepherd to lead us. If Good Shepherd hadn't been with Jelly then all she would have seen in herself were the bad things that she was embarrassed about. She tended to maximize her weaknesses and minimize her strengths. Good Shepherd reflected to her that she could be forgiven and that she was still lovable and valuable in spite of her shortcomings.

Other people make the opposite mistake of Jelly's; they minimize their weaknesses and maximize their strengths. Like Narcissus, the self-possessed youth of Greek mythology, they are so enamored with the image they see reflected back to them in the still waters that they fall in love with the image and fall into the water and languish, yearning for their ideal self. People who are absorbed with themselves in this way are actually hiding secret insecurities and inadequacies. On the outside they may look bold and proud, but inside they are scared of rejection and failure; they feel embarrassed about who they really are underneath the ideal self they try to project.

Like Jelly and Narcissus, people need a shepherd with whom they can be honest and share their real selves. God's eyes are the only perfect mirror. Yet in this life you will "see but a poor reflection" of His love.[7] You get glimpses into those eyes when you look into the eyes of godly shepherds who know you personally. It's through relationships with personal and loving shepherds that you can develop a balanced and healthy self-perception that sees the good and the not so good in yourself and still feels OK about you. You will feel OK because the good is being valued and the not so good is being forgiven.

Another way in which you can get a glimpse into God's love for you is to look intently into the mirror of the Bible —"the perfect law which gives freedom"—and continue to do this regularly, taking what you read of God's love for you and receiving it into your soul.[8] There you will discover that you are a beloved child of God, even the "apple of His eye"; you are forgiven of your sins if you have trusted His love and forgiveness through Christ.[9] In fact, the apostle John declares, "How great is the love the Father has lavished on us, that we should be called children of God!"[10]

Many people struggle to feel God's love for them in the pages of Scripture. Some open their Bible and instead of seeing God's mercy they see flames of guilt and condemnation burning them for past sins. Other people think the Bible reads like a rule book, telling them all that they should and should not do; they're bound by a yoke of legalism. Still others enjoy the praise and poetry of the Psalms without reading those passages that show that a mature faith is an emotionally honest one. They misuse other portions of Scripture so that their open Bible becomes a lid that pushes down on their unwanted feelings of depression, anger, insecurity, inadequacy, and the like. Then there are those who call the Bible irrelevant to life, perhaps because they're reading from an old and hard-to-understand version or because they don't know where to start reading.

I think of the Bible as God's letters of love to me. In its pages God demonstrates His forgiveness of my past, present, and future sins. I understand God's commandments and instructions to me not as "shoulds" or "should nots" but as they are—God showing me how to live in a way that will be most fulfilling for me. After all, He made me. He knows the kinds of things that will make me happiest and help me to function best.

Read the Bible as a book full of examples, exhortations, and instructions that permit you to feel and to struggle, thus promoting recovery. Seen in this way, the Bible makes a pretty good mirror to reflect back to us how God sees us.

Personal Reflections

1. If you were in Jelly's place and you looked into the still waters at yourself through your own eyes, what would you see? Take some time this week to write down what you think are your strengths and your weaknesses.

_____

_____

2. Later this week ask a friend to make a similar list of your strengths and weaknesses. Note how this added perspective helps to sharpen your insight into yourself.

_____

_____

3. Are you more like Jelly or more like Narcissus? Do you

tend to devalue or overvalue yourself? (On the inside Jelly and Narcissus are a lot alike, but on the outside they are opposite. People who are like Narcissus are actually compensating for the fact that they feel like Jelly on the inside.) Check the traits below that describe you. (You may have some in both columns.)

Jelly	*Narcissus*
☐ Lack confidence	☐ Overconfident
☐ Maximize your weaknesses	☐ Minimize your weaknesses
☐ Minimize your strengths	☐ Maximize your strengths
☐ Self-critical	☐ Self-aggrandizing
☐ Insecure	☐ Self-sufficient
☐ Easily discouraged	☐ Ambitious

4. What do you see when you look at yourself in the quiet waters of God's unconditional love? In your heart how do you suppose God feels about you?

_____

_____

5. What kinds of things do you see when you look into the mirror of Scripture? If you have committed your life to God and trust Scripture, read what the Bible says about your identity in Ephesians 1:1-14. Reflect upon your identity in Christ as:

- A saint
- One who has grace and peace
- Chosen
- Freely given glorious grace
- Forgiven
- Blessed with every spiritual blessing
- Adopted by the Father
- Redeemed from a destructive lifestyle
- Lavishly given wisdom, understanding, and grace
- Given the Holy Spirit as a deposit of your inheritance

Jelly took a leap of faith when she jumped into the quiet waters. At first all she saw reflected to her were the unwanted parts of herself: insecurities, sins, and shortcomings. But then she dared to believe in Good Shepherd's forgiving love for her; she jumped into the water, washed off her dirty coat of wool, and scrubbed away her shame and guilt. She learned to accept the bad in her without shame because she was loved, forgiven, and in the process of being transformed into a beautiful, pure white sheep.

Jelly's leap of faith into the quiet waters of Good Shepherd's love demonstrated her emerging new perception of herself. For the first time she was able to accept the unwanted parts of herself as OK; she didn't have to pretend to be someone she was not. Rather than banishing her bad parts into her unconscious, she was able to accept the fact that they are there and then bathe herself in Good Shepherd's forgiving love. Jumping into the quiet waters also indicated Jelly's emerging new perception of Good Shepherd. Because she believed in his love and forgiveness for her and his valuing of her, her picture and esteem of herself improved. Only by experiencing that kind of gracious and unconditional love from someone whom she respected could Jelly begin to be healed of her guilt and shame.

Guilt and shame are emotions that cripple your self-perception. They follow and amplify each other's effects like lightning and thunder. First comes guilt exposing your actions under bright light and pointing a critical finger at you. Then comes shame thundering down on your sense of self.

Guilt is the feeling of "I've done a bad thing. I shouldn't have done that." Typically guilt arises when you or someone else criticizes and condemns your actions. It's a self-punitive and angry response to having violated a standard or expectation and tends to leave you depressed and discouraged. Guilt accepts no solutions except _penance:_ you must be punished and you must make up for this bad thing you've done. When you then try to "do better next time" you feed into a vicious cycle of trying to measure up, failing, feeling guilty, trying to measure up.

Shame is the feeling of "I'm a bad and unacceptable person. I shouldn't be who I am." It leaves you with your head hung low, feeling embarrassed about who you are. Shame accepts no solutions except _pretense:_ you must become (or at least look like you've become) someone different than you are in order to be accepted. It also generates a vicious cycle. You try to be who you should, people may accept your ideal but false self, you feel praised but empty because people don't really know you and if they did you're afraid they wouldn't value you, so you try to be who you should.

After she tried to butt Wanda, Jelly felt guilty for what she had done in jealousy. She also felt ashamed of herself and so she walked away from Good Shepherd's forgiving acceptance with her head hung low. Her guilt said, "How could you do such a terrible thing? You should know better! You don't deserve to be forgiven. You should have been kind to Wanda." Her shame said, "You're a bad sheep. You don't belong in Good Shepherd's flock. You're not worth being loved."

Fortunately, at the quiet waters Jelly felt something very different. When she looked initially at her reflection in the waters she felt the similar pangs of guilt and shame. Then she looked into Good Shepherd's compassionate eyes; he made her feel lovable in spite of her faults. The Shepherd of the Psalms declares to us as well, "I have loved you with an everlasting love, I have drawn you with loving-kindness"[11]

Once Jelly felt his love, she had hope of change. She didn't feel hopelessly guilty anymore, as if her error could never be erased even if she did do better next time. Nor did she feel like an awful and unlovable sheep. Instead, she was convicted in that she felt sad that she was so insecure and didn't know Good Shepherd's mercy and love. Her sadness came from hurting Wanda. She wanted her insecure places filled with love. She wanted her sins forgiven. She wanted to be different.

This sense of conviction might be called "godly sorrow" as it is very different from the "worldly sorrows" of guilt and shame.[12] Godly sorrow is the feeling of sadness about our sins and the pain they cause us and others. It carries with it the hope of restoration and change. It's a dark cloud with a silver lining. Conviction like this enables us to look honestly at our faults, accept that they are there, and look for the grace to receive forgiveness for wrongs and healing for hurts.

Godly sorrow promotes your recovery from painful and unhealthy patterns of living. It fosters an accurate self-perception that lets you look at both good and bad in you. That which is genuinely good and authentically you is to be valued, whereas that which is a pretense, an expectation that you tried to measure up to, is to be discarded. That behavior that feels "bad" only because somebody labeled it that way may be worthy of keeping, while that which hurts you or somebody else needs to be cleansed by bathing yourself in God's grace.

You respond out of godly sorrow rather than guilt or shame when you take the leap of faith. This week try to join Jelly by taking the leap of faith into the still waters and bathing yourself in Good Shepherd's loving grace for you. It's a scary leap, but in the end you will feel much better than living in penance or pretense.

Personal Reflections

1. Reflect on the extent to which you value the good in you. For instance, how do you respond to compliments? Check the responses that apply to you:

☐ Accept it with a "thank you"   ☐ Pass the credit to another person
☐ Discount it   ☐ Change the subject
☐ Gloat   ☐ Am surprised
☐ Gobble it up   ☐ Embarrassment
☐ Awkward silence   ☐ Defer all the credit to God

What do your responses tell you about the degree to which you value yourself?

2. It's tempting to try to hide the bad parts of ourselves rather than deal with them. Yet hiding our bad parts only perpetuates them. Guilt and shame encourage us to hide our bad parts, but godly sorrow encourages us to bring our badness into the light in order to be forgiven by God. Check any of the following defense mechanisms that you tend to use to hide your badness. Then pray that God would give you the courage to follow Jelly's example by admitting your faults and then jumping into the still waters of God's love.

☐ Pretending to be someone you're not
☐ Hiding unwanted feelings
☐ Intellectualizing or spiritualizing your faults away
☐ Repressing your badness into your unconscious
☐ Blaming your badness on others
☐ Trying to redeem yourself by doing better next time

☐ Escaping from pain into compulsive behavior patterns

3. Set aside some time this week. Write down the names of the significant people in your life: Mom, Dad, stepparent, grandparent, other relative, spouse, friend, boss, pastor, counselor, and so on. Then write beside each name any positive things that those persons identified in you. What aspects of you did they value? What messages helped you appreciate yourself just for you? What messages, though "positive," actually encouraged you to try to be somebody you weren't just to please them?

4. Another day this week do the same exercise as above, listing the *negative* things that people rightly or wrongly identified in you. What things were you unjustly criticized or shamed for? In what cases did someone "speak the truth in love"[13] to you, helping you identify and deal with a weakness?

5. Last week you evaluated your strengths and weaknesses. This week reconsider this list. Take a day this week in which you think only about your strengths. Reflect on these good parts of you throughout the day and try to value them. Think about how they are good for you and for others. Thank God for working to develop these in you.

6. Take another day this week to consider your weaknesses, the "bad" and unwanted parts of yourself. Evaluate these "bad" traits. Are they truly bad? Do they disrespect you or others? Put a check mark beside those that are truly bad and unhealthy and think about the ways in which they hurt you or someone else. One by one picture yourself taking these bad parts to God. Take the leap of faith into the still waters of God's love. Bathe in His forgiveness. Remind yourself throughout the day that God knows about these parts of you and He still loves you.

Our Understanding of God

"He leads me beside
quiet waters."

Psalm 23:2*b*

The key to the sheep's well-being is their ability to depend upon Good Shepherd. Without him they cannot care for
their basic needs for food, water, and rest; they're left to wander about going nowhere; and they have to hopelessly fend
for themselves against wild animals. Sheep who trust a caring shepherd are happy and productive. Why do some sheep
trust their shepherd and some don't?

Wanda was learning to trust Good Shepherd because
she experienced his goodness. Jelly took her leap of faith
after seeing compassion in Good Shepherd's eyes. On the
other hand, Imp didn't trust the shepherd. He ran in front of
Good Shepherd and didn't listen to his warning not to drink
the contaminated water. He blamed the shepherd for his
own folly. Imp didn't really know Good Shepherd yet; he
needed to learn to trust in his shepherd's goodness.

Similarly, we won't trust God and surrender our hearts to
Him until on a feeling level we understand God to be good
and loving, with our best interests at heart. This is not a matter of simply believing intellectually that "God is love."[14]
Many people think that God is loving and will say that they
have made a decision to turn their will over to His care, yet it
hasn't made a significant difference in their lives. These
same people may be very religious, active in church, and
spend time regularly in prayer and Bible study. But unless
their relationship with God is a personal one in which they
come to feel Christ's love and to trust Him from their hearts,

their spirituality will lack depth and will have little positive impact in their lives.

This was the case for Jerry. He was a committed Christian who was devoted to serving people and spreading the gospel. He knew Scripture backwards and forwards. In fact, for years he had taught Sunday school classes and Bible studies. He knew all about God's love, but inside he felt depressed and fought gnawing pangs of inadequacy.

"I just don't feel like I'm a good enough Christian," he told me one day. "I don't do as much for the church as I should. I should be a man of prayer, but I'm not. I should be a more godly example at home and in my business. And what really troubles me is that I'm a leader in the church. I feel like a hypocrite!"

"What do you feel when you're alone with God in prayer?" I asked.

"What do you mean, *feel?* I don't think I feel anything. I just tell God about decisions I need to make or family or friends who have a need."

"But what about you and God on a personal level?" I persisted. "Do you feel God's love for you? How would it feel to call Him Daddy? Could you picture yourself being held by Jesus? Do you ever pause during a busy day and find yourself spontaneously smiling as you think about how much God cares for you?"

The blank, empty look in Jerry's eyes answered my questions. His relationship with God was emotionally dead. He experienced God as being like his emotionally absent and workaholic father. He regarded God as distant and hard to please. He needed to receive God's love and grace in order to come alive emotionally and to be freed from his guilt.

Little by little Jerry started to come alive emotionally when over time he saw that I meant it when I asked him, "How do you feel?" We discovered how sad and empty he felt inside underneath all the things he was doing and how guilty he felt if he didn't do what he should. He learned to feel his feelings in the "here and now" rather than analyzing them and trying to "fix" them. In doing this he became more open and accepting of himself.

At the same time Jerry learned to trust God on a deeper level. He started to emotionally differentiate his heavenly Father from his earthly father. He was experiencing the truth of the apostle Paul's words "For you did not receive a spirit that makes you a slave again to fear, but you received a Spirit of sonship. And by him we cry, '*Abba*, Father.'"[15] Now in his prayers Jerry expressed to God his hurts and his struggles. In the Bible he discovered anew the compassion of Jesus for hurting people. And as he felt better about himself he became more interested in the needs of his family and people at church.

Do you experience God's love for you? Do you sense personally His care and His guidance in your daily life? For a vibrant spiritual life, you may need to share your feelings with a shepherd or a friend, someone who has received God as his or her own Shepherd. That person can be God's eyes of compassion to look into our souls, to be God's listening ears to hear our hurts, and to give us Jesus' hand to hold as we walk the path of our life.

"We know and rely on the love God has for us" when we feel loved by others in the name of God. Our trust in God as a loving God can grow when we are receiving His love though people we trust. Living in God's love in this way changes how we see ourselves; we feel lovable and valuable.[16]

Personal Reflections

1. What is your reaction to the idea that you will tend to experience God as being like your parents and others who

have been significant in your development? Only when you work through the issues with these people in a healing process can you become more open to experience God as He really is, a loving Good Shepherd.

2. Meditate this week on 1 Corinthians 13:4-8, part of the famous love chapter in the Bible. In the past you've probably been told to read "I am patient, I am kind . . ." But before you do that put God's name in there and read, "God is patient with me, God is kind toward me . . ." This is consistent with the principle that "we love because He first loved us"[17] and will help you to consider your need for God's love. For each of the following fourteen characteristics of God's perfect love read "God . . ."

- is patient and available
- is not jealous of me
- is gentle and not rude
- loves me unconditionally
- forgives me
- protects me from harm
- disciplines fairly and in love

- is humble and on my level
- praises me
- does kind things for me
- is considerate of my struggles
- supports my dreams
- respects and encourages me
- is someone I can count on

3. One day this week rate from 1 to 10 (with 10 being highest) the extent to which you felt loved as a child in each of those fourteen ways by your father. Go back to the list of loving attributes above and designate a column as "F" for father and write in the rating number beside each attribute. (The purpose of this exercise is not to blame your dad for your difficulties in knowing God's love for you, but to identify the good and the bad that you received from him so that you

can face reality and be thankful for the good and forgiving of the bad.)

4. Later this week do the same rating for the extent to which you experienced your mother's ("M") love.

5. Do the same for God ("G"), but base it on your current experience of God's love. Note the areas of God's love that are the hardest for you to receive. Are these connected to any unresolved issues with your parents? You might put a check mark by these areas and pray that God would begin to heal these. Pray also that He would reveal those aspects of His love to you in your relationships and in your devotional life so that you can love others as He has loved you.

NOTES

1. 1 John 2:15-17.
2. Romans 12:21.
3. Psalm 63:1.
4. Isaiah 55:1.
5. John 4:14; 7:37-39.
6. Luke 10:41-42, italics added; the story begins in verse 38.
7. 1 Corinthians 13:12.
8. James 1:22-25.
9. Galatians 4:6; Deuteronomy 32:10; Psalm 17:8; and Colossians 1:13-14.
10. 1 John 3:1.
11. Jeremiah 31:3.
12. 2 Corinthians 7:9-11.
13. Ephesians 4:15.
14. 1 John 4:16.
15. Romans 8:15. *Abba* is an Aramaic term used in Jesus' day to indicate affection for a father, such as *Daddy* and *Papa* are used in the English language.
16. 1 John 4:7-19, 21.
17. 1 John 4:16.

"Made a searching and fearless moral inventory of ourselves. Admitted to God, to ourselves, and to another human being the exact nature of our wrongs."

STEPS 4 and 5,
Alcoholics Anonymous' Twelve Steps

———————————

"He restores my soul."

Psalm 23:3a

STEP 4

Confession of Sin

Good Shepherd was gazing into the still waters when he noticed that the water had been changing from light blue to a deeper and darker blue. He sighed in the late afternoon sun, knowing he must leave this peaceful place and head back to the ranch. He looked around him at all his sheep lying beside the still waters. They too had become very relaxed. He took in one last deep breath of the misty air, held it in his lungs for a long time, and then exhaled, all the while listening to the gentle roar of the waterfall.

Good Shepherd softly tapped each of his sheep one by one on the shoulder and helped them to their feet. Once Good Shepherd rounded up the sheep, they all started their walk back to the ranch. Imp was having trouble walking, though, because he was still feeling sick from the contaminated water he drank. Good Shepherd stopped the flock and looked back at Imp. The other sheep also looked over their shoulders. Staggering back and forth, Imp looked like he was drunk. He zigzagged so much that he was hardly moving forward. A few of the sheep couldn't hold back their giggles.

One of the larger ewes, named Wobble, became very impatient watching Imp stagger around and hold up the whole flock. She wobbled and swayed up to the staggering Imp and spoke sharply. "Imp, do you realize that you are holding up the whole flock! If you weren't so foolish as to drink that dirty water we'd be almost home by now! Stand up tall and stop swaying back and forth! It drives me crazy just watching you! You're a pitiful sight."

Imp was already feeling guilty about holding everyone up. When he looked up at Wobble and saw her stern, impatient look, he dropped his head in shame. Just then Good Shepherd came over to them. He looked at Wobble and set her straight saying, "Wobble, you have enough problems of your own. I don't think you need to be worrying about Imp. He's already learned his lesson."

Turning to Imp, Good Shepherd reached down, put his hands underneath Imp's stomach, pulled with all his might, picked him up and put him across his shoulders. A collective gasp rose from the flock; the sheep were doubly shocked. They wondered how the shepherd could carry such a large ram on his shoulders. Their greater surprise, however, was that Good Shepherd was so patient and tender with Imp, who had been such a problem.

The other sheep began following Good Shepherd and Imp across the barren field toward the ranch's green pasture. After walking awhile, Good Shepherd noticed his shadow suddenly disappear, so he stopped walking and turned to look over his shoulder at the sun. It had just slipped under the snow-topped Table Mountain. Good Shepherd had an eerie feeling. Something wasn't quite right, but he couldn't figure out what.

Instinctively, he started to count his sheep aloud, "One, two, three, four . . . Hmm. That can't be. One, two, three, four. . . . I'm one short!" Frantically he looked all around, but the other sheep was not to be found. Then he looked into the sky and saw a vulture swirling around in the distance. "Wobble must have fallen down!" he shouted. Terror swelled in his heart. He dropped Imp, gathered Imp and the others in a huddle, quickly surrounded them as best he could with tumbleweeds and bramble, and then started running back toward Table Mountain.

Good Shepherd was sprinting as fast as he could, hoping he wouldn't be too late. He looked back into the sky and spotted two vultures swirling. They were slowly swooping downward in long, wide loops. Then they would ascend once more to repeat their ominous dives. A mixture of excited hope and panic now squeezed Good Shepherd's heart like a vise closing in on a piece of soft wood.

"Wobble must still be alive!" he cried. "But I must hurry and get to her before it's too late!"

As he sprinted in the general direction of the swirling vultures, he heard a faint, "Baah-aah-ahh. Baah-ahh-ahh." His keen ears were like a radar, and he slightly adjusted his course. He was getting closer; Wobble's cries were getting louder and louder. Finally, in the distance, he could see Wobble. She was flat on her back, rolling back and forth, deep in a hollow. Her fat stomach stuck out, and her stubby forelegs and hind legs pointed straight into the air as she flailed helplessly back and forth. Wobble had fallen down and couldn't get up again by herself. If it wasn't for the seriousness of the situation it would have made for a wildly funny sight.

"Shoo! Shoo! Go away!" Good Shepherd started screaming as he waved his arms in hopes of scaring the vultures. Finally he reached Wobble and pulled up his stride. _She's still alive! The vultures haven't attacked yet._

Huffing, puffing, and panting, Good Shepherd rolled Wobble out of the hollow in the ground and onto her side so that her digestive system could push out the gasses that built up as she lay on her back. Then he started to rub Wobble's legs and body to restore her circulation. Had she been on her back much longer, her limbs and body would have become numb from the lack of circulation. Then she wouldn't have been able to flail her legs, and the vultures would have then made their attack and eaten dinner.

Still panting, Good Shepherd looked into Wobble's relieved eyes and said, "I'm so glad I found you in time!" He kissed Wobble on the nose and then, rubbing Wobble's large stomach, he grabbed hold of a gigantic handful of her dirty wool and remarked, "You remember what I said to you when you were condemning Imp? I told you that you had your own problems to deal with. Well, this is what I meant. Look how thick and heavy your wool is. It's time we shear that off for the coming summer. It's also time you look at your heaviness and your wobbling tendencies. You know you really do take after your mother. Maybe this summer I'll put you on rations to help you trim down."

Wobble smiled up at Good Shepherd. She knew he was right. He had a way of correcting her with such gentleness and tender love that she knew he had her best interests at heart. *I'll apologize to Imp as soon as I rejoin the flock,* she thought.

Good Shepherd and Wobble walked briskly side by side back to the other sheep. They were hurrying to beat the darkness back to the ranch.

Sin: The S Word

> "He restores my soul."
>
> Psalm 23:3a

Wobble was a typical sheep in that she was prone to wobble and fall down. Sheep fall down for many reasons: because they're too fat, heavy with lamb, carrying a heavy coat of thick wool (which gets extra heavy when it's full of dirt, sticks, rocks, or moisture), or overtired and prone to rest in a soft hollow in the ground. When Wobble fell, she couldn't stand again without help. Her body was too fat and her limbs were too stubby; she was unable to fight against gravity and right herself.

Wobble dealt with her weakness by trying to ignore it; she felt ashamed when it was pointed out to her that she wobbled like her mother. When she saw Imp staggering, her unconscious mind figured out the perfect way to get rid of her shame: she projected it onto Imp!

Looking at Wobble we have to laugh because we too are prone to wobble and fall down. Falling down is part of our humanness, yet many of us, like Wobble, have trouble admitting to our proneness to fall down. We cringe when it comes to making a searching and fearless moral inventory of ourselves.

Many people I know who are in Twelve Step recovery groups have told me that Step Four is the hardest step for them. This is where they get stuck. Some people spend months doing and redoing this one step. The list of follies, foibles, and personal issues to take inventory of seems endless. The wreckage they leave behind seems too great to calculate.

To take moral inventory and admit to our wrongs means taking responsibility for our moral failures. It's the "wrong" part, the "moral" part of this step that we choke on. Sin is the bad "S word." Because of family upbringing or church experiences many people confuse sin with shame. A mother punishes her daughter for spilling milk on the kitchen floor. A father tells his son he is "bad" for yelling at mother. A youth pastor condemns those teenagers who drink and "get physical" with the opposite sex. When you've been corrected in these ways, taking responsibility for your moral faults and confessing your sins is tantamount to saying, "I am a failure. I am a worthless, horrible, unlovable person." Therefore, rather than confessing your sins you'll tend to hide them in shame.

The other problem we have here is in our concept or definition of what sin is. If the concept of sin that I frequently hear implied were to be put into a dictionary it might sound something like this: "Sin: a willful choice to act in a way that is disobedient, rebellious, or obstinate and which has the consequence of separating you from God's love."

The problem with the above definition of sin is that it is incomplete and based on two half-truths. Sometimes sin is a willful disobedient behavior. But is it always a conscious choice? Does it have to be a behavior? No, nor do we have to act like "rebellious teenagers" to sin.

And what about the "separate you from God's love" part? It's true that the Bible indicates that my sin and your sin would send us both to an eternity separated from God's love. And it's true that when we sin we are walking away from God's love for us. But that does not mean that God doesn't love us anymore. His unconditional love and free grace is still able to reach us in the midst of our sinful state.

Sin can be better defined like this: "Sin: the inborn tendency in human nature to fall short of God's standard of perfect righteousness; it is manifested in conscious or unconscious choices, thoughts, motives, character traits, or actions; it is hurtful to oneself, to another, and to God; sin reflects a failure to receive God's love, which He freely extends to us even though we have failed to live rightly and to follow His guidance."

This second definition requires a far greater scope of moral responsibility; it means that we need to search our souls and confess unseen sins of thoughts and motives that haven't yet been expressed in obvious behaviors or character traits. It acknowledges the reality that every minute of every day unfound and unconfessed sin and sinful tendencies remain in the dark corners of our souls. This means that sin is far more severe than we sometimes think. But the good news is that sin isn't shame-based; in God's eyes we are worthwhile, lovable, and forgivable. Thus we don't need to hide our shortcomings. Instead, we can confess our sinfulness and received God's forgiveness for our wrongs.

If you read Jesus' famous "Sermon on the Mount" you will see that Christ defines sin as beginning with an unconscious attitude of the heart that often leads to behavior that is hurtful to yourself or others.[1] Although the Bible reveals that God is sometimes angry and frustrated with repeated sin, God also is consistently compassionate and merciful toward sinners. He knows, after all, the damage sin does to the sinners and those in contact with them. Thus, it's not a matter of "Will God still love us?" but, "Will we turn from our sinful ways and admit that we need God's grace?"

Really, sin is a lot like falling down. Like sheep, we wobble around in this life, slip and fall flat on our faces, hurting ourselves and often bringing somebody else down with us. Wise old Solomon observed this. He said, "Though a righteous man falls seven times, he rises again."[2] This means we sin again and again and yet, because we accept the grace of God to restore us after we fall, we're considered righteous anyway. Those who received God's grace through Christ are in a learning process, being gradually transformed into God's likeness.[3]

It's hard to use the "S word" by taking inventory and admitting to your wrongs. But it doesn't have to be degrading if instead of believing you're a worthless person who should be ashamed you can begin to look at yourself through God's eyes of knowledge and love. Then with sorrow and conviction you can admit that you've fallen down again, you've missed the mark of perfection. To do this you need to work through your issues of shame caused when family or religious leaders called you a "bad" person because of your mistakes and sins.

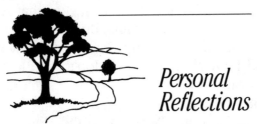

Personal Reflections

1. Perhaps like Wobble you tend to project your sins onto others. Jesus gave us a nugget of pure wisdom when He said, "Why do you look at the speck of sawdust in your brother's eye and pay no attention to the plank in your own eye? . . . First take the plank out of your own eye, and then you will see clearly to remove the speck from your brother's eye."[4] This week consider the planks in your own eye. One way to do this is to note the specks in other people's eyes that really bug you! What problems or traits of others do you tend to be critical of? Ask your spouse or a close friend for help in identifying the things you complain about. Make a list of these things.

———————————————————————————

———————————————————————————

2. Review your list of complaints and criticisms about others. One by one carefully ask yourself, "Why does this bother me so much?" Probably you're projecting your own wobbling onto others, and you need to trim off some fat. Maybe these are tendencies of yours that you need to con-

fess. (Look closely because they'll be hard to see.) Or perhaps you are seeing in others traits of a parent who in some way hurt you. If so, then you need to begin confessing your unresolved anger and hurt about those issues.

3. Go back and re-read the two definitions of sin that I proposed this week. Which is closest to your concept of sin? Is sin connected to shame for you? Do you feel so embarrassed of your moral faults and inadequacies that you tend to hide them?

4. Do you have a definition of sin that focuses only on your behavior? Read what Jesus has to say in Matthew 5:17-7:6. He describes a number of sinful tendencies that start in your heart.[5] Check off the sins below that you need to confess.

- ☐ Unresolved anger
- ☐ Unfaithfulness
- ☐ Wanting revenge
- ☐ Pride in your abilities
- ☐ Playing the martyr
- ☐ Worry

- ☐ Lust
- ☐ Judging others
- ☐ Unresolved conflict
- ☐ Faithless prayer
- ☐ Greed, wanting more
- ☐ Saying yes or no insincerely

WEEK 15
"Oh, Conscience!"

"He restores my soul."
Psalm 23:3*a*

The grandmother of a friend of mine says, "Oh, conscience!" when she feels pangs of guilt over doing something she "shouldn't" do. That describes how Wobble felt as she lay flat on her back, limbs flailing in the air. If we were to attach an electrode to her little sheep brain and tune in to listen to the self-talk of her conscience it would have sounded something like this: *I blew it! How could I be so stupid to get myself stuck in this hollow in the ground? If only I hadn't fallen down! Oh, I'll never get up again! I'm just too fat! I'll lay here until I die—unless the shepherd finds me. Oh, if he finds me I'll really be in trouble.*

Wobble had a harsh conscience with high self-expectations, which she tried very hard to live up to. She was critical of herself and anyone who didn't do as he should. She felt miserable when she didn't measure up to her set of rigid expectations. To avoid those pangs of guilt she tried not to look at the "bad" parts of herself. Instead, with self-righteous pride, she tried to focus on how well she followed the shepherd's directions and how strong and competent she was.

Interestingly, Wobble was like Imp. Not only did she sway when she walked, but she too had an impulsive side. That was a consequence of her self-righteousness and her unwillingness to look at her "bad" and unacceptable parts. Her impulsiveness was a contradiction to, and a reaction from, her more typical compulsive and perfectionistic self. This came out when she fell down and then gave in to the temptation to roll over onto her back in a soft hollow in order to give herself a short break from following hard after Good

Shepherd. She planned to lie on her back for only a minute and then run and catch up with the flock. Well, "pride came before the fall" for Wobble because she couldn't get back up. There she lay, flat on her back and feeling guilty. All she could do was flail her legs and cry, "Bahh-ahh-ahh!"

People who struggle with compulsive behaviors can't stop doing the things they know they should not do. For instance, Sid, married to a beautiful woman and the father of two model children, had been having an affair for two years. The more he tried to stop himself from going back to this woman the more trouble he had saying no.

Talking with Sid, I learned he was leading a double life. He was an elder in his church, seemingly committed to his Christian faith and his family; he did what he should and he put the needs of others before his own. Yet, he also lived the life of an impulsive sinner; he did as he pleased, regardless of how it affected others.

There was a split in his conscience. Usually it was legalistic, compulsive, driven to do all that he should, and determined to please God and others. The legalistic side tried to conceal sin and look pure on the outside. The impulsive side was his attempt to escape this oppressive and depressing way of life. This side of him thought only of himself and on an impulse would gratify and indulge himself without thought of the consequences of his sin.

Sid's biggest mistake was in thinking, _I'll be all right If only I can get rid of this sinful side and stay committed to do what is right._ That may sound wise to you, to do all that you should, to be committed, to strive to please God and others. The problem was that in Sid's supposedly Christian side there was no room for his needs or for God's free grace; it was legalistic, driven by guilt, and self-righteous. The impulsive side was mostly a reaction to and an attempt to be free from the compulsive side. In that sense the two sides to Sid were like the two sides of a teeter-totter. To be on either extreme was unbalanced and sinful.

Sid needed to balance his teeter-totter and avoid the extremes of legalism and license. He needed to live in grace and truth, putting aside pretenses and being honest about his behavior. Instead of telling himself to follow all sorts of rules or just throwing up his hands and doing as he pleased, he needed to be free to do what he believed was good for him, balanced by what was good for others.

Sid needed a mature conscience that was free of demands and impulses and would guide him in terms of what would be most fulfilling. He also needed to understand that God the Shepherd would forgive him of wrongdoing.

Good Shepherd modeled this kind of a conscience to Wobble. When he found the fallen Wobble he showed a gracious and forgiving heart, which was concerned for her well-being. With tenderness he helped relieve her gas pain and restore her circulation. With gentle firmness he corrected her to encourage her to learn a lesson and then helped her back on her feet. He disciplined her by trimming her excess wool and putting her on a diet so that she wouldn't be as likely to fall again.

Our Shepherd's balance of forgiveness and correction, grace and truth, is what we need to develop a strong conscience. People with strong consciences have a sense of what is both self-respecting and other-respecting.[6] This is much better than living with a conscience that is driven by guilt or impulse.

Personal Reflections

1. If your conscience were a teeter-totter with legalistic tendencies on the right, impulsive tendencies on the left, and grace and truth in the middle, how would it be balanced?

Which side do you lean to? How far? Does your teeter-totter swing back and forth?

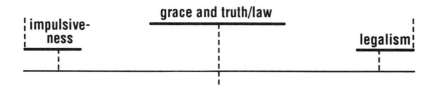

2. Some people say that your conscience is the "voice of God." Actually your conscience is an "internalized parent" that carries expectations and standards that were passed down to you in childhood from your parental figures and the church—standards that may not reflect what the Bible teaches. So consciences vary in terms of how accurately they speak God's voice. Think about the formation of your conscience this week, and when you can set aside some time complete the following sentences:

As a child my father thought I should _____

_____

My father expected me to _____

_____

He thought I should not _____

_____

He got angry at me when I _____

_____

3. Another day this week think about your mother's impact on your conscience and complete the following statements:

When I was a child my mother thought I should _____

_____

My mother expected me to _____

_____

She thought I should not _____

_____

She got angry at me when I _____

_____

4. If you attended church during your formative years do the same evaluation for the church staff, including ministers and Sunday school teachers.

The church thought I should _____

_____

The church expected me to _____

_____

The church thought I should not _____

_____

The church got angry at me when I _____

_____

5. Some time during the next few days think about the things from your past that you feel guilty about. Write those things down. Then talk to your Good Shepherd about those areas and try to picture Him responding to you in mercy as Good Shepherd did to Wobble. To symbolize God's forgiveness to you, erase the guilt-inducing things you wrote down.

_____

_____

WEEK 16

Identifying Your Generational Patterns

"He restores my soul."
Psalm 23:3*a*

Maybe you have seen the little people called Weebles®. They are children's toys bearing the slogan: "Weebles wobble, but they don't fall down!" A child can push on a Weeble person and he will wobble around, sway so far back that he looks like he is going to fall, but then he will pop right back up. Well, Wobble was no Weeble! And neither was her mother.

Wobble took after her mother. She had her mother's tendency to wobble and fall down. Just like her mother, when she started to fall she was "a'gonna go alllll the way over!" And then she'd roll onto her back and be unable to get up! Unlike the Weebles, she stayed on her back, helplessly flailing her legs back and forth.

Wobble hated it when people called her "a chip off the ol' block." She didn't like to admit that she was like her mother. She made the mistake of refusing to deal with the ways in which her mother's faults affected her and were passed down to her.

Like Wobble you probably have had passed down to you various unresolved issues and sins of your parents. This can mean two things. In some cases you will have a struggle just like your mom's or dad's. In other cases, you'll seem to have opposite characteristics because a trait of Mom's or Dad's bothered you so much that you determined not to be that way. In either case you're still being adversely affected by your parents' faults.

Generational patterns are various, and their consequences can be numerous. For instance, an alcoholic father can contribute to his child's similar abuse of alcohol. Or the child might develop some other addiction (i.e., to drugs, food, work, or unhealthy relationships) in order to cope with pain and stress. Another child in this family might become a teetotaler who doesn't go near alcohol and gets angry and self-righteous about those who do. Other children from such a family might develop feelings of being lost and neglected, insecure about the unpredictable tension in relationships, fearful of disappointing others, or guilty about their need for attention. Still others might become codependent on their alcoholic father and anyone who is like him so that they try to fix people's problems and rescue them from trouble. Or a child may have great difficulty trusting and counting on other people because his father was so unreliable and inconsistent.

Other examples of generational patterns in which sins are passed down might include family members who suffer emotional, physical, or sexual abuse; divorce; infidelity; emotional neglect; lack of healthy communication; a controlling parent matched with a passive parent; a perfectionistic parent; an inadequate parent who is insecure and needs reassurance; or a physically or emotionally absent parent. The reality is that whatever your parents were like they had some good and some bad qualities. Consequently, for better or for worse, their character and their treatment of you has greatly affected the formation of your personality.

Your question should not be, "Have my parents' unresolved issues and faults affected me?" but, "What do I do about the effects their sins did have on me?" As Wobble would attest, ignorance is not bliss, because patterns will tend to be passed down, except as you work through your issues with your parents. Many people, especially in the young adult years, make the mistake of idealizing their parents and blaming themselves for any problems they've carried into adulthood. Other people make the opposite mistake of blaming their parents for the issues that emerge from their childhood.

A centuries-old antidote exists to free us from the sins and the pain of our parents: we need to confess the sins of commission and omission of our parents and others significant to us.[7] This may sound like blaming your parents for your problems or setting yourself up to judge and criticize others, but that is not the intended meaning. Neither is this idea a license to gossip and slander your parents' faults. Instead, confessing the sins of your parents means taking responsibility to deal with the effects of their sins against you. Obviously, no parent is perfect and even the best of Christian parents will make mistakes and sin against their children; their own unresolved issues and weaknesses of character and lifestyle will impact their children who depend upon them.

Therefore, no matter how much people you trusted may have sinned against you, as an adult you still need to take responsibility for your life. You need to deal with your anger over the ways in which your parents' attitudes and actions adversely affected you. You need to begin the healing process for your wounded places. And as you deal with the effects of your parents' sins upon you, you should not forget the good and loving effects they had upon you.

Admittedly this is a difficult task. It's especially hard because it often means working through resentments from the distant past that may be unconscious. Ideally, our families of origin would have provided a relational environment of "speaking the truth in love,"[8] combining emotional honesty with love and respect. Parents would model to their children the humility and courage of consistently "taking inventory" of themselves and confessing to their wrongdoings. As it was, many of our parents had characteristic ways of hiding their faults from themselves and others and were not open to confrontation, but were defensive when others were angry with them.

In such families, the children—who want to see their parents as good and loving anyway—typically will defend and idealize their parents, blame one and idealize the other, or escape emotionally from the family system. For these children the "sun goes down on their anger"[9] and frustration night after night until as adults they begin to break the generational patterns and deal with the issues. To the extent that you take responsibility to confess and work through your parents' ills that have been passed on to you, you can begin to reverse your generational patterns and pass down love and blessings to your children and others.[10]

Personal Reflections

1. One of the Ten Commandments is "Honor your father and mother."[11] Some people interpret this as "I should please my parents and do what will make them happy." This attitude prevents them from dealing with their parents' sins. One definition of *honor* in Webster's dictionary is "a keen sense of right and wrong." What do you think about this? Could it be honoring to your parents to confess their sins? How would it be; how might it not be?

_____

_____

2. When you were a child, what was your family's attitude about anger? If you were angry about something, how did your parents respond to your feelings? To some people, expressing anger seems bad or sinful. Yet, the apostle Paul says we need to learn to "be angry and sin not" by expressing our anger truthfully and respectfully. He warns us not to repress our anger and become resentful.[12] For the responses to your anger, below write an "M" beside those that were true

of your mother and "F" beside those that were true of your father.

___ Got angry at me   ___ Punished me

___ Threatened me   ___ Made me feel guilty

___ Felt guilty themselves   ___ Cried and felt hurt

___ Let me have my way   ___ Cold silence

___ Tried to control my feelings   ___ Ignored me by getting busy

___ Listened and understood   ___ Admitted to any wrong doing

___ Made necessary adjustments   ___ Helped me to express my anger in appropriate ways

3. Think about how your parents' responses to your anger have influenced your feelings about confessing your parents' sins against you. How do you feel when you look at the effects your parents' weaknesses and sins had on you? Check the responses below that are true for you.

☐ I minimize my parents' faults to protect them.

☐ I tend to blame them for my struggles.

☐ I feel anxious at the thought of being angry at them.

☐ I feel sad about the caring I did not receive.

☐ I feel guilty for "judging" them.

☐ I don't have a right to be angry at them because I've sinned too.

☐ I should focus only on the good they've done for me.

☐ I don't remember my childhood.

☐ I don't feel angry about the ways they hurt me.

4. Set aside some time this week to confess your own sins of commission and omission. Read Galatians 5:19-23, which contrasts sinful fruit[13] and righteous fruit.[14] *Check* the

sins you struggle with and *circle* righteous fruit that is *not* well expressed in your life.

SINFUL FRUIT

- ☐ Sexual immorality
- ☐ Impure sexual thoughts
- ☐ Unresolved conflict
- ☐ Uncontrolled anger
- ☐ Quarreling
- ☐ Drunkenness
- ☐ Resentful dislike of another
- ☐ Controlling others

- ☐ Lustful indulgence
- ☐ Putting anything above God
- ☐ Jealousy
- ☐ Selfish ambition
- ☐ Criticism
- ☐ Wild partying
- ☐ Hating or despising another

RIGHTEOUS FRUIT

love	joy	peace
patience	kind acts	goodness
faithfulness	gentleness	self-control

5. Later this week go back to the lists of sinful fruit and righteous fruit. Consider how your sins of commission and omission are related to your difficulties in working through your issues regarding the effects of your parents' sins on you. Write an "M" beside the sinful fruit and the unexpressed righteous fruit that describe your mother. Do the same for your father using an "F."

6. Make one day this week a day of thanksgiving. Note the sins that are not big struggles for you and consider the righteous fruits that God has developed in you. Then consider the blessings that your parents passed on to you. Thank God for the sins they did *not* pass on to you and for the good fruit they did pass on to you.

120

Confessing Your Sins to Another

> "He restores my soul."
> Psalm 23:3a

When Good Shepherd found the fallen Wobble he rejoiced. He kissed her on the nose and shouted with joy. And he rubbed her legs and stomach to restore her circulation. Then with gentleness and firmness, graciousness and truthfulness, he helped her to look at her wobbling tendencies, her temptations to slough off and lie down in a soft hollow, her dirty and heavy excess wool that needed to be cut off, and her extra weight that needed to be trimmed so that she wouldn't fall again.

Good Shepherd restored Wobble's soul; he forgave her sins, put her back on her feet, and helped her learn how to stay on her feet.

When Wobble looked at her own sinfulness and received Good Shepherd's forgiveness, something changed inside her. His love transformed her conscience from being perfectionistic and condemning to being gracious and honest. She didn't need to project her badness onto Imp anymore. She had the courage to face her own weaknesses because she knew she was loved and forgiven. She didn't want to harbor resentment toward the staggering Imp in her heart. Instead she felt compassion for Imp. She saw him as a fellow struggler in need of mercy. Because of these changes in her heart, she later confessed to Imp her sin of being critical towards him.

We must admit that we also are wobblers. We fall down and can't get back up without the help of a shepherd. We need someone to hold us accountable and to look at our shortcomings. We need other people's feedback to see ourselves accurately. We need to feel forgiven by someone we respect in order to forgive ourselves.

Have you looked at your sinfulness and weaknesses this month? Have you considered specific issues that you struggle with? Looking at the truth of our sins is dangerous. We must look with loving compassion, which seeks to understand and not to judge; we need to display gentle mercy, which seeks to forgive and not to condemn.

Confessing your sins becomes destructive if it's not done with compassion and mercy. Most people I know who are beginning their journey of recovery do not have loving compassion or gentle mercy for themselves. Instead, they tend to be critical of themselves and struggle to forgive themselves for their mistakes. When they see their shortcomings they feel ashamed, bad, and unlovable. As a consequence they have ingrained and habitual tendencies to cover up their faults.

Condemnation and judgment from others or yourself will never bring you to confess your sins. *Only the goodness and grace of God can inspire you to confess your sins rightly and truly.*[15]

Self-condemning people are stuck on this step of confessing their sins until they develop a relationship with a compassionate and forgiving shepherd who can "restore their soul." Jesus is just such a shepherd. He says to us, "I am the good shepherd. The good shepherd lays down his life for the sheep."[16] Jesus gave up His life for us. He was accused of things He didn't do, ridiculed, abused, and rejected; He even was betrayed by a friend. He understands our pains because He has experienced them.

In the epistle of Hebrews, Jesus is described as a high priest who is able to "sympathize with our weaknesses" because as a man on this earth He too was sinned against and felt hurt and angry. He too was tempted to sin "in every way, just as we are—yet was without sin."[17] Jesus has compassion for your hurting places, your temptations, and your struggles with sin. Furthermore, He is forgiving. He has the right and the ability to forgive our sins because He lived a sinless life before God; He sacrificed His holy life for you and me by allowing Himself to be crucified and punished for our sin, and then He rose from the dead to conquer sin and death.[18]

Do you experience God as compassionate and forgiving? What do you feel when you approach His throne to confess your sins? Remember, Jesus is there, His nail-pierced hands extended to you. He says to you, "Tell me about your hurts and your sins. I want you to know that I understand how you feel and that I share in your struggles. I want to forgive you and to help you back onto your feet."

It may be hard for you to feel God's compassion and mercy in your heart. For this reason God uses people to remind us of His love. In order to "be reconciled to God" we need "ambassadors" for Christ to receive His appeal of love.[19] We're best able to feel God's compassion and mercy for our sinfulness when we find a shepherd committed to God to whom we can confess our struggles and receive the message of God's forgiveness. His sensitivity and the strength of His encouraging arm can pull us to our feet once more.

The beauty of this kind of confession is that it works! When you confess your struggles to a caring shepherd your soul experiences cleansing and restoration. It was this kind of purifying honesty and cathartic confession Jesus was referring to when He pronounced, "Blessed are the pure in heart; for they will see God."[20] We see God as a God of loving forgiveness when we purify our hearts by confessing our shortcomings and issues with someone we trust and respect.

Personal Reflections

1. Who in your life serves as a human shepherd? Do you have a friend or counselor whom you respect and trust to share your issues and your sinful struggles with? If not, then this week start praying and looking for God to help you develop such a relationship.

2. If you were Wobble and you had fallen and gotten stuck on your back, how would you have felt? When you make a mistake or fall into a sinful pattern how do you respond? Check the responses below that apply to you.

☐ Impatient with self   ☐ Critical of my mistake
☐ Self-condemning   ☐ "I'll make up for it"
☐ Try to get up on my   ☐ Try not to think about
own   it
☐ Make excuses   ☐ Make a "joke" out of it
☐ Blame somebody else   ☐ Seek forgiveness
☐ Worry about the con-   ☐ Have compassion for
sequences   myself
☐ Try to learn from my mistake

3. Picture yourself fallen down like Wobble. Imagine Good Shepherd running to save you from the vultures, rejoicing that he's found you, kissing you, rubbing your legs to restore your circulation, and then gently trimming your excess wool and helping you to slim down so you won't fall so easily. Perhaps others have not been so kind to you when

you've fallen down. How have your shepherds and fellow sheep responded to you when you've fallen?

_____

_____

4. Set aside time one day this week to meditate on Psalm 51 in which David, the poet of Psalm 23, confesses to God his sins of adultery and murder and prays for God to restore his soul. Note how he searches deeper than his outward behavior and looks into his heart and prays for "truth in the inward parts." Elsewhere, he prayed similarly, "Who can discern his errors? Clear me [purge me] of hidden [unconscious] faults."[21] Make this your prayer.

5. Jesus is the Good Shepherd come to earth. Search your heart today to see whether you have truly given your heart to Christ, the Good Shepherd. To you, His beloved sheep, your Shepherd says, "For God so loved the world that he gave his one and only Son, that whoever believes in him shall not perish but have everlasting life."[22]

NOTES

1. The Sermon on the Mount is recorded in Matthew 5-7.
2. Proverbs 24:16a.
3. 2 Corinthians 3:18.
4. Matthew 7:3,5.
5. Mark 7:20-23.
6. Romans 14:1-23.
7. Leviticus 26:39-42.
8. Ephesians 4:15.
9. Ephesians 4:26.
10. Exodus 20:5-6.
11. Exodus 20:12.
12. Ephesians 4:15, 25-27.

13. Other passages listing sinful fruit include Exodus 20:1-17; Mark 7:20-23; and Ephesians 5:3-5.

14. Other passages listing righteous fruit include Romans 5:1-5; 1 Corinthians 13:4-8; James 3:13-18; and 2 Peter 1:5-9.

15. Romans 2:4.

16. John 10:11.

17. Hebrews 4:14-16.

18. Isaiah 53:4; Hebrews 9:28; 1 Peter 2:24; 1 John 3:5.

19. 2 Corinthians 5:20.

20. Matthew 5:8.

21. Psalm 19:12, *Amplified Version*.

22. John 3:16.

"Were entirely ready to have God remove all these defects of character. Humbly asked Him to remove our shortcomings."

STEPS 6 and 7,
Alcoholics Anonymous' Twelve Steps

"He guides me in paths of righteousness for His name's sake."

Psalm 23:3b

Delayed Gratification

Good Shepherd delights to hear the birds chirping their love songs. All around him on this lush spring day, the green blades of grass stretch toward the sun, the flowers spread an array of radiant colors, and the tree buds burst forth with new growth.

Winter is but a memory. For the sheep it had been a season of getting to know Good Shepherd up close and learning to follow his guidance. They had learned to trust him and to take in his goodness as they graze at the home ranch. During winter they were learning to lie down and rest in the soft green pastures and to see themselves in the quiet waters of his love, the love that satisfies their thirst. They also began to learn from their mistakes, often falling down and then watching Good Shepherd help them back on their feet.

Now the pastures have all been grazed to exhaustion. The sun is getting hotter and the temperatures are on the rise. So with the strength of all they've learned this winter from Good Shepherd, the sheep are ready to move forward to newer and higher ground. There fresh pasture and moderate temperatures await for the summer months.

Good Shepherd looked over his flock as they grazed on the ranch's pasture at the base of the snow covered mountains. His attention focused on Table Mountain, where he and his sheep would spend the summer. Then he took in a breath of the fresh spring air and began to sing:

> *Hey, hey! Spring is in the air, I say!*
> *My darlings, it's a new day.*
> *So let us hop, skip, and play.*
> *We will take a new path today.*
> *Come with me,*
> *This is the way!*

Good Shepherd's happy idea of taking a new path met with a mixed reaction from the sheep audience. Some loved it and had been itching to get up and go somewhere. Others were confused and didn't know what to think because they didn't know what was ahead. Some were excited because they had heard from the older sheep about the wonderful mountain plateau where they would spend the summer. Still others were scared to take the new path because they'd heard chilling tales of past dangers encountered in the Valley of the Shadow of Death.

One of the fearful sheep was named Timi, a timid little lamb who liked it at the home ranch. She had a little friend named Blue Bell who grazed on the other side of the white picket fence over in the neighbor shepherd's pasture. All winter long they had played games together at the fence. They hopped up and down to see who could reach the top of the fence. They darted back and forth from one fence post to the other to see who was faster. They whispered to each other between the rails of the fence. They played hide and seek too and all sorts of other games fit for two little sheep.

This would be Timi's first journey through the valley to the high country. After Good Shepherd had rounded up everyone it was time to get little Timi and leave. When Good Shepherd reached down to pick her up, he saw big tears rolling down the little lamb's face.

"I don't wanna leave home! I wanna stay and play with Blue Bell!" Timi sobbed.

Stooping down, Good Shepherd looked right into Timi's eyes and said, "It is sad to say good-bye to someone you love. We love you too, Timi, and we cannot leave you here. There would be no one to take care of you. Soon it will be getting very hot, and you wouldn't want to be here. I have lots of things I want to show you. Then we'll come back home after the summer, and you can spend next winter with Blue Bell."

As Good Shepherd picked up Timi and draped her across his broad shoulders, Timi nodded good-bye to her friend. She kept repeating to herself Good Shepherd's words, "We'll come back. We'll come back."

With Timi atop Good Shepherd's shoulders, they were finally on their way down the path. As usual Imp was up at the front of the flock anxious to see what was ahead. At his side was a ram named Doody. Some of the sheep jokingly called him "Do-do" for short. He didn't like it because it reminded him of the "bird doo" that sometimes landed on his face! "Do-do" was an appropriate nickname for him, though, because he was a doer. He did whatever he was told. In fact, Doody was a very busy young ram. He was always doing something: grazing here or there, helping other sheep find shady spots, comforting troubled sheep, and helping Good Shepherd keep all the sheep together.

As they were walking along the path, Good Shepherd tried to point out some of the pretty sights to Doody, but

Doody missed them because he was too busy. Some of the more playful sheep were singing and dancing to Good Shepherd's spring song:

Hey, hey! Spring is in the air, I say!
My darlings, it's a new day.
So let us hop, skip, and play. . . .

Doody thought that was silly; he wanted no part of such senseless frolicking and singing.

Imp spotted a fork in the path just ahead and thinking they were almost "there"—he didn't really know where they were going—he rushed ahead of Good Shepherd. When he arrived at the fork he saw that the path to the right was narrow and wound up a hill. It was full of rocks that had to be stepped over and looked like it hadn't been trodden much; little blades of spring grass were growing on it. But to the left Imp saw a broad, flat, and well-worn path. He could see that many sheep before him had walked that path. He even thought he could smell the lush green pasture and the beautiful flowers ahead.

Imp was so excited he started to salivate. In moments he was prancing ahead down the broad path.

He hadn't walked very far when his ears perked up and he heard Good Shepherd's voice behind him: "No! Imp, don't go down that path! It's not what you think. Turn back and follow me!"

Imp stopped at once. He turned around and saw Good Shepherd with the others back at the fork in the path and got a sick feeling in his stomach. *Oh, the dirty water! That was awful! I think I'd better listen to Good Shepherd this time.* He retreated back to the flock and then they all started climbing the narrow path.

WEEK 18

Moving to New Ground

"He guides me in paths of righteousness for His name's sake."

Psalm 23:3*b*

Timi didn't want to move to new ground. She was afraid to leave home. She didn't want to leave her friend Blue Bell behind. She was terrified of what might be ahead if she went down the path. She had heard scary stories about cougars jumping out of the shadows and all the sheep needing to huddle in dark caves during storms of giant hail. And she was afraid that she wasn't strong enough to climb the steep mountain paths ahead.

All sorts of excuses held Timi back from the things ahead that she feared. She was unaware that the summer sun at the home ranch would brown pastures and evaporate water holes. Summer would bring horrendously annoying insects. She also didn't know about the beautiful places ahead she would explore, the delicious green grasses and cold spring waters she'd find in the high country, and the wonderful things she'd learn. Her fears would have caused her to miss all this if she hadn't put faith in Good Shepherd's words to her and believed that he had a good plan for her.

Like Timi, we too have lots of excuses to halt our progress on the path of recovery. We're not entirely ready to have God remove all our defects of character. We're hesitant about humbly asking God to remove our shortcomings. So instead of moving forward in our recovery from a wounded and unhealthy past we may stay where we are and:

- fearfully hide our issues lest anyone see them
- blame others for our struggles

133

- isolate from those who can help us in fear of being hurt
- hopelessly give up because we can't see the path's end
- feel sorry for ourselves and look for others to pity us
- wait for God or someone to miraculously rescue us
- look for answers without feeling our pain
- intellectualize or spiritualize our problems away
- project our problems onto others and then "help" them

These are just some of the ways that people avoid the process of recovery. Recovery is truly a long and painful process. It means one step forward and two steps backward, then two steps forward and one step backward and one more step forward. If you stick to the processes of understanding, relating, grieving, confronting, and forgiving, then eventually you will make progress. But you will feel pain and fall down along the way. The path of recovery and growth is definitely a narrow, uphill path with slippery curves to be careful on and rocks to avoid stepping on.

Thinking about the painful and difficult process of recovery reminds me of a young woman named Patty, who had recurring panic attacks. Her self-talk sounded like a recording of her mother through a loudspeaker: "You shouldn't feel that way. . . . Smile and stand tall because people are always watching you. . . . Be strong so that you can be a good Christian and please God."

Patty's soul was a volcano of seething, boiling emotion. Yet on the outside she displayed the calm strength of a beautiful mountain. She pressured herself to maintain her composure at all times. She forbade feelings like fear, sadness, insecurity, loneliness, and anger from her demeanor. When she experienced such feelings she pushed them back down. Her unconscious mind was like a storage shed full of unwanted and rusty old tools. She kept repressing her unwanted feelings back into the storehouse until it was full and then she'd stick some more in there.

Finally the pressures in her emotional storehouse would begin to boil like a pot of water with the lid held down. When the lid blew the panic attack seemed to come from nowhere. Little or seemingly no external pressures were required. That's because her stress was internally imposed. It was hard for her to grasp, but her recovery from her panic attack disorder was a paradox. She thought the way to avoid panic again was to repress her uncomfortable feelings back into the storehouse of her unconscious. Actually, the path to recovery was in feeling her fears and distresses.

I guaranteed her that if she tried and kept trying to have a panic attack by feeling her feelings she'd never have one! And I was right. The more Patty became honest with herself and faced her uncomfortable feelings, the less frequent and the less intense were her panic attacks.

Similarly your own progress of growth and change will follow your willingness to step out of the darkness of aging defense mechanisms and weak excuses and into the light of being honest about what you're feeling and struggling with. This is a very God-like thing to do, as "God is light; in him there is no darkness at all. . . . If we walk in the light, as he is in the light we have fellowship with one another, and the blood of Jesus, his Son, purifies us from all sin."[1]

Solomon described these narrow "paths of righteousness" and honesty that our shepherd leads us down: "The path of the righteous is like the first gleam of dawn, shining ever brighter till the full light of day."[2] The process of recovery is one in which your future becomes brighter and brighter as you take steps forward. In the beginning, though, you probably won't see that hope-inspiring first gleam of dawn. Instead, you're likely to feel lost in the dark skies and stormy clouds of the night that you are trying to escape.

Personal Reflections

1. This week think about the path of recovery ahead of you. How do you feel as you approach what's ahead? Do you identify with Timi's fears of leaving the familiar and moving to new ground? Maybe you're having some trouble working at the process of change. What excuses hold you back in your recovery journey? Check those that apply to you.

☐ I can't make the time.　　☐ It's too painful.
☐ I'm too busy.　　　　　　☐ It won't work.
☐ I've tried and got no-　　☐ I don't have pressing
　 where.　　　　　　　　　　issues.
☐ I don't have help.　　　　☐ Others need my help.
☐ I already "know" all　　　☐ I don't know how to
　 this.　　　　　　　　　　 change.

2. One day this week pause for some quiet and uninterrupted time to "walk in the light" of honesty and truthfulness by feeling your emotions and reflecting on your struggles. Complete three "I feel" statements describing how you feel at that moment.

I feel _____

_____

I feel _____

_____

I feel _____

_____

3. What feelings are most uncomfortable for you? What feelings are hardest for you to share with a friend? From the

list below, identify and circle the feelings you try not to feel. These are the feelings you repress into the storehouse of your unconscious. Begin to monitor these feelings in you and see if you can't catch yourself before you banish them to the dark corners of that storehouse.

anger	confusion	helplessness
fear	insecurity	inferiority
sadness	inadequacy	not being in control
embarrassment	aloneness	dependency/trust

4. Have you seen the first gleam of dawn on your path of recovery? Do you have hope of feeling better about yourself and that your life is more manageable? What is the goal you're working toward? Write down your vision for recovery.

_____

_____

WEEK 19

Choosing Between Two Paths

"He guides me in paths of righteousness for His name's sake."
Psalm 23:3*b*

Imp was so anxious to get to the new pasture that when he saw the fork in the path he ran ahead of Good Shepherd. He thought they were almost there. Actually they'd just begun. Standing at the junction, Imp was forced to choose between two paths: the broad path, which was flat, easy, and well-worn, or the narrow path, which wound uphill, was full of rocks, and had not been traveled much. Predictably, Imp went with his first impulse and raced down the easy path.

Up to this point Imp was acting like his old impulsive self. Just as when he drank the contaminated water, Imp dashed in front of his shepherd and took the quick and easy route to getting what he thought he needed. But then a miracle happened. When Good Shepherd called out to Imp and told him to stop, Imp listened. And he got a sick feeling in his stomach—a wonderful, *sick* feeling! He remembered the contaminated water that was "not good for him" and how sick it had made him. The last thing he wanted was to repeat that fiasco!

Imp showed his emerging new self by listening to Good Shepherd's voice and turning around to join him and the others on the narrow and difficult path. Imp trusted that in the end the hard road would be the best road for him. Instead of continuing to react impulsively to his momentary whims to indulge himself, he responded to what he thought was right. He followed his shepherd's leading to the path of righteousness, the right path for him.

In your journey of personal growth you will also come to forks in the path at which you'll have to choose between one of two paths. The broad path will offer pleasure, ease, and escape from your troubles, and it will seem that "everybody is doing it." The narrow path, offering rightness, will bring difficulty and painful struggles, and it will seem you're all alone on it. The fork in the path is a test because it offers a temptation. Can you say no to momentary, pleasurable impulses? Can you say yes to pursuing what will be good for you in the long term? Taking this step will add another important tool for your recovery journey: *delayed gratification.*

It's a step of faith in the dark, however. Remember that usually people don't see "the first gleam of dawn" right away. Imp saw an easy path and a hard path. He imagined that the easy path would lead him to the high country's lush pastures, cold spring waters, and breathtaking views of mountaintops and valleys. After all, everybody before him seemed to have taken that path. What Imp didn't know was that the broad path actually led to a barren wasteland. Though its fields were green in the spring, they would soon be overgrazed by the multitude of sheep and fried to a golden brown by the hot summer sun. It was the narrow path that led to the unseen high country.

There are many examples of the broad path and its appeal. A line of cocaine will make you feel good fast. A sexual encounter will help you feel loved and not alone. A dozen cookies will numb out your depression. A night in front of the television will distract you from internal anxieties and put you to sleep. Even some seemingly good deeds are part of a deceptive broad path: a ten-hour day of hard work and a job well done will help you feel adequate; a day full of errands or projects will make your life seem significant; and a meticulously clean house will help you feel like your internal world isn't really such a mess.

Consider other broad roads you may travel. Giving to someone who is needy will relieve your guilt. Gossiping with a friend will hide your awkward feelings of not connecting and will create an instant sense of closeness between the two of you. Getting on a soapbox to criticize the "other side" who is wrong will discharge some of your anger. More knowledge and insights will help you to feel in control and to detach from messy, painful feelings inside. The list could go on and on. The temptation most days is for us to take one of these easy paths, which is not the best path.

Perhaps you're asking, "What's wrong with the easy path? Some of those examples don't seem so bad." The problem is that *the broad path is a lie.* It promises to give you what you need by offering love, esteem, peace, intimacy, and other good things, but it doesn't deliver.

Oh, the broad path does deliver some sort of pleasure or gratification of an impulse. And it delivers the freedom to escape from internal discomforts. But a huge fishhook hides inside that tasty bait. The pleasure is fleeting, and so is the escape from discomfort; you'll need to go back for more again and again. Before you know it you may be addicted.

When you go down the broad path you're neglecting to process and understand your feelings and to think about what is truly good for you *before* you act. You're reacting out of an impulse rather than responding out of a need. You're choosing comfort in the short term over growth in the long term.

Jesus pointed out that relatively few people follow His example and walk the narrow path in life.[3] Those on it are walking one step at a time through their life's struggles, seeking to deny selfish gratifications.[4] The narrow path involves distinguishing between needs and impulses and between wants that are good for you and wants that are not. As you retrieve unconscious feelings, you can understand how you feel and what you need. This requires continually asking for what you need and continually seeking for what is good for you, instead of seeking selfish gratifications that can never satisfy.[5] It's the path of the upright who see where they're going and give thought to their ways so that they "act out of knowledge."[6]

Personal Reflections

1. "We all, like sheep, have gone astray, each of us has turned to his own way," Isaiah wrote.[7] We're all like Imp in some ways. That's because delayed gratification is not a naturally human characteristic. We instinctively choose the path of ease and pleasure, not the path of difficult growth and painful recovery. Which of the following broad path examples are temptations for you?

☐ Abusing alcohol or drugs

☐ Overeating

☐ Overworking

☐ Perfectionistic cleaning

☐ Venting anger

☐ Zoning out with the TV

☐ Sexual indiscretions

☐ Overbusyness

☐ Intellectualizing feelings

☐ Gossiping

2. This week try to become aware of the feelings or issues that can quickly influence you when you encounter a fork in the path. From the list below identify what you feel just before you start prancing down the broad path. Begin to monitor these feelings so that you can follow Imp's example of thinking before you act and listening to your Shepherd's guidance.

- depressed
- insecure
- needy
- lost
- hopeless
- anxious
- angry
- confused
- lonely
- unloved
- bad about yourself
- out of control

A Walk with Your Shepherd _____

3. Broad paths pretend to meet your needs, but really
don't. Look underneath your impulses and ask yourself,
"What is it that I really need?" Identifying your needs can
help you to overcome temptations to react to your impulses.
Listed below are some basic emotional needs. Set aside
some time this week to pray to God, asking for what you
need most right now.

- empathy
- joy
- guidance
- forgiveness
- significance
- respect

- strength
- affirmation
- peace
- security
- stability
- patience

- hope
- acceptance
- companionship
- encouragement
- discipline
- unconditional
  love

4. It's important that you identify the consequences of
your impulsiveness. Like Imp, we need to remember the sick
feeling in our stomachs when we drank from polluted potholes. This week consider the destructive consequences to
the broad paths you've walked down in the past.

5. Are you at any forks in the road this week? What decisions are you facing? Those decisions are like gates that
open to one path or the other. Consider Jesus' words: "I am
the gate for the sheep. . . . Whoever enters through me will
be saved. He will come in and go out, and find pasture. The
thief comes only to steal and kill and destroy; I have come
that they may have life, and have it to the full."[8] Ask God to
help you make decisions that are good for you.

142

WEEK 20
The Path That Seems Right

"He guides me in paths of righteousness for His name's sake."

Psalm 23:3*b*

Doody was a sheep devoted to doing what he thought his shepherd wanted him to do. He stayed on the path, following close to Good Shepherd; there was no worry about his wandering impulsively down a broad path. He lived up to his nickname, "Do-do," as he was quick to busy himself by doing things for other sheep: comforting the troubled, helping the wanderers stay on the path, and doing anything else that could help Good Shepherd. Doody seemed to be on the right path. He appeared to be the model sheep.

But Doody was missing something. He was so busy trying to do everything he could to please Good Shepherd and help the other sheep that he neglected to enjoy the journey. He was missing out on the shepherd's goodness. He was working so hard he didn't have time to sing and dance and play with the other sheep who were reciting Good Shepherd's spring song. Doody didn't see the grandeur of the trees, nor did he feel the warmth of the morning sun overtaking the chill of the night, nor did he stop to smell the fragrant and beautiful wild flowers along the way. Doody's senses were dulled because he had neglected them for so long.

What Doody didn't know was that, if he would just open himself to enjoying Good Shepherd's love and the beauty of the journey, he would have joy instead of tiredness as he helped Good Shepherd. Instead of serving out of duty and obligation he would serve because he wanted to. Instead of trying to give to others what he wished he had received, he

143

would give to others so that they could enjoy what he was already enjoying. Doody needed to have his senses awakened so that he could enjoy the journey.

We all want to enjoy our lives and to appreciate goodness and beauty. Yet many of us do not. Doody's senses were dulled for the same reason that the senses of all obsessive-compulsive people are dulled: they lose themselves in a world of thoughts and activity in order to avoid painful feelings.

Sharon is the mother of three children and an attorney. She strives to be a loving mother and a good wife and to maintain an immaculate home. She works long, hard hours representing her clients as best she can. She also has dedicated herself to serve God and is active in speaking to women's groups and helping in various church ministries. Clearly she is a very busy woman.

"I don't know how you can keep this pace!" I told her one day.

"Well, you know that 'idleness is the devil's workshop,' " she replied simply.

It's true that she was busy doing "good" things. What she didn't know, however, was that the good is always enemy of the best, the urgent the enemy of the important, and busyness is just as much the devil's workshop as idleness.

My friend was on the path to burnout. She couldn't keep doing all that she "should" and neglecting her needs for things like rest, play, and relationship. It would catch up to her. Underneath her outward life, which was so full of activity, was an empty soul. Sharon was detached from her feelings—her senses were dull, which is the way she wanted it! She wanted it that way because in spite of her confident appearance she felt inadequate inside. She was driven to do all that she did to prove that she was significant. She needed other people to need her so that she could feel important and so that she could "lose herself" in helping them. That way she wouldn't feel the depressing emptiness and deflating inadequacy that lodged in her soul.

Even Sharon's Christianity was dead. She was like the legalistic Pharisees and teachers of the law in Jesus' day who kept the commandments to the minutest detail. They prided themselves in doing all that they should but didn't realize that they were "straining a gnat and swallowing a camel"; in their rigid adherence to the law they missed the whole point of the law, which is to show us our need for God's forgiving grace.[9] They cleaned the outside of the cup and dish but not the inside; their lives looked good on the outside but their hearts were full of pride, greed, jealousy, and other unconfessed sins. They covered up the emptiness and deadness of their spirituality with self-righteous acts.[10']

Like Doody, Sharon, and the biblical Pharisees, Do-Gooders have no idea what it means to "process feelings" and to "work through emotional issues." Usually their feelings are unconscious. From time to time, if they dare to slow down, do-gooders may feel the _guilt_ that pushes them forward and forward, the _resentment_ of giving help that is not appreciated, the _inadequacy_ that must be overcome, or the _nervous energy_ that won't let them slow down. Sometimes they recognize the depressing and empty feeling that pushes them "back to work." But they don't feel their feelings very deeply or for very long before their internal taskmaster yanks them around the neck from behind and pushes them back into doing all they should. Although they are enslaved to this taskmaster, they are grateful that he distracts them from uncomfortable and unwanted feelings inside. And besides, they can take pride in all that they "do-do."

As you can see, there are problems with this rigidly narrow path, which at first glance seemed right. Indeed, according to the old proverb, "there is a way that seems right to a man, but in the end it leads to death."[11] Your feelings, which are such an important part of who you are on the inside, get

145

ignored on this path of life. Yet they are what's driving you into an overcommitted lifestyle that destroys intimacy, fun, and rest and motivates you out of "shoulds" instead of love and grace. This actually is a lot of "doo doo!"

The only way out of this lifestyle is to make a drastic change. Obviously this includes working less hours and not helping as many people. But it also means getting out of the think-do mode, where you just do what you think you should. Instead you must enter a feel-think-do mode. Take the time and energy to slow down and attend to your feelings, wants, and needs, reflect on their meaning, and then do.

During the initial period you will experience the uncomfortable feelings that you have been flushing into your soul as if it were a toilet. As you persevere, however, you will begin to discover a whole new life. My attorney friend Sharon did just that. In addition to feeling tears and fears, insecurities and angry feelings, she was learning how to play and have fun with her children, to experience romantic moments with her husband, to receive from God without doing anything, and to work because she wanted to, not because she had to.

Personal Reflections

1. This week consider the prophet Isaiah's words "Our righteous acts are like filthy rags."[12] Then meditate on Colossians 2:20–3:4, where the apostle Paul expanded on this principle. He exhorted the Christians in Colosse to set aside all their rules and regulations and their disciplined life of doing all they "should" and instead to focus their minds and hearts on all that God has done graciously for them in Christ.

Do you sometimes "do what you should" as a means to serve God?

2. Do you identify with Doody and Sharon? Does your lifestyle sometimes fit that of a "Do-Gooder"? Take some time to reflect on the feelings that Do-Gooders neglect to process. Note any of the feelings that push you to work harder, help more, or do better. This week, instead of reacting this way, try to respond to your emotional needs.

☐ Guilt, which pushes you to give more and more
☐ Resentment of giving so much that isn't appreciated
☐ Inadequacy, which drives you to work harder and harder
☐ Nervous energy, which won't let you slow down
☐ Depression or emptiness, which you avoid by going back to work

3. Some day this week set aside time to identify your "shoulds." Write down three things that you feel you "should do" even though you're not sure you really want to do them.

I should _____

_____

I should _____

_____

I should _____

_____

4. Later this week visit a park, forest preserve, or some other setting in which you're surrounded by God's creation. Pray that God would awaken your senses to all that is around you. Walk through God's creation and one at a time focus on each of your senses: look at the grandeur of the trees, touch a flower or a running stream, listen to a squirrel scamper, fill

your lungs by breathing in through your nose and smelling, put a blade of grass in your mouth and taste it. As you do these things, tune your spiritual ear by listening to what God has to teach you. As you return home, pray that God would help you to remember this experience as a metaphor for experiencing your life. Then during the rest of the week practice experiencing and taking in God's goodness at home, at work, at play, and in church.

5. Some time this week observe a young child at play and prayerfully reflect on Jesus' words "Unless you change and become like children, you will never enter the kingdom of heaven."[13] You may have regular contact with a young child; otherwise get together with a relative or a friend, or simply visit a nearby playground. Note how free children are to play, discover new things, and enjoy what they're doing.

WEEK 21

Getting Out of the Rut

"He guides me in paths of righteousness for His name's sake."
Psalm 23:3*b*

Overgrazing destroys a pasture. If a flock of sheep continually grazes and regrazes the same pasture, the area will wear out and become unproductive. Some sheep who are tended by careless shepherds literally wear ruts into the ground as they walk back and forth in search of forage. With time sheep trails erode into deeper gullies that fill with urine, feces, and stagnant water. What was once a lush green pasture can turn into a toxic waste dump if the sheep aren't tended by a shepherd.

For this reason Good Shepherd planned a careful rotation of pastures for his sheep to graze on. He planned ahead and kept his sheep on the move from one pasture to another. He didn't let his sheep get stuck in one pasture, wandering in circles, ruining the land that was their sustenance.

As it is with sheep so it is with people. If you're not taking steps forward to work through your emotional struggles then you're probably being carried backwards by those same struggles. Your unresolved issues quickly generate repeating patterns in which your history repeats itself again and again until you find yourself "stuck in a rut."

Jack's life affirmed the truth of the proverb "As a dog returns to its vomit, so a fool repeats his folly."[14] He walked into my office even looking like a dog with his tail between his legs. When he sat down he dropped his head and mumbled, "I'm so discouraged. My marriage just isn't working—but I don't want to go through another divorce."

After hearing descriptions of Jack's three marriages and his childhood, I knew that Jack was stuck in a foolish rut. He was an adult child of an alcoholic mother, and all three of his wives were addicted to something. His first wife was a religious addict who detached herself from her many troubles by absorbing herself in Bible reading and church work. His second wife was an overeater who ate to cope with stress. His third wife was an alcoholic who, just like his mother, drank when she was depressed.

Looking at Jack, his head still dropped in discouragement, I commented, "You're still trying to rescue your mother!"

His head shot up. "What do you mean?"

"Your mother was an alcoholic. You married a religious addict, then an overeater, and now an alcoholic," I explained. "You've spent your life trying to connect with and take care of needy women."

Jack's eyes lit up and he said, "I guess you're right. I do have a need to take care of troubled women and to help them manage their lives. It makes me feel strong and confident and helps me forget about my own problems. But maybe it's a false sense of strength because inside I feel lonely and inadequate."

Jack started to find his way out of the rut of continually getting into unhealthy relationships with addicts and other dysfunctional people when he made a concentrated effort to look at his own issues of emotional detachment, lack of intimacy, and self-esteem problems. He addressed the anger and pain still remaining from his relationship with his alcoholic mother, and he began the forgiveness process. He became more in touch with his feelings, learned how to relate effectively with other people, and began to esteem himself. As a result, he was able to break the repeating pattern of entering codependent relationships.

The narrow path has no ruts, for few people walk that path. But the broad path, so heavily traveled, contains a deep rut that's hard not to fall into and equally difficult to escape. It's the easier and more tempting route. Fortunately, God is faithful, and when you feel tempted go back to that past behavior or feel that you can't get out of a situation He provides you with a "way out so that you can stand up under the temptation."[15]

An important ingredient in the way out is truth. In order to avoid being revisited by past problems and temptations you need to deal with your past. Past patterns repeat until they are honestly addressed.

Although God certainly forgives our past sins and encourages us to forget our past sinful ways, he doesn't mean for you to pretend that you don't have a painful history, nor for you to neglect to learn lessons from your past. Imp demonstrated the wisdom we need (and avoided the plight of the dog who re-eats his vomit only to throw it up again) when he remembered his past impulsive mistake of drinking the contaminated water and turned off of the broad path and onto the narrow path. We need such wisdom too.

Personal Reflections

1. Usually I hear people say, "Why bring up the past?" What do you think? Is it helpful and worthwhile to review your history and identify repeating patterns in your life? Do current feelings about past events need to be experienced, understood, and resolved or should they just be forgotten, intellectualized, or in some other way banished into the dark storehouse of your unconscious?

2. Are you stuck in a rut you can't seem to escape? This week consider a defect of character or a shortcoming you are stuck in and want God to help you out of. Which of the following do you struggle with?

☐ Codependency
☐ Isolation
☐ Impulsiveness
☐ Emotional detachment
☐ Unresolved anger
☐ Anxiety

☐ A critical spirit
☐ Low self-esteem
☐ Perfectionism
☐ A compulsive behavior
☐ Depression
☐ Relationship problems

☐ Fear of being assertive to express your needs or wants
☐ Needs to please other people even at your own expense
☐ Another issue _____

3. Consider the items you have checked above. You may have some repeating patterns from your past. Write down when it was that you struggled with any of these before. Note the types of situations and circumstances in which the issue(s) was a problem.

_____

_____

_____

4. One day this week set aside some time to reflect on your past. What forks in the road have you encountered? Which paths did you go down? To help you with this you might get out old photo albums or reminisce with a friend or a family member.

Sing a New Song

> "He guides me in paths of righ-
> teousness for His name's sake."
>
> Psalm 23:3*b*

Good Shepherd seized the moment of spring and sang out a new song to his sheep:

> *Hey, hey! Spring is in the air, I say!*
> *My darlings, it's a new day.*
> *So let us hop, skip, and play.*
> *We will take a new path today.*
> *Come with me, this is the way!*

His song reflected his enthusiasm for life, his appreciation for the beauty of creation, his anticipation of taking a new path, and his freedom to enjoy life.

Some of the sheep were singing and dancing with Good Shepherd even as they climbed the windy, narrow, rocky path. They found laughter even in the midst of their stress. But there was no fun for Doody on his path; he missed having Good Shepherd's joy because he was so busy doing all he should. Imp too would have missed out on the fun had he not heard Good Shepherd's voice from behind, calling him back. Little Timi also would have missed the merry ride on Good Shepherd's shoulders if she hadn't faced her fears and headed toward the high country.

For each of these sheep Good Shepherd had something new in store. It was time for a new beginning. Time for Doody to stop doing and start enjoying. Time for Imp to resist gratifying his impulses and think about what would be truly good for him. Time for Timi to face her fears of the valley ahead and press on to discover the wonder of the high country beyond.

Recovery from the effects of a painful past is really another way of saying, "It's time for a new beginning!" No matter what the pains and struggles of your past, nothing appeals more than heading off in a new direction and finding healing for past hurts and beginning to change past destructive patterns.

Yes, change is painful, but it is also wonderful. There's the delight of beginning to have hopes fulfilled and needs being met. There's excitement in discovering new truths about yourself, others, God, and life. There's richness in becoming alive emotionally and experiencing more joy in your life. There's satisfaction in gaining self-control over your compulsive behaviors. And there is peace as you learn to be patient with the process. The freedom to be yourself during the recovery process comes as you encounter God's forgiving grace.

The more you experience the fulfillment of these joys the easier it is to delay gratification when you get to the junction in the path and say no to the pleasures and ease of the broad paths and say yes to the challenges of the narrow path.

Have you looked at your journey this way? If there isn't freedom to laugh and play and hope along the path of change and growth—as painful and difficult as that path is—then you won't get very far along. Truly, "the joy of the Lord is our strength"[16] when it comes to the journey of recovery. The joy of arriving at the beauty and wonder of the high country keeps us persevering on the path through the valley and up the mountain path. The only way to endure suffering and difficulty is when there is also the freedom to rejoice. Moments of spontaneous and unexplainable joy on the path of recovery are like interludes of repose that encourage us to keep going.

I'll never forget the day I was driving down a country road with an orange grove to my right and fields of strawberries to my left. I was reflecting on some sad feelings when I suddenly burst out into spontaneous laughter and started hitting my hand wildly on the steering wheel as I laughed to myself: *I'm depressed, but it's OK for me to feel that way! I'm sad about some things I need to work through, but I won't be sad forever!*

The reason I'll never forget that day is because I didn't use to give myself the freedom to feel what I felt, much less laugh about a struggle. I used to literally "work through" my issues, with the emphasis on *work*. It was delightful to realize that I could find enjoyment in the working-through process.

Perhaps it's because of my own transformation in this area that I get a special thrill when these kinds of joyous moments occur as interludes for my clients in their journeys of working through painful issues in therapy. Sometimes they feel guilty about it, as though they shouldn't enjoy their therapy because it's supposed to be hard work. But what they learn is that the laughter of a cheerful heart is good medicine for the soul,[17] and it breaks up the long, hard journey of recovery.

The challenge of recovery is in finding a balance between facing the reality of your painful struggles and seeing the blessings along the way. The twenty-third Psalm has a way of helping us find this balance, as it is at once an arduous and painful journey and also a delightful balm of repose. Therefore, it should come as no surprise that David, the author of this psalm, developed a nice balance in his own life between pain and praise. He carried a spear and a harp with him in his own life's journey. He also carried stylus and tablet to record his experiences—both bad or good—along the way.

In Psalms we read about David's own journey of recovery. There are psalms of joyous praise and happy thanksgiving as well as psalms of agonizing despair, angry complaints, fearful ruminations, and unmet longings. Psalms of victory and progress mingle with psalms of defeat and failure. In David's day all psalms were recited and sung in the community. Most of today's communities of faith wouldn't dare to sing out the painful psalms! But David did. And he had a way of holding onto hope, love, faith, and even joy despite being in the midst of suffering, and he did this without denying or repressing his pain. His faith was honest in addressing life's struggles and injustices, and it was also free to enjoy the goodness of God.

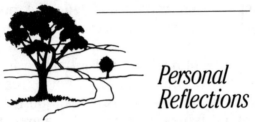

Personal Reflections

1. Perhaps you are in need of a new beginning. What are some things that you would like to put behind you? Write these down in a psalm of petition.

2. This week "sing to the Lord a new song!"[18] As the apostle James said, when we're happy we can sing a song of praise to God.[19] Take some time to write a psalm of thanksgiving for the things that you're thankful for. Praise God for these things.

3. One day this week read Psalm 69. Note how David expresses feelings of being overwhelmed, depressed, ashamed, rejected, afraid, stuck, alone, helpless, angry, and distressed (verses 1-29). Yet, he also sings to God, gives Him praise, glory, and thanksgiving, and has faith that God will hear him and deliver him (verses 30-36). Follow David's example and write a psalm like this in which you sing out of your pain.

4. Some time in the next few days get together with a friend who is also participating in a recovery or growth process. (If you can find someone who has a long face about his

recovery, then it'd be all the better!) Speak to your friend in psalms, hymns, and spiritual songs and encourage him or her to do the same for you.[20] If you have trouble making up your own, then turn to Psalms. Share one psalm of praise that seems appropriate. Also try to find a psalm of pain that expresses some of the feelings that you're struggling with and recite this to your friend.

NOTES

1. 1 John 1:5, 7.
2. Proverbs 4:18.
3. Matthew 7:13-14.
4. Luke 9:23.
5. Matthew 7:7-12.
6. Proverbs 21:29; 13:16.
7. Isaiah 53:6.
8. John 10:7-10.
9. Matthew 23:24.
10. Luke 11:39; Matthew 23:27.
11. Proverbs 16:25; 14:2.
12. Isaiah 64:6.
13. Matthew 18:2-3.
14. Proverbs 26:11.
15. 1 Corinthians 10:12-13.
16. Nehemiah 8:10.
17. Proverbs 17:22.
18. Psalm 98:1.
19. James 5:13.
20. Ephesians 5:19-20.

"Were entirely ready to have God remove all these defects of character. Humbly asked Him to remove our shortcomings."

STEPS 6 and 7,
Alcoholics Anonymous' Twelve Steps

"Even though I walk through the valley of the shadow of death, I will fear no evil, for you are with me."

Psalm 23:4a

STEP 6

Perseverance

The narrow path wound to the left and up a bluff. The sheep seemed to pant in unison as they slowly followed the shepherd.

"Come, my children!" Good Shepherd said, and he slowed his pace only slightly. At the top of the bluff he and his sheep stopped and looked ahead. "Oh yes, here we are. It is lovely, isn't it?"

Below them lay the Valley of the Shadow of Death. Its floor, a deep, dark green, contrasted sharply with the brilliant white snow-capped mountains that rose above it on all sides. The steep mountains dropped sharply into the valley, creating the look of a shallow canyon. A crystal-clear blue stream divided the valley and sparkled with reflected rays of sunlight.

"What a wonderful sight!" Good Shepherd exclaimed. The sheep had been hiking along the narrow path for many hours, withstanding the hot sun and holding back their appetite, waiting and waiting for the sight of water and pasture. Now their cries stopped, half in awe, half in fatigue.

Once the flock entered the valley, however, their voices rose again, this time with great expectations. Sheep were chattering back and forth, excited about the respite to come. Older rams and ewes were telling the young lambs story after story about the famed valley. The vivid "can you top this?" stories slowly changed into less exciting, more terrifying "watch out!" warnings.

The change in mood was amplified by an abrupt change in the weather, typical of this valley. Dark storm clouds blew in and suddenly overtook the sunny blue skies. The temperature dropped quickly, and a chill filled the air. The wind picked up speed and made increasingly loud howling, whistling sounds as it swirled through ravines and trees.

The flock scurried for shelter, trying to beat the storm. No one felt hungry anymore, just afraid. Little Timi was terrified. Her little legs could hardly keep up with the rest of the sheep. Rams and ewes were passing her right and left in the frenzy to find shelter. She didn't know where everyone was going. And she couldn't get her mind off the last story about the big, black, hungry bear!

Suddenly, a shadow fell across her path and danced back and forth. Timi's heart fell into her stomach, and she gasped. "It's the hungry bear! He's after me!"

Just then a trio of sibling sheep, the Doubters, approached Timi. They had been trailing the flock ever since the sheep left the home ranch. They were not part of Good Shepherd's sheepfold but tended to "hang out" on the outskirts of the flock. He had invited them to join his sheep in the past, but they had doubted his sincerity.

As was their forte, they now seized on the negativity of the situation and pounced on Timi like three little demons fanning the flames of her fears of the unknown. The oldest, Pessamissi Doubter, gently but firmly went on and on to Timi. "You could never outrun a bear! You can't get away from a hungry bear!"

Pessamissi's brothers, Skep and Critter, were less gentle than their sister. Skep, in his usual skeptical frame of mind, told Timi, "The flock is going to leave you behind. You'll never make it to the shelter." With a critical tone Critter added, "If you didn't walk so slow maybe you could keep up with the others!"

Timi's fears overtook her to the point of tears. "Oh, Pessy's right!" she sobbed. She fell in a heap, crying. At this point the Doubters felt guilty and began to pity poor little Timi. Pessamissi spoke for the clan and said, "Oh, Timi, don't cry. That'll just make things worse. We didn't mean to hurt you. We were just pointing out the difficulties here. This is such a horrible situation—not just for you but for us too! We'll all get caught in this storm! We'll probably die here! I don't know why we even entered the Valley of the Shadow of Death! Why does your shepherd always lead his sheep through here? The other flocks don't take this path."

Timi had tried to bury her head in the grass and not even listen, but she could not shut out the words of doubt. The more she heard the more she cried. She felt abandoned and lost. Pessamissi's words were like a broken record spinning around in her mind, "We'll die here! We'll die here! We'll die here!" Timi mumbled under her breath, "Why *did* Shepherd take me here anyway? I left home and followed him. Now he's left me behind—forgotten me. I'll never get back home!"

Meanwhile the storm was quickly overtaking them. A bolt of lightning momentarily brightened the darkening valley. No sooner did the darkness recover when thunder cracked and rain started pouring down.

Good Shepherd and the rest of the sheep were getting soaked. Quickly, they reached the edge of the near mountain and ducked underneath a wide overhang of rocks. The trees just outside the cave made a nice windbreak. Boulders and brush at the cave's opening formed a fence that almost closed out the circle. They had a natural sheepfold!

Good Shepherd was still settling the sheep when he realized that Timi was missing. Immediately, he ran out into the rain. He ran only fifty yards when he found Timi and the Doubters huddled in the wet grass. Seething with anger, Good Shepherd reprimanded the Doubters.

"Why did you do this to Timi? You skeptics and doubters! You hang on the outskirts, never joining the flock because of all your negativity and fault-finding. And then you prey upon this poor lamb's fears! C'mon, little Timi. I have a warm, dry, and safe place for you."

Good Shepherd picked up Timi and quickly headed for the shelter. Timi was shaking and shivering, partly from cold, partly from fear. She looked up at her shepherd and stammered out, "I'm—I'm so-so sc-sc-aaared! I-I d-don't like th-this v-v-val-ley at all! Can't we g-g-go back ho-home?"

Once underneath the shelter, Good Shepherd sat down with trembling Timi and put her in his lap. He rubbed and rubbed her wet, chilled body to dry and warm her. Looking into Timi's scared eyes he reassured her. "I'm glad you're here with me now."

Then pointing toward the tree that had cast the dancing shadow across Timi's path, Good Shepherd said to Timi, "See that big tree out there blowing in the wind?" Timi nodded. "That tree makes a shadow that looks just like a big black bear! And look just to the left of the tree. See the Doubters? They're soaking wet and freezing in the rain because they don't have faith. Stay close to me on our journey through the Valley of the Shadow of Death, and I'll help you to face your fears and doubts. I know it's hard for you to understand now, but when we get to the high country you'll look back on this stormy night and feel that it was worth going through."

Timi's rapidly beating heart gradually calmed as she listened to Good Shepherd's soothing voice and felt the warmth of his rubbing her body. She snuggled into his lap and listened to the pitter-patter of the rain, which eventually put her to sleep.

Good Shepherd had positioned himself so that he was lying across the opening to the sheepfold. On his sides were boulders and brush. In front of him his sheep slept peacefully underneath the rocks jutting out from the mountain. Behind him was the dark, stormy valley. As usual, he slept with one eye open and one ear alert. His right hand rested on his rod at his side.

WEEK 23

What's Lurking in the Shadows?

"Even though I walk through
the valley of the shadow of
death I will fear no evil,
for you are with me."

Psalm 23:4*a*

The Valley of the Shadow of Death is a scary place for the sheep. The days there are shortened and darkened by long shadows, as the sun rises late and sets early in the valley encircled by mountains. These shadows have an eerie feel of death in them. That's because the sheep are hemmed in by mountains on all sides. They are trapped; there is literally nowhere to run or hide. They're at the mercy of storms that can unleash flash floods and predators that can easily overtake the defenseless sheep.

Timi was especially anxious about being in the valley. Even before she entered the valley, she remembered the scary stories that the older sheep told her. Then came the thunderstorm and her struggle to keep pace with the flock as they scurried for shelter. Then there was the dancing shadow of a hungry bear! And thanks to the Doubters she was afraid she had been abandoned in the rain by Good Shepherd.

Her fears of the unknown and of worst-case scenarios grew until she couldn't persevere and go on anymore; she fell to the ground crying and trembling. She tried to shut her ears and keep from hearing the Doubters' negative thoughts, but their words stayed in her mind because she agreed with them. She didn't calm down until Good Shepherd helped her out of her anxious state by comforting her with his peaceful presence. She appreciated how he helped her to turn her anxiousness into specific fears and doubts that she could face.

Anxiousness is a common symptom that pushes people into recovery. Anxiety can be debilitating, yet it tends to be so vague and pervasive that many people find it difficult to articulate clearly what it feels like. Anxiety often means feeling the pressures of expectations to measure up to, commitments to keep, unfamiliar situations to deal with, unresolved interpersonal conflicts to face, or simply squeezing lots of things into a little time. Anxiety becomes particularly troublesome if you lack the internal resources to cope with the stress. Instead of acknowledging and processing your feelings of fear, anger, confusion, or shame, you try to ignore them and push them down into your unconscious. There they fester and grow.

Some people are so detached from their anxious feelings that they wouldn't even know they had a problem, except for their growing inability to continue normal life. They develop many symptoms of repressed anxiety, such as an ulcer, spastic colon, headaches, body pains, frequent sickness, panic attacks, compulsive behavior, phobias, avoidance of certain situations, irritability, racing thoughts, and nightmares. They may even experience "blanking out" spells, forgetfulness, or difficulty sleeping. Anxious people like this need to face whatever is lurking in the shadows of their unconscious mind. During anxiety, we feel the terrible tension of trying to push down (repress) feelings that want to come up.

Michael, a thirty-six-year-old salesman, told me that he became anxious whenever he had to give a presentation to a group of potential clients. Hiding in the shadows for Michael was the pressure of having his sense of self-worth hanging in the balance.

"You know, they have the power of the thumb over me," he explained one day. "My clients can give me a 'thumbs up' or a 'thumbs down,' based on what they think of my presentation." How Michael felt about himself as a person was wrapped up in his performance. We discovered that apart from his successes he didn't feel valuable. His anxiety was the result of his unconscious feelings of shame trying to find their way into consciousness by "pushing up" against his defense mechanisms, which were masking his feelings of shame.

A young woman named Cynthia told me she felt anxious whenever she talked to her mother on the phone. Lurking in the shadows was her discomfort with conflict and her anger. Her mother had control over her sense of well-being, as Cynthia felt good about herself only when her mother was happy with her. She expended tremendous amounts of energy trying to keep her mother from getting upset with her and trying to hide her own anger at her mother over being controlled by her. Her anxiety was the result of her unconscious fears of being abandoned by her mother and her unexpressed anger at her mother. Those fears and anger were trying to "push up" against her own tendencies to repress uncomfortable feelings.

As Timi learned from Good Shepherd, the cure for anxiety is to look at and recognize what is in the shadows. This is exactly what anxious people like Michael and Cynthia don't want to do. Their "cure" for anxiety is to repress it. That will work only a little while, until the anxious feelings accumulate and can be ignored no more.

Some people believe the apostle Paul's words "Do not be anxious about anything" mean that they shouldn't feel anxious. However, if you finish reading that verse you'll discover the plea "but in everything, by prayer and petition, with thanksgiving, present your requests to God."[1] That is anything but an injunction to repress your anxieties. Instead it is saying, "Feel all your anxieties, talk to God about what it is you're anxious about, and learn to trust Him to help you work through your uncomfortable feelings." Paul followed his own advice. He talked about how it felt to be persecuted, beaten, stoned, thrown in jail, shipwrecked, hungry, and in such situations he was often found praying to God.[2]

When we stop repressing our feelings and put the necessary time and energy into feeling what it is we're anxious about, God can guide us through His Holy Spirit. He seeks to help us grow emotionally and spiritually by gently pushing our unconscious feelings and issues up into our conscious minds. And when we face the unknown truths about ourselves that lurk in the shadows of our unconscious, our anxiety will begin to dissipate.

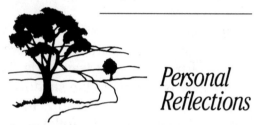

Personal Reflections

1. Do you experience any of the symptoms of repressed anxiety described in this week's reading? Put a check beside any that apply to you:

☐ Ulcer   ☐ Spastic colon   ☐ Headaches
☐ Frequent   ☐ Racing   ☐ Compulsive-
    sickness   thoughts   ness
☐ Phobias   ☐ Panic attacks   ☐ Irritability
☐ Nightmares   ☐ Forgetfulness   ☐ Body pains
☐ Difficulty sleeping

2. Sometime this week set aside a time for prayer. Pray Psalm 139:23: "Search me, O God and know my heart; test me and know my anxious thoughts." Take some time to be quiet and to listen. Then write down your anxious thoughts that the Holy Spirit is pushing out of the dark shadows of your unconscious mind into the light of your awareness.

3. When we are stressed out or going through a hard time, our shortcomings or character defects often emerge. How do you react when you're walking through the fears and difficulties of a valley? Check the responses below that apply to you.

☐ Lose your temper   ☐ Isolate from others
☐ Get depressed   ☐ Overeat
☐ Develop a fear or pho-   ☐ Become perfectionis-
    bia   tic
☐ Abuse a substance   ☐ Become workaholic

4. Set aside some time this week to reflect on your fears. Perhaps, like Timi, you're having trouble persevering due to anxiety. As Timi learned, the best way to deal with anxiety is to look at whatever is lurking in the shadows and scaring you. If you don't shed light on the shadows they may turn into attacking bears. Identify any of the following pressures you're facing.

☐ Dealing with someone's criticisms or negativity
☐ Measuring up to expectations at work or at home
☐ Entering an unfamiliar or new situation
☐ An unresolved conflict with someone
☐ Having too much to do in too little time
☐ Worrying about money, or a personal or family problem

5. Go to God in prayer and "cast all your anxiety on him because he cares for you."[3] Let this time of prayer become a shelter for you in the midst of the storm. Get into a comfortable chair and use the "palms up, palms down exercise." Prayerfully, consider each anxiety one at a time. Approach the altar of God with your palms up, figuratively carrying your burdens, and then turn your palms down to help you picture yourself releasing your burdens to God.

Through the Valley

"Even though I walk through
the valley of the shadow of
death, I will fear no evil,
for you are with me."

Psalm 23:4*a*

Believe it or not, the Valley of the Shadow of Death is the quickest and easiest route to the glorious high country where the sheep will graze for the hot summer months. The valley turns into the ridgeline path that leads directly to the top of Table Mountain. Good Shepherd knew from experience that the ridgeline was the most direct path and had a manageable grade for the sheep to climb. The valley is also a good route to Table Mountain because it offers the sheep lush green grass to eat and a running stream to drink.

For these sound reasons Good Shepherd chose this path for his sheep. However, the sheep did not understand these things. All they knew was that the path through the valley is long and dangerous and then turns steeper as it heads up the ridgeline. They tired from walking and climbing on the long, hard path, and they feared being surprised by a storm or a predator.

With prodding from the Doubters, Timi feared that she'd be left behind in the valley by Good Shepherd and would die in the freezing cold rain or be slaughtered by the big black bear. When Timi's fears overwhelmed her, the Doubters could only offer her pity, telling her they felt sorry for her and that she shouldn't cry. She was stuck in her fear until Good Shepherd retrieved her out of the rain and brought her to shelter, where he dried and warmed her wet, chilled body.

Good Shepherd really was with Timi in the valley, for he understood her fears and helped her face them. Timi was able to persevere because she trusted that her shepherd was with her, would stay with her, and was leading her to a good place.

Like Timi we need help to persevere in our recovery through pain and difficulty. We need a shepherd who is compassionate with us, who will feel our struggle with us and offer us the comfort and encouragement we need. That kind of shepherd is hard to find!

It's easy to find people like the Doubters who will pity you, feel sorry for you, and acknowledge what a horrible situation you're in, yet won't share in your pain. Other people will share in your pain, even to the point of getting lost in it with you, but are unable to help give you the encouragement and strength you need to work through your difficulty. Some people will try to rescue you from your difficulties by giving you answers, advice, or trying to do for you what you need to do for yourself. None of these helpers are truly helpful. When you're in a valley of the shadow of death you need someone to be with you in your struggle and to encourage and strengthen you so that you can persevere through to the other side.

Perseverance and working through painful struggles are not natural traits for most people. Many of us manage our lives by insisting on such things as instant coffee, microwaves, fast food restaurants, fax machines, express mail, car phones, answering machines, one-day dry cleaners, one-hour photo developing, news briefs, and instant bank tellers. We also want aspirins, antacids, "miracle cure" seminars, how-to-have-it-now books, and maintenance-free relationships. We want what we want *now*. And we want it easy. We don't want to work for it or struggle through it. If it takes work we want someone else to do it.

The "instant coffee approach" to emotional and spiritual growth just doesn't work. "The path of life leads upwards for the wise."[4] Growth is a long and difficult uphill climb. It requires perseverance, struggle, working through, continual maintenance, trusting others who can help, not getting what you want when you want it, waiting and hoping, falling down and getting up again, making mistakes, learning by trial and error, and continuing one step at a time.

At this point you probably are not jumping up and down exclaiming, "I'm ready! Where I can I sign up for recovery!" Few are excited about this kind of growth. Only a masochist would be.

We don't naturally enjoy struggling. So why do the writers of Scripture again and again say things like, "Consider it pure joy, my brothers, whenever you face trials of many kinds."[5] I know of only two good reasons to rejoice in suffering. And to be honest they're usually not good enough to cause anyone to feel happy while he is hurting.

The first reason is that persevering through difficulty improves our character.[6] During hardship we can see our defects of character and humbly ask our shepherd to remove our shortcomings. There's no quicker or better path to learning and growing than to go through the valley and study ourselves in the "school of suffering." Through this painful process we become better, healthier, and stronger people. That outcome eventually will feel good for you, and it also means you will have more to give to others.[7]

Second, when you've been through a period of suffering you come out of it with a renewed appreciation for and enjoyment of life and all the little things that you otherwise take for granted. It's like having a second chance at enjoying and appreciating life. These two reasons for enduring hardship can give you the hope that is an "anchor for your soul"[8] on the stormy, troubled seas of your life.

*Personal
Reflections*

1. Instead of comforting and encouraging Timi's faith, the Doubters only worsened her hurts and fears. This week consider how your friends and family respond to you when you're in a dark valley and hurting. Check any of the following statements that have been true of your experience.

☐ My friends are too busy and hurry past me.
☐ They offer me pity from a distance.
☐ They share in my feelings to the point of getting lost in them and have no strength or encouraging comfort to offer.
☐ My friends give me quick advice or easy answers.
☐ They try to rescue me.
☐ They offer blank expressions and a shrug of the shoulders.
☐ They show compassion (feels what you feel with you).
☐ They give encouragement (have strength and courage that empower you to go on).

2. If, like Timi, you've been sinned against when in a valley of need or difficulty then consider God's promise "It is mine to avenge; I will repay."[9] It's best to be angry when you are sinned against and then to release your anger to God and put your trust in His justice.

3. Are you tempted by "instant coffee approaches" to growth and recovery? Have you tried to get to the high country without going through the valley? Take some time this week to reflect on your history of attempts at emotional and

spiritual growth. Write down the easy answers that didn't work.

_____

_____

_____

4. Set aside some time in one of the next few days to meditate on Hebrews 12:1-3, which describes you as being in a relay race. Abraham, Moses, David, and others who trusted God have run before you and have passed the baton down the line to you. They are now part of the "great cloud of witnesses" who are cheering you on. In running your leg of the relay, fix your eyes on Jesus, who is ahead of you. He understands your struggles because He too ran a race with struggles in it and He can empower you to finish your race because He ran a perfect race.

5. In the passage above, the writer said that Jesus "for the joy set before him endured the cross." Take some time this week to consider the cross that you are carrying, a burden that you alone bear. Write down one or two of these crosses. Then think on what joy is set before you. What's the benefit to you in carrying this cross? What is God trying to teach you? In what ways is He changing you for the better?

_____

_____

_____

6. Meet with a friend (hopefully one who can be a compassionate and encouraging shepherd) and discuss your feelings about your cross and "the joy that is set before you."

WEEK 25

Is God Really with Me?

"Even though I walk through
the valley of the shadow of
death, I will fear no evil,
for you are with me."

Psalm 23:4*a*

Timi was afraid that Good Shepherd had abandoned her
in the Valley of the Shadow of Death. She thought she'd have
to face the big black bear and the thunderstorm on her own.
It seemed that her only companions were Pessamissi, Skep,
and Critter, and all they did was increase her fears and leave
her crying and trembling in the shadows with a cold rain
pouring down on her.

Timi hadn't yet developed a trust in Good Shepherd that
she could cling to even when she couldn't see him with her
eyes. She hadn't spent enough time with her shepherd, getting to know his love and letting him into her heart. She
hadn't yet internalized his caring presence in such a way as
to feel that he was with her in spirit even when he wasn't
physically next to her. Good Shepherd invited Timi to stay
right at his side through the valley so that she could begin to
understand his care for her. Then she would eventually be
able to persevere through difficulty even if he wasn't physically right at her side.

In this sense little lambs are a lot like little children. Out
of sight literally means out of mind. If mommy isn't visible to
her one-year-old baby, then to the baby mommy seems not
to even exist in that moment. Some of us have a childish
faith in this sense. We have trouble trusting that God is really
with us when things don't look right in our lives.

174

This was the case for Shirley. She was seeking recovery from the devastating effects of having been dropped in and yanked out of one bad foster home after another during her elementary school years. She would just start to bond with a parent, and then she'd feel abandoned again. In some homes, even the bonds were weak due to different kinds of abuse. Shirley was verbally criticized in one home, told she was an intrusion in another, and seemed never to please her foster parents in a third. In the final foster home her parents were so detached that they didn't even know she was drinking and smoking pot.

Because of those feelings of abandonment, Shirley could not develop relationships of trust or feel that people were being sincere. Consequently, when it came to feeling loved by people "out of sight was out of mind" for her—she doubted they cared when they were away from her. This was all the more true in her relationship with God.

In our relationship with an invisible God most of us share Shirley's distrust. God is invisible. That presents a difficult problem when it comes to internalizing and holding onto His love.

Ironically, while we're in a valley of the shadow and God seems farthest away, we most need God's hand to hold. That's why David chose this point in the Psalm 23 poem to change the pronouns referring to himself and God, respectively, from "me" and "he" to "I" and "you." Instead of speaking indirectly in the third person about his journey and his relationship with God, David now speaks personally with God, as though he's holding onto God's hand. "Even though _I_ walk through the valley of the shadow of death _I_ will fear no evil for _you_ are with me," David writes. Our valleys are meant to be times in which we experience intimate contact with God.

Again, it's in times of suffering and trial that we have the most difficulty feeling that God is with us. During one of his own journeys through a valley, David said, "How long, O

175

Lord? Will you forget me forever? How long will you hide your face from me? How long must I wrestle with my thoughts and every day have sorrow in my heart? How long will my enemy triumph over me?"[10]

Going through hardship and difficulty strengthens and improves our character as a furnace refines and purifies gold.[11] It is inevitable in such trials that at times we won't "see" God with us. At such times our faith necessarily draws upon our relational history, recalling people who gave us comfort and encouragement. If your bank account is low on love then your faith won't have much to draw upon when you really need it.

On the other hand, if in the past (or just recently) you have taken in God's love through others then you will have something to draw from. In addition, if you are a Christian you have the Holy Spirit, who gives inner peace and a filling of God's love.[12] Then the apostle Peter's words will apply to you also: "Even though you do not see him now [in this time of trial and suffering], you believe in him and are filled with an inexpressible and glorious joy, for you are receiving the goal of your faith, the salvation of your souls."[13]

What is the key to perseverance? Learning to "live by faith, not by sight" so that even in difficult times you can "see him who is invisible."[14] This means internalizing and holding onto God's compassion and encouragement so that even in hardship when you are full of doubts and feel all alone you can trust by faith that God is indeed with you.

Personal Reflections

1. This week consider my explanation that "walking by faith and not by sight" refers to a personal knowing that lets

you walk with God through difficulty because you draw upon previous experiences in which God's love has been "deposited" in you by others. Some people teach that "walking by faith and not by sight" means focusing on the promises of the Bible and ignoring your negative experiences until you get what you want. What do you think it means to "walk by faith and not by sight?"

_____

_____

2. Can you identify with how little Timi felt abandoned in the valley by the other sheep and her shepherd? Have you ever felt abandoned or unnoticed by a parent, friend, spouse, or God? Write down a time or two that you felt left out and describe what it felt like.

_____

_____

3. Perhaps as you look back on your childhood you realize that often your mother or father didn't notice or empathize with what you felt and needed as a child. Have you ever felt as if God didn't notice or empathize with your feelings or needs? On a scale of 1 to 10, with 10 being the highest, rate the degree to which you have felt that your mother, father, and God have understood and attended to your emotional needs.

Mother:	1	2	3	4	5	6	7	8	9	10
Father:	1	2	3	4	5	6	7	8	9	10
God:	1	2	3	4	5	6	7	8	9	10

4. As the shivering and trembling Timi sat in Good Shepherd's secure lap in the center of a protected sheepfold, she looked into her shepherd's compassionate eyes, listened to

his soothing voice against the dripping rain, felt him rubbing her back, and believed in his love for her. This week pray that God would help you to take in and hold onto His love for you.

5. Set aside some time to meditate on Psalm 13. Are you going through a struggle in which you feel similar to David? Using the following three components of David's psalm as an example, write your own psalm of distress to God.

    1. Express your troubled feelings to God (verses 1-2):

_____

_____

    2. Ask Him for what you need and want (verses 3-4):

_____

_____

    3. Make a statement of faith and thanksgiving regarding God's anticipated response (verses 5-6):

_____

_____

6. Later this week reflect on some of the trials of fire that have refined your faith. Write down one or two of the most difficult experiences you've persevered through. How did your faith and your character grow through that trial? For each trial write down how you grew or learned something important.

    1. _____

_____

    2. _____

_____

WEEK 26

When Evil Happens

> "Even though I walk through
> the valley of the shadow of
> death, I will fear no evil,
> for you are with me."
> Psalm 23:4*a*

Evil happened to Timi. She was sinned against by the Doubters. Their negativity and criticism amplified Timi's fears. Their pity left her alone and helpless. Their doubts in the shepherd's goodness led her to doubt too. Timi stayed far behind the flock and became stuck in the pouring rain. She could have been eaten alive by a bear, but fortunately the only bear around was in her imagination.

Timi was a typical sheep who was vulnerable to having bad things happen to her. This is reality. Sheep get lost in caves, become sick from contaminated water, fall down, hurt themselves, are hurt by other sheep, get stuck in the cold rain, and are attacked by predators.

So what does David mean when he says, "Even though I walk through the valley of the shadow of death *I will fear no evil*" (emphasis mine)? To answer this question we need to consider Jesus' words "I give [my sheep] eternal life, and they shall never perish; no one can snatch them out of my hand."[15] When we entrust our souls to Jesus He protects and nurtures our souls for eternity. But in the meantime our bodies, our feelings, and even our faith may be hurt. Like sheep we are vulnerable to being sinned against and injured. Evil things do happen to us, but we don't need to fear their happening to us because our souls—our real inner persons—are safe for eternity. And God can use the bad things that happen to us for the betterment and growth of our souls.

Of course, this is a difficult perspective to maintain when you've been the victim of evil. This was the case for Sandra, a survivor of incest who was beginning therapy. Tears came to my eyes when I heard her story of being molested between ages ten and twelve by her father, who was a minister. He would go into her room at night and read to her from the Bible, fondle her and have her fondle him, and then tell her she was dirty and needed to take a bath. Sandra's shame, confusion, and anger at her father were intertwined with her feelings toward God. The same father who talked about God and ministered to people in Jesus' name abused her sexually.

"Where was God when my father walked into my room with his Bible?" she asked me. "Why did God allow my father to abuse me?" The tears in my eyes were my only answer. From the beginning of time people of faith who suffer have asked this question: "How can a God who is all-loving, all-powerful, and always present allow evil to happen to innocent children and Christians who strive to serve Him?"

Three years after beginning therapy Sandra had a different perspective on what had happened to her. She was far enough along in her recovery that she was starting to notice some good things that came out of the evil events of her childhood. She had become a woman of very deep feeling: she knew what it felt to be in the depths of despair, to boil over with rage, to be terrified, and to feel helpless. She also knew what if felt to be understood, to feel valued, to be courageous, and to feel joy. She lived her life as though she'd just been let out of jail and had so many wonderful things to enjoy. Furthermore, she had an incredible sense of compassion for other hurting people and was finding a fulfillment in her work at a home for abused children.

I don't mean to suggest that Sandra would have gladly gone through it all over again. She still dealt with consequences from this abuse. For instance, she still had occasional bad feelings when making love to her husband.

Sometimes she still mistrusted older men. And she felt sad when she thought of what a dad should be compared to what her dad was to her.

Nevertheless, her greater compassion and newfound joy shows the biblical truth that "God causes all things to work together for good to those who love God."[16] Even though she'd been suffering outwardly for so long she was now beginning to be renewed inwardly by God.[17] (Sandra developed this perspective when she was advanced in her recovery, which was years after her abuse.) It's incomprehensible to our anguished and finite hearts, but God promises that at the end of time my friend will see that her traumatic and abusive experiences were like "light and momentary troubles" when compared with the "eternal glory" she will then be enjoying.[18]

Personal Reflections

1. Feeling abandoned, discouraged, and angry in the valley, Timi complained, "Why did Good Shepherd take me here anyway?" Have you ever been through a time of suffering that left you feeling angry at God and asking Him, "Why have You let this happen to me? Where are You?" Sometimes our anger at God is based on misperceptions of Him. Other times we just don't see how anything good could come out of a situation that feels all bad. In either case, it's helpful to be honest with your anger.

2. Maybe you wouldn't dare to get angry at God or to question Him. Set aside some time this week to read the book of Job in the Old Testament. Job was the most righteous man of his day, and yet God allowed Satan to ruin him financially, kill members of his family, afflict him with boils,

and entice Job's self-righteous "friends" to condemn and abandon him when he was in despair and suicidal. In chapter after chapter—in between brief moments of astounding expressions of faith and trust—Job questions God, argues with Him, complains to Him about the injustice of his suffering, and angrily demands that God appear and answer him. Although God did open Job's eyes to his limited understanding, He didn't condemn Job. Instead, God commended Job for his honesty and his faith in difficulty.[19] Job should be one of the all-time heroes of our faith because he clung to God—even if in anger—in the midst of horrendous suffering, unjust evils, and self-righteous condemnations from his "friends."

3. One psalm that speaks to those who have been victimized by evil is Psalm 10. Set aside some time to read and reflect on the angry feelings expressed in this psalm. Note how David confronts God for apparently hiding Himself in times of trouble and how he expresses to God his nger at his abusers, asking God to take vengeance.

4. Later this week when you can, write down one or two of the most hurtful ways in which you've been sinned against. Your enemy may even be a parent or a Christian. Using Psalm 10 as a model write your own angry psalm expressing your feelings to God.

_____

_____

5. When a friend of mine was suffering endlessly without healing or deliverance, I was quite distraught by some of the foolish responses that people had to her pain. I expressed these in the following poem. Have you thought some of these things when seeing someone suffer? Have other people responded to you in some of these ways when you were suffering?

The Nine Fools

"Life has to be fair,
You must have messed up.
What did you do to deserve this suffering?"
Said one undeserving fool.

"God has nothing to do with your suffering!
It is evil and always will be;
The devil just slipped behind God's back."
Said another ignorant fool.

"Where's your faith?
If you really believed God,
He'd surely heal you today!"
Said a third misbelieving fool.

"If God let you suffer
Then He's not a good and kind God.
I can't trust a God that allows such evil."
Said yet another doubting fool.

"I don't know why you're suffering,
But I'm glad it's not me!
It's so terrible I can't bear to look."
Said the most damnable fool of all.

"If only you'll pray harder
And beseech God until you get His attention.
Then He'll finally heal you!"
Said another pridefully pious fool.

"Just give up!
You're doomed to suffer forever;
There's no healing for you."
Said one more defeated fool.

"It's the devil's fault!
He alone is responsible for your suffering!
Just rebuke the devil and you'll be free!"
Said yet another simple-minded fool.

"You should enjoy your suffering.
It's a privilege, so ask God for more.
Then later you'll enjoy your reward."
Said the last, an ascetic fool.

Nine fools did stand up and preach
Before one wise person sat with the sufferer silently in tears.
Together they searched for meaning and waited for healing.
Under the cross with the suffering Christ they sat.

NOTES

1. Philippians 4:6.
2. For examples of Paul's talking to God or others about his anxieties and stresses, see Acts 16:22-25; 1 Corinthians 4:11-13; 2 Corinthians 1:8-11; 4:8-9; 11:23-30; 12:7-10; and Philippians 4:11-13.
3. 1 Peter 5:7.
4. Proverbs 15:24.
5. James 1:2.
6. Romans 5:1-5.
7. 2 Corinthians 1:3-5.
8. Hebrews 6:19 12.
9. Deuteronomy 32:35; Romans 12:19.
10. Psalm 13:1-2.
11. 1 Peter 1:6-7
12. John 14:25-27; Romans 5:5.
13. 1 Peter 1:8-9.
14. 2 Corinthians 5:7; Hebrews 11:27.
15. John 10:28.
16. Romans 8:28, *New American Standard Bible.*
17. 2 Corinthians 4:16.
18. 2 Corinthians 4:17.
19. Job 42:7*b*.

"Were entirely ready to have God remove all these defects of character. Humbly asked Him to remove our shortcomings. "

STEPS 6 and 7,
Alcoholics Anonymous' Twelve Steps

"Your rod...comforts me."

Psalm 23:4b

STEP 7

Boundaries

The rain fell steadily throughout the night, but the sheep slept undisturbed. Later the first rays of dawn peered over the far mountain range and landed on the glistening buds of a tree; they then touched Good Shepherd's cheek. He was still lying in the opening to the rough sheepfold he had found for shelter. Opening his eyes, he looked at his peacefully sleeping sheep. The storm had moved through the valley during the night and had left a fresh smell and a cool, comfortable dampness. The quiet, calm valley contrasted sharply to the sounds of thunder and pounding that had filled the night.

Suddenly, a stick cracked and a bird began chirping frantically, flapping her wings in a hasty departure. Good Shepherd instinctively turned to face the valley and grabbed the rod at his side. Then, just ten yards in front of him, a cougar jumped out of the brush. In a split second Good Shepherd hurled his rod and hit the cougar in the head and knocked him out cold. Then he ran to the cougar, drew his knife, and slew the predator.

The commotion had woken the sheep. Fear overwhelmed them as they watched Good Shepherd hurl his heavy rod. But Good Shepherd's quick slaying of the beast brought a sigh of relief, and calm gradually returned to the flock.

Good Shepherd decided it was time to lead his hungry sheep from the night's sheepfold to the pasture just beyond the valley brush. So he rounded them up and headed for the grassy meadow. Once they saw the green grass the hungry sheep all darted toward it. They began gobbling it up to fill their empty stomachs.

Wanda was grazing next to Lone and after a while noticed a field of beautiful wild flowers just beyond the area where they were grazing. Feeling rambunctious and mischievous, she whispered excitedly to Lone, "Look at those flowers! There's red, purple, blue, yellow and white! Let's sneak off and taste them. Let's run and play in the flowers! "

Lone frowned at Wanda. "I don't think we should do that."

"Oh, c'mon, Lone," Wanda pleaded. "Don't be a party pooper! It'll be so much fun! We'll come right back. We won't even be missed."

In the bat of an eyelid they were back to their old habits, wandering from the flock and losing sight of Good Shepherd. Together they frolicked in the flowers, biting at each other's ears, rubbing noses, smiling, dancing, and chasing each other in circles. Then, as if they were at a smorgasbord, they started to sample some of the different kinds of flowers laid out on the table of the valley. One at a time they began to sniff, lick, and bite at the various flowers.

Of course, Good Shepherd noticed Wanda and Lone playing in the flowers. They were only about fifty yards away. He was concerned because he knew that some of the flowers were poisonous. Quickly, he called after them, "Yee-dee-ohh-dee-dee-ollie! Wanda and Lone, come here!" Totally oblivious, the two sheep didn't even hear his sheep call. So he grabbed hold of his rod and hurled it toward them. The rod went whistling and tumbling as it cut through the air and then landed just three feet in front of Wanda's nose.

Wanda's and Lone's heads both flung up and their ears stood straight. "What was that!" Wanda screamed.

Wanda was about ready to bolt when Lone said, "Oh, that's Good Shepherd's rod. Listen, he's calling us. Let's go! We shouldn't have sneaked away."

When Wanda and Lone had rejoined the flock Good Shepherd pulled them aside. "You two have forgotten the lessons you learned about wandering away from me. Wanda, don't you remember the cave you got lost in? And Lone, don't you remember the coyote that almost ate you alive when you were grazing alone? Some of those flowers are poisonous and will make you very sick if you eat them. So stay here at my side and play close by me so I can protect you."

Then Good Shepherd led all the sheep toward the stream so they could drink. On the way he retrieved his trusted club. Once at the stream, Good Shepherd noticed that Jelly had flared up. She had been watching Wanda and Lone and was quite jealous of Wanda because she too was fond of Lone. Good Shepherd made eye contact with Wanda and then pointed at Jelly. Without words, he was warning her to be careful and to trust him.

Only moments later, Jelly went up to Wanda and picked a fight with her by kicking up dirt in her face. Wanda decided that she had had enough of Jelly's aggressiveness, so ignoring Good Shepherd's warning, she backed up and then rammed into Jelly with a strong head butt.

Good Shepherd quickly broke up the fight and swatted each of them on the bottom with his rod. He gently and carefully checked them both to see if they had injured each other.

Then he looked at them sternly and said, "You two need to learn to get along!"

Turning to Jelly he said, "Jelly, I think you forgot the lesson you learned at the quiet waters. Remember how you saw yourself through my eyes of love and had your shame washed away so that you saw yourself as worthwhile? You realized that you didn't need to have what Wanda and others had in order to be happy. I want you to think on these things so that you can get control of your jealousy problem."

Then, looking at Wanda, Good Shepherd said, "Wanda, you also have forgotten some lessons. Just a few minutes ago I told you that I would protect you. And remember how I protected you when Jelly tried to head butt you? Stay close to me and trust me to defend you. I know you're frustrated with Jelly, but you need to control your temper and let me deal with Jelly's behavior. "

As the sheep grazed the rest of that day, Lone, Wanda, and Jelly each thought about the things Good Shepherd said to them. They felt his loving concern for them and knew that these things were important.

Finding a Safe Place

"Your rod... comforts me."
Psalm 23:4*b*

The sheepfold at the side of the mountain was a safe place for the sheep. The mountain, boulders, and brush formed a horseshoe-shaped fence. Good Shepherd himself acted as the gate that closed off the sheepfold. He lay down in the opening at night so that the sheep couldn't get out and predators couldn't get in without going over his body. Right at his side he had his rod, the club that symbolized the shepherd's strong protection of his sheep.

Good Shepherd's rod was like a sixty-yard extension of his arm; he could throw the heavy club that far with amazing accuracy. His rod had struck the attacking cougar square in the head, knocking the animal out before it could get through the sheepfold boundaries to the sheep. Later Good Shepherd threw the rod just beyond Wanda and Lone, who were more than fifty yards away, and the accurate throw landed only feet in front of them, getting their attention and pulling them back "in bounds," away from the poisonous flowers.

Boundaries are like gates that keep the bad out and let the good in.[1] Good Shepherd kept predators out of the sheepfold but extended the sheepfold and let the green pasture and the stream in. Even as he extended the sheepfold, though, he was careful to protect his sheep from extending the boundaries to the area infested with poisonous flowers.

People need the safety of boundaries just as much as sheep do. They need to be able to say yes to things that are good for them and no to things that are bad. They need to learn the difference between good and bad. Healthy boundaries help to create a safe environment in which you are free to be and to express yourself. Without boundaries we wander into trouble or find ourselves at the mercy of a predator.

Many people in recovery look back on their childhoods and recognize that others have violated their essential boundaries. A father criticizes his teenage son for making an error and does so in front of his Little League friends; another father punishes his nine-year-old daughter in anger, whipping her harshly and leaving red marks on her bottom. A mother refuses to believe her daughter's story that her uncle got in bed with her last night; a frustrated mother discloses her marital problems to her adolescent daughter; an adolescent girl isn't allowed to lock her bedroom door. Meanwhile, a grandfather insists that his eleven-year-old granddaughter take off her bathing suit outside and hose off the sand from the beach that is all over her body; she tries to cover her naked body with her hands as she runs to the bedroom where her clothes are.

Crossed boundaries like these make home an unsafe and insecure place for the children who have been violated. Children need adult shepherds who not only respect their feelings by not crossing their boundaries, but who also help them establish protective boundaries. Parents do this when they teach their school-age children to look both ways before crossing the street. Another example is the mother who tells her four-year-old daughter, "Honey, these parts of your body here and here are special and private and not for anyone else to look at or touch. If someone tries to look at or touch you there, then you tell them no and then come talk to me about it." Similarly, a father protects his nine-year-old son who has been teased by neighbors by compassionately listening to his son's feelings, expressing anger at the neighbor's wrongful behavior, and then empowering his son with encouragement and preparation so that the son can learn to defend himself.

When parents respect their children and help them set and maintain protective boundaries, they express an important part of God's character. God desires for us to have healthy boundaries by being our refuge and our fortress, keeping us safe and secure.[2] He is the defender of the victim and will avenge the perpetrators of abuse.[3] He hears the cries of the afflicted and offers them encouragement. He is a father to the fatherless and a defender of widows; and He receives those who feel forsaken by their father and their mother.[4]

When David cried to God on behalf of the victimized who had not yet been helped, God replied, "Because of the oppression of the weak and the groaning of the needy, I will now arise. . . . I will protect them from those who malign them."[5]

God's ultimate answer to those who have been treated unjustly and had their boundaries crossed came in Jesus Christ. When you feel violated remember your Good Shepherd who laid down His life for you.[6] He hung on a cross naked, beaten, bruised, insulted, and abandoned by the same people He healed, fed, cried with, taught, and died for. Jesus was victimized; His boundaries were crossed. And then He overcame His abusers and conquered sin and death so that now He can help you to do the same.

Personal Reflections

1. This week think of your personal boundaries as being like a gate that lets in what is good for you and keeps out what is bad for you. How well does your gate work? To what extent are you able to discern people who are trustworthy and receive good things from them? How effective are you in protecting yourself from being hurt by unsafe people?

2. Consider that Jesus, as our Good Shepherd, lays down His life for us to become the gate to our sheepfold. As the

gate, Jesus wants to help us with our decisions. The instructions and commands of God's Word show us what we need to say yes to and what we need to say no to. How well do you follow God's guidance?

3. Consider the following protective boundaries that you needed your parents to help you establish and maintain. Rate from 1 to 10, with 10 being excellent, the degree to which your parents taught you these things:

____ Your room is private (lockable door, people knock to enter).

____ Other people may use your belongings only with your permission.

____ The private parts of your body are not to be looked at or touched by others until you're old enough to give consent.

____ You deserve to be talked to respectfully.

____ As a child you don't need to worry about your parents' marital, work, and financial troubles because they're handling them.

____ It's not your responsibility to make Mom or Dad happy.

____ It's not right for anyone to hit you.

____ You were told "no" when you wanted to do something that was bad for you or others.

____ You were told "yes" when you needed something that would be good for you or others.

____ You have the right to say yes to things that are important to you and to have your desires respected, unless your parents help you see that those things really are not good for you. (That exception is different from their saying no just because they're the boss.)

4. One day this week meditate on Psalm 25. Pray that God would bring healing to the areas in which you have been shamed by people who crossed your boundaries (verse 2). Also pray that God would teach and guide you, helping to protect you from having your boundaries crossed in the future (verses 4-5, 20-21).

Waiting for God's Vengeance

"Your rod ... comforts me."
Psalm 23:4*b*

Many people are unaware that sheep are not always meek and mild. They can be aggressive with one another if they aren't having their way. This was especially true for Jelly. Her angry jealousy flared when she saw Wanda and Lone affectionately rubbing noses and nibbling on each other's ears as they frolicked in the flowers. Later at the stream Jelly picked a fight with Wanda by kicking dirt in her face.

The last time Jelly had picked a fight with her, Wanda wisely restrained herself and trusted in Good Shepherd to defend her and to discipline Jelly. Not this time! Wanda was foolish enough to lose control of her temper and knock the chip off Jelly's shoulder by giving her a head butt. Wanda would have been flattened by Jelly, who was far bigger and stronger than she was, except that Good Shepherd rushed in to break up the fight. Wanda didn't trust Good Shepherd to protect her and to measure out justice. Consequently Wanda was disciplined along with Jelly.

Perhaps you can identify with Wanda. Have you ever taken matters into your own hands and sought revenge against someone who sinned against you? Even people who are usually quite patient and tolerant can lose control of their anger when they are sinned against by someone they trusted.

Other people make the opposite mistake. When they are sinned against they make no effort to protect themselves. Instead, they act like a roly-poly worm that curls into a ball and plays dead. Showing no resistance or boundaries, they simply let their perpetrator of abuse step on them or kick them.

196

Frequently, people think that being a doormat is being a good Christian and will cite Jesus' words "If someone strikes you on the right cheek, turn to him the other also."[7] However, Jesus was speaking about a personal disagreement and our willingness to forgive a sinner, even showing him acts of kindness when he insults us. He was not excusing lies and personal attacks. When the Pharisees accused Jesus of doing a miracle by demonic power, He defended Himself and accused them of demonic influence.[8]

Furthermore, the whole context of what Jesus is saying when He talks about "turning the other cheek" is that it is not good to seek revenge. David knew this principle well. As a shepherd his sheep learned to trust in his rod to protect them and to measure out justice. As a loyal servant to King Saul, David himself learned to trust in his Shepherd's rod of justice when Saul suddenly turned on him and threw a spear at his head. David fled (he didn't let Saul sin against him),[9] and, as a fugitive whom Saul was trying to kill, David twice could have easily killed the king, but both times he spared him.[10] His words to his enemy were "I have not wronged you, but you are hunting me down to take my life. . . . May the Lord avenge the wrongs you have done to me, but my hand will not touch you. . . . May he vindicate me by delivering me from your hand."[11]

When we follow David's example and resist the temptation to repay evil for evil by taking revenge, we "leave room for God's wrath." And God promises, "It is mine to avenge; I will repay!"[12] David's angry words in Psalms teach us another important lesson. David didn't sit on his hands while he waited for divine retribution. Instead, he located his tablet and in a prayer psalm expressed to God his anger over being sinned against; he also asked God to deliver him and to punish his enemies.[13]

What is God's response when, like David, you're sinned against? God is enraged at those who abuse you or violate your boundaries. "He was angry. Smoke rose from his nostrils; consuming fire came from his mouth. . . . He parted the heavens and came down. . . . He shot his arrows and scattered the enemies. . . . He reached down from on high and took hold of me; he drew me out of deep waters. He rescued me from my powerful enemy."[14] And God promises that He will champion your cause, bring justice and vengeance, and deliver you. He doesn't promise when He will do this, however. You may have to wait.

The most common way in which we observe God's vengeance on the person who sins against us is when over time we see that "a man reaps what he sows."[15] "The trouble he causes recoils on himself; his violence comes down on his own head."[16]

David's faith in God really shone in that not only did he resist taking revenge on Saul and wait for God's justice, but he went the "second mile"[17] and responded to Saul's mistreatment by being kind and gracious in return. David knew that when you're kind to your enemy "you will heap burning coals on his head"[18] and instead of being "overcome by evil" you "overcome evil with good."[19] The old adage is true: "The best revenge is to live well."

Personal Reflections

1. This week think about your characteristic ways of responding when you're sinned against. Perhaps like Wanda you have some defects of character that emerge. Check any of the following ways in which you respond to being sinned against and then humbly ask God to remove your shortcomings.

☐ Lose your temper   ☐ Take revenge
☐ Ignore the situation   ☐ Be a "doormat"
☐ Slander them behind   ☐ Become resentful
    their back

2. Who has sinned against you recently? How were you sinned against? Follow David's example of resisting revenge and pray to God about this matter, expressing your anger to Him and asking for His justice and deliverance. Then over the next few days "heap burning coals" of kindness on this person's head.

3. Take some time this week to consider some of the ways in which you have been abused or violated in the past. Perhaps you have some unresolved anger over these things. If so, follow David's example in the imprecatory, or cursing, psalms and write an angry psalm to God in which you:

    1. express your anger over being sinned against:

    _____

    _____

    _____

    2. ask God to deliver you from the hurtful conse-
       quences: _____

    _____

    _____

    3. make a statement of faith about God's coming
       vengeance: _____

    _____

    _____

4. One day this week read Psalm 18. David wrote it when Saul and his armies were trying to kill him. What does this psalm have to say to those who have been victimized?

WEEK 29

Learning to Say No

"Your rod ... comforts me."

Psalm 23:4*b*

Lone hadn't learned to think for himself. He hadn't learned to "just say no" to things that weren't good for him. As a result he let Wanda talk him into sneaking away from Good Shepherd to play in the field of wildflowers. He wanted Wanda to like him so he joined in her mischief. Had he done his own thinking he would have remembered his coyote scare and the lesson of staying close to Good Shepherd and probably would have said no to dangerous play.

Lone didn't do his own thinking and didn't say no to Wanda because he had a problem setting boundaries and being separate. Inside he felt so lonely and insecure that he would do almost anything to be liked by Wanda and the other sheep. By needing to please Wanda he gave her the power to determine his worth and value. Often he would exhaust himself trying to please others until he couldn't take it anymore and then he'd isolate from them. Lone needed to learn to stand on his own.

Good Shepherd stepped in and set a boundary where Lone didn't. He did this by throwing out his rod to stop Lone from eating the poisonous flowers. Good Shepherd's rod formed a perimeter that confined Lone so that he could go no farther. Interestingly, that confining rod was a comfort to Lone; it also pointed out to him his character defect of being a "sheep-pleaser."

Like Lone, many of us are people-pleasers who have trouble saying no. Perhaps only toddlers don't have trouble saying no. The other day I walked Beth, my one-and-a-half-year-old niece, over to the park near our home. I asked her if she wanted to swing and she exclaimed, "No! No! No!"

Then I asked her if she wanted to slide and she repeated, "Mm-hm! Mm-hm!" She went down the slide, looked at me, raised her arms up for me to pick her up, and demanded, "Maw-or! Maw-or! "

Little Beth knew what she wanted and didn't want. She was in an important stage in her development in which she was exercising control over her environment. That's a very healthy thing, although she still needs lots of parental guidance in learning to discern what is good and what is bad for her.

Betty was active in "Co-dependents Anonymous," a twelve step group for people who are dependent upon being in relationship with someone who is dysfunctional. She shared with me her struggle to say no to men. She had been through a few different relationships in which her needs to please the man she was dating got her into trouble. She drained her savings account "to help get one guy out of a jam," loaned her car to another boyfriend, only to see it totaled, gave up an opportunity for a job promotion because it was threatening to an insecure boyfriend, and attempted without success to straighten out a drug abuser.

After becoming enmeshed with the drug abuser, Betty finally admitted that she had a problem with boundaries.

"Hmm, you call that 'setting boundaries'?" she asked me one morning. "Well, I guess I do have a problem saying no. I want to give to men and please them."

"Yes, and you want to rescue them in order to feel secure and know they like you," I answered. "You depend upon having a relationship with a guy whose life is messed up in order to feel needed. By becoming consumed with trying to fix a boyfriend's problems, you are able to distract yourself from your own issues."

Eventually Betty started saying no to her temptations to engage in codependent behavior. At first this was very uncomfortable for her because it meant becoming aware of her own character defects, which primarily involved her insecurities and feelings of low self-worth. As she progressed in working through these issues she gained an increased sense of self-respect and had a new capacity for deeper and healthier relationships with others.

How do people like Betty learn to follow Jesus' advice to "Simply let your 'Yes' be 'Yes' and your 'No,' 'No' "?[20] How do you learn to set boundaries? Some people think the way to set boundaries is to simply determine to do what is right. Actually that encourages legalistic pride.

The apostle Paul explains that only the grace of God can "teach us to say 'No' to ungodliness and worldly passions, and to live self-controlled, upright and godly lives." [21] The only way to say no to that which is bad for you and to be self-controlled rather than other-controlled is to receive God's unconditional and free grace. His love allows you to live in honesty and integrity.

His grace forgives our sins and values our person such that we begin to be more self-respecting, which lets us establish boundaries around what is good and right for us.

God's grace is received through faith in Christ's forgiveness expressed at the cross where He was crucified and rose from the dead. Faith is our way of saying, "Yes, Lord, I am a sinner who needs your forgiving grace." It also means saying, "No, I don't want to sin because it isn't good for me."

Personal Reflections

1. Do you identify with the way Lone followed Wanda into the poisonous flowers even though he knew better? Do you sometimes follow others into trouble? Will you try to

make others happy even if it isn't good for you? Check any of the statements below that are "people-pleasing" behaviors of yours.

- ☐ Joining others in destructive behaviors
- ☐ Sacrificing what's important to me to please others
- ☐ Agreeing to do things that I don't want to do
- ☐ Doing for others what they should do for themselves
- ☐ Hiding my feelings that might hurt someone
- ☐ Wearing myself out serving and helping others
- ☐ Letting people cross my boundaries verbally, emotionally, physically, or sexually

2. Exercise your "no muscle" this week by saying no when you're tempted to appease someone. Think before you say yes to someone. This will help you be more self-controlled rather than other-controlled. Then you can freely offer yourself to serve God and others. If you cannot say no, then you cannot really say yes.

3. Have you ever played the codependent role in a relationship with someone who is dysfunctional; that is, someone who is addicted, compulsive, can't hold down a job, is emotionally unstable, or has deep insecurities? Cite an example or two and note what personal issues your codependency enabled you to overlook.

_____

_____

4. Some time this week consider whether one of your parents had some codependency traits and how that affected you. Perhaps this person had high expectations for you, was emotionally detached from you, tried to control you, or took your struggles and feelings personally. Or he or she needed you to be his source of strength or comfort.

WEEK 30

Dare to Be Disciplined

"Your rod . . . comforts me."
Psalm 23:4*b*

The shepherd's rod protects the sheep in another way: through discipline. Sheep are prone to do foolish things like wander away from the fold, drink bad water, lie down in a hollow in the ground, or fight with each other. In such cases there are negative consequences such as getting stuck in a cave, becoming sick, being traumatized by hungry vultures, and being injured.

Despite the negative consequences of their foolish actions, sheep are slow to learn and will often make the same mistakes again and again. Wanda and Lone wandered away again, and if not for Good Shepherd's rod they would have eaten poisonous flowers. Jelly picked another fight with Wanda, and they would have hurt one another if Good Shepherd had not stepped in with his rod.

Good Shepherd's typical style of discipline was to use the negative consequences of the sheep's foolish behavior as their own punishment. He would focus his attention on the foolish sheep, and with tenderness and firmness he would give correction by pointing out how that attitude or behavior was not good for them. Then he would explain specifically what *was* good for them.

For instance, after breaking up the fight between Wanda and Jelly, Good Shepherd swatted them each on the bottom with his rod; yet he checked them gently and carefully for injuries. His rod was not of rage but loving correction. His words of correction told them what was hurtful about their behavior and reminded them of how they had been satisfied by his love in the past. Good Shepherd's discipline was firm and loving, and it had the sheep's welfare as its focus.

In the Bible we read warning after warning in which God says, "Don't be like this. Don't act in this way. These things are not good for you. Remember my love for you, and be this way and do these things." Yet, in spite of God's love for us and His guidance to us, we still sin and get ourselves into trouble.

Like Wanda, we too are slow to learn. In the heat of the moment we too are prone to react foolishly rather than responding with our Shepherd's past provisions and warnings in the forefront of our minds. Thus we make the same mistakes again and again and need to be disciplined by God. Such discipline helps to remove our character defects and our shortcomings.

Many people cringe when they think of God's disciplining them. It conjures up images of an "out-to-get-cha" police detective God who is waiting around the corner in a dark alley, watching for you to stumble. When you walk by His corner you trip, and this tough-cop God jumps out, shakes His finger in your face, and yells, "I caught you! You sinned again! You're gonna really get it this time!" People who are used to being punished harshly by angry or controlling parents may unconsciously picture God this way.

Other people shrug their shoulders with indifference when they think of God's disciplining them. They have images of God as a "nice guy" who just wants them to be happy, or a "wise old man" who is usually distant and uninvolved. In either case, this God is permissive when it comes to discipline. He is like an indulgent, pampering parent or an absent father.

The reality is that "the Lord disciplines those he loves."[22] But He first comes to us in a personal and caring way. In time we develop trust in His love for us, and out of that background He disciplines us. This is very different from being disciplined by someone you don't know or trust. Discipline apart from loving relationship is damaging.

The purpose of God's discipline isn't to control you and "keep you in line." Instead, "God disciplines us for our good."[23] He has your best interests at heart. He is training and teaching you so that you will "produce a harvest of righteousness and peace."[24] To live rightly and to be at peace is good for you. That doesn't mean that it doesn't hurt to be disciplined. It does. Even God says that His discipline is painful.[25] (That's why it is so important that we really know that we are loved by the one who disciplines us.)

When we allow ourselves to be disciplined and taught by God we "share in his holiness."[26] God alone is holy: He is morally perfect and completely separate, or self-existent. Any holiness we develop comes from God and what He has done for us, and it comes gradually over time as we open ourselves to His grace and His truth.[27] You need God to discipline you because you can't discipline yourself to become holier.[28] You can discipline yourself to be more religious, but your religion will be like that of the Pharisees: self-righteous, legalistic, and empty on the inside.

As One who is holy and separate, God never seeks to control us with His discipline. He does not take responsibility for our lives in such a way that He needs to coerce us to be holy so that we don't make Him look bad or hurt His feelings. The wise God wants to guide and direct our lives; yet at the same time He has given us the freedom of choice. We are responsible for our own lives, and therefore we will experience the hurtful consequences of our sins.

Personal Reflections

1. This week consider the way your parents used the rod of discipline when you were a child. Were they good role

models of the Lord's discipline—disciplining with love, and for your instruction and benefit? To the extent they were, thank God. Then note any ways that they fell toward unhealthy extremes of being permissive or punitive. Where either parent exhibited the following problems, indicate that with an "M" for mother or an "F" for father. (They probably leaned in one direction or the other but may also have swung back and forth in some areas. The latter case, of being inconsistent, is the most damaging of all.)

Permissive	Punitive
____ loose boundaries (rules)	____ rigid boundaries
____ few boundaries	____ many boundaries
____ indifferent	____ angry, even harsh
____ indulgent, pampering	____ stingy, restrictive
____ controllable by you	____ controlling of you
____ overlooking	____ condemning
____ too soft and easy	____ harsh or abusive

2. What kind of discipline has been conveyed to you in your church experiences? Denote that in the blanks above using a "C."

3. Set aside some time this week to reflect on the impact your parents and your church experiences have had on your experience of how God disciplines you. Then rate your experience of God (not the biblical reality of who He is) in the table above. Place a "G" for God in the categories that reflect how you have imagined God to be.

4. Meditate on Hebrews 12:7, which says, "Endure hardship as discipline." This is a difficult concept. Write down two or three hardships (painful or difficult experiences) that you have been through recently. Ask God to show you what He is trying to teach you in these situations. Perhaps they

reveal some defects of character or shortcomings for you to pray about and work on. Maybe they are consequences of past sinful choices.

NOTES

1. John 10:9.
2. Psalm 16:1, 5, 6, 9.
3. Psalm 7:10-17.
4. Psalms 10:17; 64:5-6; 27:10.
5. Psalm 12:5.
6. John 10:11, 14-15.
7. Matthew 5:39.
8. Luke 11:14-20, especially verse 19.
9. 1 Samuel 18:10-11; 19:9-10.
10. 1 Samuel 24 and 26.
11. 1 Samuel 24:11-12, 15.
12. Romans 12:17, 19; Deuteronomy 32:35.
13. There are more than thirty "cursing psalms," and most of them were written by David. Including Psalms 5, 7, 9, 10, 13, 16, 21, 23, 28, 31-36, 40-41, 52, 54, 55, 58, 59, 68-70, 109, 137, 139, 140.
14. Psalm 18:7-9, 14, 16,17.
15. Galatians 6:7.
16. Psalm 7:16.
17. See Matthew 5:41.
18. 1 Samuel 24:10, 17; Proverbs 25:21-22.
19. Romans 12:20-21.
20. Matthew 5:37.
21. Titus 2:11-12.
22. Hebrews 12:6.
23. Hebrews 12:10.
24. Hebrews 12:11*b*.
25. Hebrews 12:11*a*.
26. Hebrews 12:10.
27. Hebrews 2:11*a*; 7:26; 10:14.
28. Isaiah 64:6.

"Were entirely ready to have God remove all these defects of character. Humbly asked God to remove our shortcomings."

Steps 6 and 7,
Alcoholics Anonymous' Twelve Steps

"Your . . . staff comforts me."

*Psalm 23:4*c

STEP 8

Accountability

The sheep had spent a few weeks grazing in the Valley of the Shadow of Death. Good Shepherd had been slowly leading them through the valley, following the stream. Each afternoon as the shadows lengthened, Wanda and her friends recalled the dangers of the storm and the cougar. These thoughts brought a mixture of pangs of fear and sighs of relief. In the valley Wanda, Jelly, Lone, and the others were learning to find comfort by staying close to Good Shepherd. They were also gaining strength for the journey ahead as they grazed in the lush valley and drank from the running stream. Good Shepherd wanted his flock to be well prepared for the remainder of the upward climb to Table Mountain.

One particular morning was much hotter than the previous days. Good Shepherd realized that summer was fast approaching and it was time to head up the ridgeline path to

Table Mountain. Once the sheep reached the mountain, they could breathe in cool air and graze at a banquet table of grasses, plants, and flowers. Good Shepherd looked at his trusty staff. Years ago he had cut down the long and slender sapling and then shaped it into a cane, carved a hand grip on it just below the hooked end, and smoothed it out. Now he was ready for the annual trek and so were his sheep. He rounded them up one by one, tapping each on the side with the staff. Then he pointed his staff toward Table Mountain.

The older sheep recognized this familiar ritual. The moving staff signaled his unspoken words: "Go on and I will follow close behind." One by one, beginning with Imp and then Wobble—the eldest ram and ewe respectively—the sheep all assembled in single file and started climbing the ridgeline path. Good Shepherd was last in line. This way he could easily keep watch over his sheep as they climbed the steep, narrow, winding, and rocky path.

As Good Shepherd and his flock climbed the ridgeline path he marked their forward progress with his staff, poking it into the ground with each step. Along the way, he often stretched forward with his staff to touch various sheep who started to stray off of the path.

Suddenly, just ahead of him and around the corner of the winding path, Good Shepherd heard the crashing of sliding rocks and dirt and breaking tree branches accompanied by a shrieking "Ba-aa-ah! Ba-aa-ah! Ba-aa-aa-aa-aa-aa-ah. . . . Ehh, Oww-oww . . . Owww-wooch!"

Good Shepherd raced forward and peered from the path's edge down into the ravine. There was little Timi, fearful and helpless. She had slipped on some rocks at the path's edge and tumbled fifteen feet down the mountain until she caught in some pricker bushes.

Good Shepherd gulped when he realized that just beyond the pricker bushes the slope was sheer rock falling steeply downward into the valley below. Timi was crying, and that meant she was still alive—but barely. As painful as the pricker bushes were, Good Shepherd was glad they caught Timi's fall. They saved her life!

Good Shepherd called down to his little one. "Yee-dee-ohh-dee-dee-ollie! Timi, I see you! Don't move! I'm coming to get you."

He made his way down the ravine. He kept from sliding out of control by leaning backwards into the steep mountain, using his right hand to poke his staff sharply into the ground ahead of him and using his left hand to hold onto tree branches along the way. When he got to Timi he reached into the pricker bushes with his staff and wrapped the hook of his staff around Timi's waist. Gently he pulled her out.

Despite Good Shepherd's gentleness, prickers poked Timi and she cried out a series of pained "Ee-ow-ows." Good Shepherd winced right along with Timi, as he knew how much it hurt to be pricked. Once he had Timi out of the prickers, Good Shepherd picked her up and draped her across his shoulders. Carefully holding onto Timi with his left hand, he used his staff in his right hand for leverage as he carried Timi up the steep ravine back to the path. As he climbed he looked up to see an audience of gaping and gasping sheep peering over the edge.

When they reached the path Good Shepherd lowered Timi and checked her closely for injuries. He pulled the thorns out of her skin, and he gently rubbed his healing ointment onto her wounds and scratches. The balm began to soothe her pain and would protect her from infection. "Ah, there, there, my little one," he cooed.

Looking into Timi's eyes, Good Shepherd said, "Timi, I'm so glad you're OK. You could have died! I don't want you to get hurt again. Please be more careful to watch where you're going. You got so confident and excited about all that's ahead that you got far ahead of me and didn't watch your step!"

Now his attention returned to the sheep. They were tired from their climb the past few hours, so Good Shepherd started to look for a good resting place. Up ahead on the narrow ridgeline path he saw a more level and broader area of ground. It wasn't exactly a pasture, but there were plenty of green plants and patches of grass for the sheep to feed on. Just in front of the side of the mountain some tall cattails stood guard at a cave entrance. To the right of the cave, sheer rock dripped with little streams of melted snow from high above. *What a perfect place to set up a sheepfold for the night!* Good Shepherd thought as he guided them to the dark, yet warm, opening in the mountainside.

He perched himself on a rock outside the cave and watched as his hungry sheep fed on the green plants and grasses and satisfied their thirst in the stream. After a while, as the sun started to set, he called each sheep to himself, and one by one he counted off the sheep and had each pass under his staff for inspection. He began with Timi. He ran his hands across her little body, parting every square inch of her wool. He checked her pricker wounds and reapplied his healing oil as needed. He rubbed off the dirt and debris that had gather on her wool while grazing that evening. Then he sent Timi into the cave for the night.

Good Shepherd performed the same examination and treatment for all the other sheep. Just as he was finishing with Wobble, who was the last sheep to pass under his staff, he heard Pessamissi's familiar moans. He had not seen the three Doubters in days. Squinting to see through the dark, he could see Pessamissi crying beside Critter. Good Shepherd looked closely but didn't see Skep with them. The Doubters always traveled together. Something must be wrong.

Just then Critter blurted out between sobs and moans, "You didn't protect us! Skep was eaten alive by a wolf! What kind of a shepherd are you, anyway?"

Good Shepherd responded, "Oh—I'm so sad to hear that—that's tragic! No wonder you're so devastated! Your anger at me, though, is misplaced. I invited the three of you to join my fold weeks ago in the valley. Even now you can come into the sheepfold and join us if you'll pass under my staff."

Even the tragic death of Skep couldn't nudge Pessamissi and Critter to respond to the shepherd's gracious invitation. They didn't want to pass under the staff and be inspected. The two Doubters slept under the stars in the cold night air and cried themselves to sleep, close to the shepherd yet outside his protection. Good Shepherd and his sheep slept in the warmth of the cave.

Hand in Hand

"Your . . . staff comforts me."
Psalm 23:4c

Good Shepherd didn't go anywhere without his staff in his hand. He had personally selected a sapling that would fit his height. He shaped it and sanded it smooth, and then he carved the grip of the staff to fit his hands.

The staff had many uses. Good Shepherd leaned on it if he was tired. He walked with it. He pointed toward the mountain plateau with it to set the sheep's sights on the goal. He used it to tap a lazy sheep and get it moving. He used it to reach out and guide sheep like Wanda and Lone who were prone to wander. He used it to pull Timi out of the pricker bushes.

Good Shepherd's staff was an extension of his right hand. It enabled him to walk "hand in hand" with his sheep. It added to the one-to-one, personal touch between him and his sheep. By staying in contact with his sheep Good Shepherd was able to keep a close watch over them. He knew who was tired, who was hurting, who was endangered, who was getting off track, and who was causing problems. A tap of his staff on a sheep's side meant, "Hey, just checking in to see how you're feeling. I'm here if you need me."

On their journey through the Valley of the Shadow of Death and up the ridgeline path the sheep needed the comfort of knowing that their shepherd was with them. A tap of the staff was a good reminder of Good Shepherd's care. He was there to look after them on their journey. They could trust him to care for them. In contrast, the Doubters and other sheep who are not accountable to a shepherd wander about aimlessly, unable to take care of themselves.[1]

It's the same with people. We also need a shepherd who has gone before us in life; one who can guide us, care for our needs, tell us what to look out for in the journey ahead, and teach us how to live in a way that is good.

We don't do well if left to ourselves. We need relationships with people with whom we regularly share our needs, struggles, plans, and daily lives. And we need these people to give us honest feedback. Such relationships help us to enjoy our lives and feel that they are meaningful; they also give us perspective on how we are living. Nobody really knows himself well unless he sees himself through the eyes of others.

Sharing yourself with others and receiving their feedback are essential components in readying yourself for God to remove your defects of character. How can you humbly ask God to remove your shortcomings if you don't at the same time seek the support and encouragement of others?

I am always amazed when I meet someone who is going through life without even one significant relationship like this. Some people are just too busy. Others are so distant from their needs and feelings that they wouldn't know what to share even if someone approached them. Others are too untrusting. Others are too ashamed. Others are simply too shy. Many have friends and family who are involved in their lives, but on a rather superficial level that does not include real vulnerability. Still others have friends they are vulnerable with, but they don't take the next step of asking for honest feedback from them on how they're living.

People join twelve step recovery groups and find a "sponsor" with whom they can share their struggles and successes because of this need for a shepherd. Others join a small group in their church or find their pastor or someone they respect to disciple them. Other people meet regularly with a friend for sharing fears, hopes, and counsel, and for prayer. Still others find that they need a "professional shepherd" and consult a psychologist.

To have relationship with a shepherd who "holds you accountable" does not mean that your shepherd takes responsibility for your life. Quite the contrary, it means that *you* take responsibility for your life by discussing where you've been, where you're at, and where you're going. It's up to you to admit to your life's struggles and to share your life with someone. It's up to you to ask for feedback and perspective. It's up to you to make decisions and changes. Your friend is there to care for you, to encourage you, and to share his or her observations and experiences with you.

Though King David was himself a shepherd, first of many sheep and later of many people, he did not stand alone. He entered into relationship with others and allowed himself to be accountable to them. His relationship with Jonathan was a good example of this. They were so close as to be considered "one in spirit."[2] David received much guidance and warning from his friend when he was in difficulty. The two of them were so committed to each other's welfare that they made a covenant together.[3]

Jonathan was truly a friend to David. "A friend loves at all times, and a brother is born for adversity."[4] We too need to make a covenant with a shepherd-friend like this by asking him or her to walk hand in hand with us through our life's peaks and valleys.

Personal Reflections

1. This week consider your relationships. Do you have a shepherd-friend who shares God's comfort and encouragement with you? If not, begin praying and looking for someone like this.

2. Perhaps you have trouble committing yourself to this kind of a relationship. Check any of the following "excuses" that inhibit you from developing such relationships. This week try to set aside these excuses and find a friend to share with.

☐ I'm too busy. ☐ I'm shy.
☐ I don't trust others. ☐ I'm too embarrassed.
☐ I'm distant from my feelings. ☐ My relationships are superficial.
☐ My feedback now is condemning. ☐ No one would understand.
☐ I get simplistic advice. ☐ I can't find a friend.

3. Good Shepherd had a wonderful way of blending empathy and guidance, love and discipline, care and correction. When he walked side by side with a sheep and tapped it on the side with his staff to "check in," he communicated the love that keeps us accountable. Rate from 1 to 10, with 10 being the best, your parents' effectiveness in checking in with you to offer you empathy and guidance. Do the same to assess how well you check in with yourself and how well you check in with others, such as your children, spouse, or friends.

Mother to you: 1	2	3	4	5	6	7	8	9	10
Father to you: 1	2	3	4	5	6	7	8	9	10
You to you: 1	2	3	4	5	6	7	8	9	10
You to others: 1	2	3	4	5	6	7	8	9	10

4. Hebrews 3:13 says, "Encourage one another daily." Perhaps the best way to develop a friendship is to work at being a friend to someone else. This week try to encourage others and watch how they warm up to you.

Passing Under the Staff

"Your . . . staff comforts me."
Psalm 23:4c

Every night before the sheep entered the sheepfold to sleep, Good Shepherd called his sheep by name. One by one each passed under his staff. As the individual sheep walked by, Good Shepherd pressed his staff down onto the sheep so that from head to back its wool would be parted and he could check body, limb, and skin for any injuries or infections that needed to be treated. A sheep might have gotten cut or bitten or pulled a muscle or broken a limb. He noted if his sheep was overweight or underweight and what kind of condition it was in. He brushed off the sheep's wool with his hands to clean out dirt and debris from the day's travels. The shepherd looked so closely that he could even see if a sheep had hurt feelings!

The sheep were so used to this nightly ritual that each day as dusk overtook the daylight they would glance nervously now and again at Good Shepherd and his staff, knowing that soon their name would be called and they'd be examined. Even though Good Shepherd was gentle, it hurt to have a sore touched!

Many of the sheep, however, especially the older and more mature ones, had learned to trust their shepherd and value this accountability. They knew that when he spotted problems and corrected them that he did so in love and for their own good. They looked forward to receiving their shepherd's soothing ointment for their wounds.

On the other hand, the Doubters refused to pass under the staff and be examined. Their attitude was, "Nobody has the right to tell us what we need!" Their pride was a cover for their fear of being corrected by Good Shepherd. They doubted his love. It was these fears and doubts that kept them from joining the fold.

Of course, they really were not part of his flock, so they could not know that Good Shepherd was trustworthy. Before one is ready to be accountable to someone else, he must develop a relationship of trust. The Doubters, however, wouldn't surrender to the shepherd's accountability. As a result, they missed the protection and care of belonging to his sheepfold. Though tragic, it was no surprise that Skep was eaten by a wolf.

Lisa, a woman who had joined Overeaters Anonymous for help with her bulimia, knew the value of accountability. She called her sponsor one night after receiving a troubling phone call from her mother that tempted her to start a binge and purge cycle. Lisa took the step of "talking out" rather than "acting out" her ambivalent feelings of love and hate for her mother. She responded to her needs for maternal understanding and affirmation by calling her sponsor rather than reacting to those unmet needs by isolating and eating. She listened to her sponsor's friendly yet firm words.

"Lisa, this is an issue that food can't solve. There's nothing wrong with wanting your mother's affirmation. You need it. You just need to learn to protect yourself from your mother's criticisms."

Lisa nodded her head, listening quietly. "You are valuable; your needs are real." Lisa and Sue talked and cried together that evening. Lisa learned to bring her needs to a trustworthy friend outside the family.

Even if you're not in a twelve step group you need a shepherd such as Lisa had. You need someone you can talk with when you're feeling depressed or overwhelmed—someone to help you be accountable to do what is best when you're tempted to react out of unmet needs and engage in unhealthy or compulsive behaviors. You need someone to give you additional perspective on how you're living.

I must admit that once in a while I forget to "check in" with one of my shepherds or friends. Sometimes I become so focused on providing support and feedback for my clients, my family, and my friends that I forget my own need to be accountable. Moses did this too. In the desert wilderness he was the judge for all of the Israelites. He settled disputes between people and helped them make decisions. He held them accountable to following God's will. However, he was so busy helping people from morning until evening every day that he had no energy for himself. He was holding everyone accountable but himself.

When Jethro, Moses' father-in-law, saw that Moses was single-handedly leading the tens of thousands of people he rebuked Moses, saying, "What you are doing is not good. . . . The work is too heavy for you; you cannot handle it alone."[5]

Interestingly, Moses had been a shepherd of Jethro's flock years earlier, and he knew that sheep needed to "pass under the staff." Now Moses learned that every human must also pass under the staff, including leaders. Even those who hold others accountable need someone to hold them accountable. Because Moses had the humility and wisdom to follow Jethro's advice he learned a valuable lesson that freed his time and energy so that he could meet his own needs and continue to be efficient in his work.[6]

Counselors, ministers, leaders, parents, and other people who help to hold others accountable to do what is right and good also need people to hold them accountable. Leaders who aren't receiving regular support, encouragement, and guidance on a personal level get themselves into trouble. Good Shepherd calls each of our names, and one by one we are to pass under his staff so that he can part our wool and examine us for shortcomings and defects of character.[7] To allow God to hold you accountable certainly means privately sharing yourself with Him and listening to Him speak to you. But it also must include being accountable to other Christians who can represent God to you.

Personal Reflections

1. The book of Proverbs is a treasure house of wisdom. Many proverbs emphasize the importance of seeking advice. Set aside some time this week to meditate on Proverbs 6:23; 8:1-14; 10:8; 11:14; 12:1, 15; 13:10; 15:5, 22, 31-32; 17:10; 19:20, 25; 20:18; 25:12; and 29:1.

2. Perhaps like the Doubters you resist Good Shepherd's call to pass under the staff and be examined for injuries or shortcomings. Solomon observed that "the way of a fool seems right to him, but a wise man listens to advice."[8] To pass under the staff you need the following qualities. Check those that you need to work on.

    ____ Discernment to pick a compassionate and wise shepherd
    ____ Humility to say "I need help"
    ____ Courage to share the struggles I'm embarrassed about
    ____ Readiness to listen to feedback
    ____ Wisdom to evaluate the feedback I receive
    ____ Courage to apply what I learn
    ____ Perseverance to learn from my mistakes and try again

3. It can be intimidating and painful to pass under the staff and have your sores and defects examined and treated. That was true for Timi, Wobble, and the other sheep even though Good Shepherd was gentle and compassionate. Maybe you've had some hurtful experiences with being exam-

ined by others. Check the boxes below that describe your experiences of receiving feedback.

☐ I didn't feel under- ☐ I felt condemned.
stood.
☐ I felt analyzed. ☐ I was preached at.
☐ My adviser rescued ☐ I got simplistic
me. answers.
☐ I was told, "Get your act together!"
☐ I was told, "You shouldn't feel that way!"
☐ I was affirmed and encouraged.
☐ The advice I received needed to be followed by the adviser.

4. How do you respond when people seek your encouragement? Put yourself in the shoes of the person needing your help. How would they answer question 3 above? Ask your spouse or a friend how he feels after seeking your help.

5. Consider the distinction mentioned between reacting and responding. Do you react out of unmet needs or repressed feelings to do something impulsively without thoughtfully reflecting on what is really good for you? This week practice responding to your needs and feelings by passing under the staff and checking in with a friend. Write down your feelings that you want to be understood and the needs that you want to be met.

I feel _____

_____

I need _____

_____

6. Do you identify with Moses? He was too busy helping other people to seek the help he needed for himself! If so, decide to make the painful and difficult-to-implement step to

cut back on your responsibilities and commitments and to carve out time for your needs. Put all your commitments through the test of passing under the staff. Write them down and then later this week ask a friend to help you prioritize and cut back. Most if not all of the things you list will be "good" or you wouldn't be committed to them. But the good is always the worst enemy of the best, the urgent the worst enemy of the important.

1. _____   2. _____
3. _____   4. _____
5. _____   6. _____
7. _____   8. _____
9. _____   10. _____

WEEK 33

Learning a Lesson

"Your ... staff comforts me."

Psalm 23:4*b*

Ever since spring when it was time to take the new path little Timi has been learning lessons. First she learned to face her fears of leaving home and saying good-bye. Then she learned to look into the dark shadows in the valley that frightened her. In time she even discovered that she was safe with Good Shepherd in the Valley of the Shadow of Death.

Climbing up the steep and narrow ridgeline path she learned another lesson, perhaps the most painful one of all. Believe it or not, timid Timi had become overconfident. She was feeling so good about her new-found courage and so excited about the tableland ahead that she stopped looking where she was going. Truly, pride came before a fall[9] for Timi and she slipped down the ravine, rolling and tumbling into some pricker bushes. When Good Shepherd retrieved her out of the bushes and carried her back to safety, Timi learned another lesson about watching where she was going.

Of course, other sheep have wandered during their journey, not just Timi. Timi was perhaps knocked the hardest as she tumbled down the ravine and landed in the prickers, but many of the other sheep also have been learning from their difficulties and mistakes.

Wanda learned to trust Good Shepherd rather than wandering away and getting lost in the dark, eating poisonous flowers, or entering a fight she couldn't win. Lone learned the value of relationship because isolating from others made him lonely and left him vulnerable to enemies like coyotes and poisonous flowers. Jelly learned that her jealousy was due to her insecurity; rather than reacting from insecurity and fighting with Wanda, she began to see her value reflected in the still waters of Good Shepherd's love. Imp learned from his impulsive mistake of drinking contaminated water and later resisted the temptation to continue down the broad path; instead he followed the narrow path. After falling and nearly being eaten by vultures, Wobble learned not to project her wobbliness onto Imp, but to instead confess her shortcomings and work on her own problems.

The whole flock was learning together the values of being protected by and disciplined by Good Shepherd's rod. They were also learning the importance of the staff that held them accountable to stay on the path and examined them along the way. Some had been slower to learn their lessons than others and in many cases sheep had to re-learn again and again. But no matter how many times his sheep messed up, Good Shepherd continued to show a gracious attitude. "My righteous sheep will fall down as many times as needed to learn their lessons on how to live in a way that is right and good," he later told a neighboring shepherd. "Each time they fall I will help them rise again."[10]

At least these slow-to-learn sheep were learning and growing. Doody was one sheep who wasn't yet learning what he needed to from the journey; in seeking to do all that he should he wasn't experiencing the real meaning or joy of the process. The Doubters certainly weren't learning any lessons. Despite Skep's being killed by a wolf because he was too skeptical to trust in the shepherd's goodness, Pessamissi and Critter remained true to the family name and refused to put faith in the Good Shepherd. As outsiders looking in, they brought only fear to the sheep who were trying to obey Good Shepherd.

Many of us are like sheep, unable to learn what God is trying to teach us until we've been knocked around hard enough to stop what we're doing and take note. Instead of learning from observing others' mistakes or heeding the warnings and instructions that God gives us, we keep going in the wrong direction until the natural consequences of our unhealthy lifestyle catch up with us.

Unfortunately, few people have the foresight to address their shortcomings and defects of character before those issues cause them problems. The adrenaline-addicted workaholic doesn't slow down until he has a heart attack. The chronic worrier doesn't seek help until she gets an ulcer. A promiscuous young woman doesn't see the need to resist temptation until she gets pregnant. A man committing adultery represses his guilt feelings until his wife catches him in a lie. The anorexic continues starving herself until she faints one day and finds herself in a hospital being fed intravenously. A businessman continually represses his feelings of anxiety until he starts having unexplainable panic attacks when traveling out of town. A hurried parent keeps rushing around trying to keep up with an overcrowded schedule until she gets into her second car accident in a week. A depressed woman covers up her sadness with smiles until she finds herself obsessed with suicide.

For such people it takes falling into a pricker bush at the bottom of a ditch to realize that they have strayed off of the narrow path. In this sense, painful consequences to unhealthy behavior become God's microphone. We need to listen when He calls.

Personal Reflections

1. This week read 2 Samuel 11:1–12:14, the story of David's adultery with Bathsheba, his subsequent murder of her husband, and his receiving of Nathan's rebuke for his sin. If you read further in 2 Samuel you will discover the devastation that followed in King David's life: the death of the first

son Bathsheba conceived, incestuous relations between his son and daughter, another son murdering the one who violated his sister, and then that same son trying to kill David, only to accidently kill himself in his treasonous efforts.

2. Read Psalm 51 in which David confesses his sins of adultery and murder to God. Note the painful consequences to his sin that David experienced.

3. When you were little your mother and father probably taught you to "look both ways before crossing the street." As simple as that lesson is, like Timi we often forget to watch where we're going and then we meet trouble. This week consider your current lifestyle. Write down one or two shortcomings or character defects, which, if you're not careful, could cause you to fall down into some pricker bushes.

1. _____

_____

2. _____

_____

4. What lessons have you learned so far as you've taken this journey of "a year in the life of a sheep"? You are more than halfway through the one-year journey. Write down two or three lessons you've personally learned as you've read and thought about the other sheep in the Psalm 23 journey.

1. _____

_____

2. _____

_____

3. _____

_____

The Counselor:
Firm but Gentle

"Your . . . staff comforts me."
Psalm 23:4c

Good Shepherd realized that some sheep like Timi would become overconfident, step out ahead of him, fall off the path, and need to be rescued by his staff. Therefore, Good Shepherd made sure his staff was soft and smooth; indeed the staff stayed so soft that Good Shepherd used it to cradle a newborn lamb as it was coming out of its mother's womb. His staff was also strong enough for him to reach out with it to guide his sheep up the ridgeline path and keep them on the straight and narrow.

The softness and strength of Good Shepherd's staff worked together when he examined his sheep by having them pass under the staff at night. He'd part their wool to look for injuries, infection, or dirt. Because of his persistent and regular examination of his sheep Good Shepherd always knew the condition of his flock. Surely no sheep could pull the wool over *his* eyes! At all times he knew who needed healing, who needed cleansing, who needed warning and instruction, and who needed correction. He knew when to be firm and when to be gentle.

We need to be accountable to the Good Shepherd of our souls by being regularly examined. That is why God sent Jesus Christ to be our "Wonderful Counselor."[11] Jesus showed us the way to live, and He taught us the counsel of God. When He ascended back to His Father in heaven, Jesus sent His Spirit to be our indwelling counselor and "Comforter."

As our Comforter the Holy Spirit comes alongside us to empathize and to encourage us to live in a manner that is right and good for us.[12] The gentle but persistent compassion of the Holy Spirit is evident in that He comes to us, He draws us to Himself, He loves us, He suffers with us, and He helps us to overcome.[13] The Holy Spirit, who indwells all Christians, guides us along the path of truth by teaching us how to live rightly and by reminding us of who Jesus is and what He has done for us.[14]

Just as the softness and strength of Good Shepherd's staff came together when he parted his sheep's wool and examined them, so also the Holy Spirit's compassion and guidance into truth together can part our defenses against being honest and search our souls. Such soul-searching is positive, for by it He convicts us of our shortcomings and our defects of character and any other ways in which we have "missed the mark" of a life of faith in God's saving grace. His conviction comes with the hope of salvation, not the despair of condemnation.[15] It brings the compassionate grace of God that forgives and heals us, and it brings the enlightening truth of God that guides and encourages us.

Many people do not know the Holy Spirit this way, as a constant companion and ever-present comforter. Many Christians do not experience God as comforting them with grace and guiding them into truth. A young woman had a child out of wedlock, struggled to feel forgiven for her past promiscuity, and doubted that God would guide her steps and help her manage, because she had disobeyed Him. Grace and truth had not come together for her. Similarly, a college graduate who was plagued with feelings of inadequacy couldn't find a job. "Doesn't God care about how I feel?" he questioned me. "Will God ever answer my prayers and open a door for my career?" he continued.

They needed to know God's comfort; and Good Shepherd's staff suggests how God reveals His Spirit to us. The staff is an extension of the shepherd's arm and the means for him to care for, guide, and examine his sheep. As the staff is to the sheep so the Bible is to us. The Bible is an extension of God's voice and a means for Him to show us His grace and truth and to convict us where needed. Through His Holy Spirit, God spoke truth to the biblical writers, revealing who He is and how we can have a relationship with Him, as sheep to a good shepherd.

The heart of Scripture is the gospel, the good news that in Christ God has first loved us. He has forgiven our sins and called us to a life in which we glorify Him and enjoy Him forever. Also the Scriptures give us God's written revelation of Himself and His guiding laws to us—truthful principles, not legalistic conditions of worth. His words of truth are like a lamp to our feet and a light to our path.[16]

Gospel and law come together when we read God's Word and let the Holy Spirit—our indwelling Comforter and Counselor—use the Scriptures to reveal the sinful thoughts and attitudes of our hearts and to motivate us to approach God's throne of grace with confidence to find mercy in our time of need.[17]

Personal Reflections

1. Set aside some quiet time this week to pray David's prayer in Psalm 139:23-24: "Search me, O God, and know my heart; test me and know my anxious thoughts. See if there is any offensive way in me, and lead me in the way everlasting." Listen to the searching Spirit's "still, small voice" to you within your spirit. If you hear words of grace and truth that are consistent with Scripture, then you're hearing right. Perhaps, though, you hear only static, as on an out-of-tune radio. If so, then after your quiet time of prayer come back and check any of the following issues that make it hard for you to hear God:

☐ Guilty conscience   ☐ Worries
☐ Undone daily respon- ☐ Feeling bad about
   sibilities   yourself
☐ Depressed mood   ☐ General anxiousness
☐ Obsessive thoughts   ☐ Intruding images or
                                 fantasies
☐ Lack of relationship with God through His Son, Jesus Christ

2. When you shop for Mother's Day cards you probably have read many that said things like, "Mom, you were always there to comfort me when I needed you. You're so understanding and compassionate. You care about what I need. I've always known that I could trust you with my most sensitive feelings." Rate on a scale of 1 to 10, with 10 being highest, the extent to which this was true of your childhood experience of your mother. Then note any similarities in the extent to which you experience God's spiritual comfort through the Holy Spirit.

1   2   3   4   5   6   7   8   9   10

3. Similarly, when you inspect Father's Day cards you may have read many that said things like, "Dad, I have always respected and admired you. You're so wise. I sure have appreciated the wisdom and guidance you've given me over the years. You've been such an encouragement to me, and you've shown me how to live a good life." On a scale of 1 to 10, with 10 being the highest, rate the degree to which this describes your childhood experience of your father. Then note any similarities in the extent to which you experience God's spiritual encouragement.

1   2   3   4   5   6   7   8   9   10

4. Set aside some time this week to meditate on John 15:1-17, in which Jesus likens God to a keeper of a vineyard,

Himself to a vine, and us to branches on the vine. Allow God's Word to discern the thoughts and attitudes of your heart. How are you doing at "abiding in the vine" by letting Christ's powerful love flow through you?

NOTES

1. Matthew 9:36.
2. 1 Samuel 18:1.
3. 1 Samuel 18:2-3; 19:1-2.
4. Proverbs 17:17.
5. Exodus 18:13-18.
6. Exodus 18:24-26.
7. Ezekiel 20:37.
8. Proverbs 12:15.
9. Paraphrase of Proverbs 16:18; 29:23.
10. Paraphrase of Proverbs 24:16.
11. Isaiah 9:6.
12. John 14:16, 26; 15:26; 16:7, King James Version.
13. John 6:44; 16:7; 1 John 4:19; Hebrews 4:15; 1 John 5:4-5 20.
14. John 14:26; 15:26.
15. John 16:8; Romans 8:1.
16. Psalm 119:105.
17. Hebrews 4:12-16.

"Made a list of all persons we had harmed, and became willing to make amends to them all. Made direct amends to such people wherever possible, except when to do so would injure them or others."

STEPS 8 and 9,
Alcoholics Anonymous' Twelve Steps

———————————

"You prepare a table before me in the presence of my enemies."

Psalm 23:5a

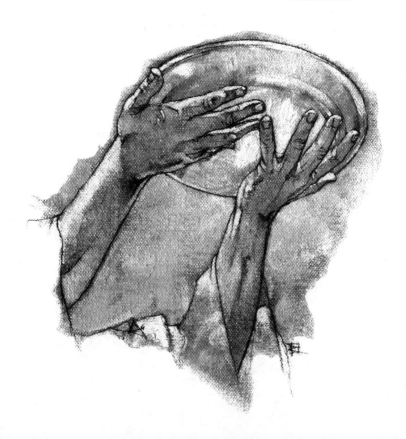

STEP 9

Forgiveness

One morning, before the first gleams of dawn, Good Shepherd awoke. He could sleep no more, roused by his anticipation of the sheep's arrival at Table Mountain. He stepped out of the sheepfold and stretched his arms into the starry night sky. Squinting to see in the starlight, he gathered some brush to close off the opening to the sheepfold. Then he headed up the ridgeline path, being careful with his steps lest he trip in the dark. In a few minutes he was above the timberline, and he could see the dawn's purple light breaking forth to light his way. The path went up a little further and around a corner.

"Ah, the tableland! We're here!" exclaimed Good Shepherd.

In all directions he beheld breathtaking views of mountain peaks and valleys against an orange sunrise. No trees or mountains could block the sun here. Good Shepherd stood before the grassy plateau and breathed in the cool, fresh mountain air.

"Hmm," he sighed, and again inhaled deeply. "This is the high country! We're at the top of Table Mountain!"

Knowing that his sheep would awaken shortly and wonder where he was, he quickly got about his business of preparing the table for his sheep. He inspected the meadow just in front of him. It looked like good grazing. He noted some patches of poisonous weeds here and there in his immediate vicinity, and he plucked them out and put them into a pile to be burned later. He found a nearby watering hole fed by a little creek. It was overgrown with grass and filled with debris. He pulled out the tall grass and then cleared the water of sticks and rocks.

In the distance were other basins and slopes that would need to be checked and prepared in the same way. He would need to plan a summer grazing program for his sheep so that he could move them from pasture to pasture. There was plenty of time for all that later, though.

This will get us started, he thought. *I'd better hurry and get back to my sheep. They will be so excited. We've finally arrived!*

Good Shepherd ran back to the path and headed back down the mountain to the sheepfold. As he ran he was smiling and broke out into spontaneous song, shouting joyfully:

> *Yee-dee-ohh-dee-dee-ollie!*
> *Yee-dee-ohh-dee-dee-ollie!*
> *Yee-dee-ohh-dee-dee-ollie!*
> *The table is set, my loved ones!*
> *It's time for us to have some fun.*
>
> *Ram, ewe, and lamb arise.*
> *Come see my surprise.*
> *No more climbing up!*
> *We are at the mountaintop.*

The sheep woke to Good Shepherd's song, growing louder and louder as he got closer to the sheepfold. They heard his excited tone and started stirring. Good Shepherd was huffing and puffing when he arrived at the fold. Still, he gladly threw open the bramble door, repeating his chorus.

The table is set, my loved ones!
It's time for us to have some fun.

Good Shepherd pointed his staff toward the plateau and the flock enthusiastically bounced forward in a jolly parade to the tableland.

It's no wonder there was so much excitement and energy among the sheep. Many weeks of walking through the fears of the Valley of the Shadow of Death and climbing up the narrow ridgeline were finally about to culminate in their arrival at the much anticipated Table Mountain. The final path to the top was short, but to the sheep, especially to young lambs like Timi who had never been there before, the last trail seemed to take an eternity.

Imp was leading the way, of course. He wasn't impulsive or independent about it, though, as now and again he looked over his shoulder at Good Shepherd and waited for his nod of approval indicating that Imp was still on the right path. Good Shepherd was in the back nudging the trimmer, but still wobbling, Wobble forward.

Imp reached the top many minutes later, and he started dancing and let out a shout. "Yippie! We're here! It's even better than I remember. Oh, how I love the summertime!"

Wanda and Lone were close behind and quick to join in on the prancing and dancing and laughing on the grassy table. When Timi reached the top she just stood there with heart pounding and jaw wide open in amazement at the beauty of the high country. Jelly went right to the watering hole to slurp up the clean, cold mountain water.

About the time that Timi and Jelly joined the three sheep in dance, Doody arrived. He had been trying to help Good Shepherd with Wobble (not that Good Shepherd needed the help, but it made Doody feel good), and when he reached the top and saw the dancing he interrupted the celebration. "It's time to get to work," he grunted, "Let's set the table."

Good Shepherd smiled at Doody and chuckled, "Relax, Doody. Join the dance. I've already set the table for you!" Good Shepherd nudged Doody playfully and started to dance himself. Somehow Doody was moved out of his stuffiness and actually joined in the merry-making. He even began to laugh aloud when Wobble made up a dance called "Wobble's Tobble on the Table Top," in which she threw herself into a tobbling roll on the ground and landed back on her feet. Pretty nimble-footed for an ewe who not too long ago could hardly even stay on her feet!

Later that day, after they were all danced out, the sheep grazed peacefully as Good Shepherd watched over them. They were enjoying the tableland without fear of the enemies that surrounded them. Good Shepherd marveled that even Timi was at ease. The enemies around the table included poisonous weeds, wolves, coyotes, cougars, and snakes. The sheep, however, were at peace. They knew Good Shepherd had prepared the way by setting the table and that he and his rod of protection were close.

Jelly was grazing next to Wanda, enjoying the tableland and her shepherd's goodness, when she found herself reminiscing on her experience at the still waters during the past winter. The pure mountain water she slurped at the watering hole earlier that same day must have triggered the memory. She remembered how Good Shepherd saw her jealousy and her mistreatment of Wanda and forgave her and loved her. She got a warm feeling inside. Then she looked at Wanda and realized that she had never apologized to Wanda for either of the two episodes.

Mustering up her courage, Jelly rubbed shoulders with Wanda and said, "You know, I have a jealousy problem that Good Shepherd has been helping me with. For a long time I've been jealous of you. I'm sorry for how aggressive I've been with you. I want to understand more of how hurt you must feel. I hope you can forgive me. I want to change, so please confront me when you see me acting out of jealousy towards you."

Wanda was very moved, as were several other sheep listening in. With tears forming in her eyes, Wanda said, "Thank you, Jelly. I forgive you. I want to apologize to you too. In spite of the way you picked a fight with me, I was wrong in giving you that head butt. Please forgive me too."

Soon other sheep were following Jelly's and Wanda's examples. Wobble asked for and received Imp's forgiveness for bad mouthing him. Lone asked for and received Timi's forgiveness for stirring up her fear in the valley. It was a moving sight that brought tears to Good Shepherd's eyes.

This was truly a great start to the summer! The only clouds in the sunny skies were Pessamissi and Critter, who were hanging out near the edge of the tableland. They still were interested in the journey but could never join, doubting Good Shepherd and the sheep who followed him. Earlier they had mocked the dancing sheep. Now they doubted the sincerity of all the forgiving they were observing.

Timi looked over at them and felt a painful twitch from a nerve of bitterness. She remembered how the Doubters had preyed upon her fears and mistreated her in the valley.

With Good Shepherd watching, Timi walked over to them and said, "I'm angry at you for criticizing me and doubting me and my shepherd. I want you both to know how you hurt me and magnified my fears. I'm working at forgiving you, though."

Pessamissi choked on the mildewed and soured grass she was chewing on. Clearing her throat, she mumbled between chews, "You were so afraid in the valley. I was just trying to help you."

Critter spit out a wad of the same mildewy grass and curtly defended himself, "Skep and I didn't criticize you! You were the one who was so upset! How can you talk to us this way! Don't you know we're mourning Skep's death?"

Timi, displaying her new courage, withstood their defensiveness and looking straight at both of them said, "You offended me, and I won't fall prey to your tactics again!"

He Prepares a Table for Me

> "You prepare a table before me in the presence of my enemies."
>
> **Psalm 23:5a**

For the sheep, Table Mountain was summer vacation. Not so for Good Shepherd. Preparing the table was a lot of hard work. He had to precede the sheep to the pasture. He looked for poisonous weeds and pulled them out so that the sheep could graze freely. He cleaned out the watering holes, pulling grass and removing sticks and debris so that the sheep could drink. And at all times he kept one hand on his rod of protection and one watchful eye looking out for predators.

He didn't prepare the table just once, but many times. The summer grazing program that he established required grazing in one pasture for a few weeks and then moving onto another so that the pastures didn't become overgrazed and so that his sheep would get the exercise they needed. Good Shepherd enjoyed this labor of love for his sheep. His reward was in dancing with his sheep on the prepared table!

Doody, in his self-righteousness and naiveté, was unaware how much he and the other sheep depended upon Good Shepherd's going before them to prepare the table. If he didn't go first they would have eaten poisonous plants and wandered around looking for forage. They also would have gone thirsty because of hidden or inaccessible water holes and would have been at the mercy of hungry predators. Because he preceded them and prepared the way, the tablelands were a place of bounty and cool peace.

As children you and I were like little sheep—just as dependent upon having someone go before us in life to prepare the way. We needed to graze in relationships that nurtured and affirmed us. We needed to drink in love from our parents and others. We needed guidance and protection. We needed forgiveness, not condemnation. And we needed help learning how to resolve conflicts with "enemies" and to forgive. Even as adults we still need these things.

In God's design for families this is something that parents are intended to do for their children. When you were a child your mom and dad were big people who seemed to know everything, be able to do anything, and have so much that you needed from them. For better or for worse, they were "God with skin on" to you. That's because early in a child's life parents are the main—in some cases the only—sources of God's love, joy, peace, patience, kindness, goodness, faithfulness, gentleness, and self-control.[1] These are the fruit of the Spirit that we hunger for, especially early in life when we need so much.

Yet, *all* parents fall short in expressing God's perfect love to their children; no parent is all good (or all bad for that matter). However, mother and father together can sufficiently express God's loving character to their children so that the children know and feel God through their parents. Unfortunately, many parents—even Christian parents—have limited their parenting to providing for physical needs, discipline, moral training, teaching, and doing tangible things for their children. Such tasks are important. Yet, due to their own emotional deficits, they have provided little personal caring—showing their love by being interested in and affirming their children's emotional development and unique expressions of personality. Even worse off are adult children who come from homes in which a parent showed them emotional, physical, or sexual abuse, was divorced, or was tied to an addiction.

Because you come from an imperfect background in which you were sinned against and you sinned, you now need a shepherd to "prepare the table" for you—to first love you—by stepping into your shoes to experience the world the way you do. Such a shepherd must understand the ways in which you were damaged and be willing to help you to recover from your injuries. Jesus is just such a Shepherd. In Him God became a man and was made like us in every way so that He sympathizes with our pains and our struggles and then leads us to the throne of grace to receive God's mercy and comfort.[2]

The Bible records that Jesus faced the temptations and trials that you face and yet was without sin. When He was crucified He became the perfect sacrifice for you, bearing the punishment for your sin and the sin of others against you. His work at the cross prepared the way for the forgiveness that can heal the pain of your sins and those of others against you. "By his wounds we are healed."[3]

God's whole purpose in sending Jesus was to reveal His saving grace in a personal way. That purpose remains today, even after Jesus rose from the dead and ascended back into heaven. Through people who care for us and show God's love, we can be led to graze on God's goodness. We need someone to go before us and clean out the clogged up watering holes so that we can drink in God's forgiving grace. We need to have poisonous weeds of bitterness rooted out from our souls. Then we need to work at forgiving our enemies who have sinned against us, forgiving even as we have been forgiven.

Personal Reflections

1. This week consider the table that has been prepared for you. Start by reflecting on your childhood. Who went be-

fore you to prepare your way? Write down the names of those who did the following things for you and thank God for these people. (Some lines may be blank.)

Provided for my physical needs ——————————————

Protected me from harm ——————————————————

Affirmed me emotionally ——————————————————

Encouraged me and respected my abilities ——————————

Supported my creativity and helped me discover and be me

————————————————————————————————

2. What's your reaction to the idea that for better or for worse your parents have been your main connection to God's goodness? The way in which they related (or didn't relate) with you is the foundation that you bring to all other relationships. Perhaps your foundation needs repair or even rebuilding if you're to develop a better connection with God's goodness.

3. Set aside some time this week to consider your journey with God. How has God worked in your life to improve your foundation?

The people who shepherded me are ——————————

————————————————————————————————

A time when God revealed Himself to me was ——————

————————————————————————————————

The most important lesson God has taught me is ————

————————————————————————————————

4. One day this week read one of the gospel accounts of the events surrounding Jesus' crucifixion and resurrection (Matthew 26-28; Mark 14-16; Luke 22-24; or John 18-21). Consider how Jesus has prepared the table before you in your journey.

WEEK 36

Forgive as You Have Been Forgiven

"You prepare a table before me
in the presence of my enemies."
Psalm 23:5*a*

A miracle occurred at Table Mountain. The sheep were reconciling with one another. Wanda forgave Jelly. Jelly forgave Wanda. Wobble forgave Imp. And Timi forgave Lone. Each made peace with his or her enemy.

It all started with Good Shepherd's preparing the table. Jelly was enjoying the goodness her shepherd prepared for her as she grazed on the green tableland and drank the pure, cold mountain water. Then she remembered her experience months before at the still waters and how her shepherd had forgiven her sins. This motivated her to ask Wanda to forgive her, and soon everyone was forgiving each other.

The sheep forgave as they had been forgiven by Good Shepherd. Jelly had received the shepherd's forgiveness for her jealousy-inspired aggression, Wanda for her wandering, Wobble for his wobbling, and Timi for her fearful reluctance. They each shared the forgiveness they had received from Good Shepherd with the sheep who had offended them. They were compassionate of their offenders' sins and wanted them to be forgiven as they had been forgiven for their own sins.

Forgiveness is an essential step in your journey of recovery. As Jelly's experience illustrates, it begins with receiving God's forgiveness for your own shortcomings and moral imperfections. We too need to go to the quiet waters of God's grace and take inventory of our sinfulness by looking at our reflection, admitting to God, ourselves, and others the exact nature of our wrongs, and allowing God to forgive us and remove our defects of character and our shortcomings. This often involves contacting other people—to make a list of all we may have harmed and make amends to them wherever possible.[4]

For instance, a recovering alcoholic named Larry went to his adult son and confessed his sins of being emotionally unavailable, undependable, and critical. Instead of doing this out of a need to relieve his burden of guilt, his words were motivated by love. Larry said to his son, "If I were you, I would be angry at me and feel very hurt. I know my alcoholism has affected you in negative and lasting ways. I want to be patient with the fact that it will take you time to heal. I'm committing myself to be available to you whenever you want to talk to me about your feelings about our past. Also, I want to work at being more loving to you from now on. I'm sure I will fall into old patterns from time to time, and when I do I hope you'll confront me."

You may never have abused alcohol. However, some shortcomings and mistakes probably have affected your children, spouse, other family members, and friends. Beyond admitting your shortcomings and failings to God, you must also confess your wrongdoing to those you have offended. Do you look for and respond to cues from others that indicate you've hurt them? Do you invite others to give you honest feedback? Or do you tend to overlook your wrongs and respond defensively when someone suggests that you have hurt them?

Let's face it. Forgiving someone who has abused, neglected, mistreated, or disappointed you in some way is simply not a natural thing to do. When we are sinned against we naturally hold grudges, gossip and slander our offender, seek revenge, or try to overlook or minimize our pain. We need God's help to forgive. We need to experience God's mercy, especially as it comes to us through our shepherds and friends, so that we can forgive as we've been forgiven.[5]

For Larry, his confession of sins against his son and receiving his son's forgiveness as he made amends went hand in hand with his forgiving of his own father who was abusive to him. Experiencing forgiveness for his sins from his son and from God impelled him to work at forgiving his father. So also, confronting the anger and pain he felt over his own childhood reminded him of his own sins and ways in which he passed down the sins of his father to his own son.[6]

We are like Wobble in that we fall again and again and need help rising to our feet. So do other people. Unfortunately people we love, and rely on, sin against us again and again. The apostle Peter knew how it felt to be repeatedly sinned against, which is why he asked Jesus, "How many times shall I forgive my brother when he sins against me? Up to seven times?"

Peter thought he was being more than generous in forgiving up to seven times, but Jesus answered, "I tell you, not seven times, but seventy times seven."[7] Wow! That's 490 times!

Jesus was emphasizing that _we are to forgive as many times as we're sinned against_ so that we, and perhaps even our offender, can grow in the process of becoming a perfected leader. That's exactly what God does for us. We sin against God and others far more than 490 times. And yet God forgives us again and again that we might grow and mature.

Personal Reflections

1. This week consider some of the sins that you've confessed in your walk with your Shepherd these past weeks and months. (You may want to review your personal reflections

in Step 4 of our journey, "Confession of Sin.") Do you feel forgiven or are you still condemning yourself?

2. In the parable of the unmerciful servant in Matthew 18:23-35, Jesus describes a servant who failed to receive true forgiveness because he did not work at forgiving a fellow servant as the king forgave him. The parable illustrates a two-fold principle: (1) working at the process of forgiving others points out our own needs for forgiveness, and (2) if we're not willing to forgive others then we should wonder whether we truly have accepted the forgiveness for our own offenses, because when we have, we will want to offer such forgiveness to others.

3. This week follow Jelly's example of seeking forgiveness for her sins. Set aside some time to make a list of people you have harmed. Write down your sins against each person.

1. _____

_____

2. _____

_____

3. _____

_____

4. Review your list of people you've wronged and how you have wronged them. This week set a meeting time with one of these people and make amends by saying the following things and then acting on your words. (This shouldn't be a one-time event in which you unload your guilt. Neither should it be a formula that you mechanically follow. Instead, it ought to be an attitude that you clearly and lovingly express again and again.)

1. "I am sorry that I have wronged you by . . .

   _____

2. "You may feel angry or hurt. I want to listen and understand how you feel and have felt about our relationship." (Work hard at being nondefensive and at feeling their pain during such conversations.)

3. "It may take you time to heal and to recover, and I want to be patient with you."

4. "What do you want from our relationship now and in the near future?"

5. "I want to be more loving to you. Please help me with this. If I slip into an old pattern or hurt you in some way I want you to confront me with this."

5. Think about ways in which you've felt wronged by your parents, spouse, or friends. Have they made amends to you in the way I suggested above? If so, how did it go? If not, how do you feel about that?

Pulling Out the
Weeds of Bitterness

"You prepare a table before me
in the presence of my enemies."
Psalm 23:5*a*

Unknown to the sheep as they graze on the lush grass of Table Mountain and enjoy the cool, refreshing mountain air, enemies surround them, especially the edible kind. Hungry sheep don't easily discriminate between healthy green grass and poisonous green weeds. In the summertime the grassy tablelands are dotted with weeds and wild flowers, some of which are toxic to sheep. This is one reason that Good Shepherd needed to prepare the table by pulling out the weeds before his sheep could eat them.

Pulling out the weeds was a big job for Good Shepherd. He had to search the tableland for toxic weeds here and there. His back often ached as he stooped to pull the weeds, helped by a small shovel that cut the plants at the roots. The job lasted all summer as new weeds appeared and the shepherd led the flock to different fields and meadows as part of the summer grazing program. Good Shepherd's labor of love was essential to the sheep's well-being.

I can tell you from experience that weeding is a lot of work. When I was a boy one of my chores was to weed the yard. This big job required many hours of lying in the dirt to pull weeds out of planters, squatting on my knees to yank little weeds out of cracks, and bending over and pulling with all my might to remove giant weeds from the wet and rocky ground.

Before I weeded my dad always reminded me, "Bill, make sure you pull the weeds out by the roots or they'll just grow right back." I didn't want to be back out there redoing the job, so I tried to do it right the first time and used a little garden shovel to help make sure I got the weeds out by the roots. Even when I did a good job I had to reweed in three or four weeks because new weeds would be growing again. Where they came from I never could figure out!

Many people have toxic weeds of bitterness growing in their souls. When someone points out that they seem resentful they deny it, thinking that they're being accused of being a crotchety, embittered old hag. Actually, resentment is simply old anger that hasn't been resolved. The anger may have been acknowledged before but then repressed into the unconscious without being understood, worked through, and released. Like weeds, festering old anger needs to be pulled out by the roots.

It seems simple enough to "speak truth. . . . Be angry, and yet do not sin; do not let the sun go down on your anger, and do not give the devil an opportunity."[8] It's not at all simple, though, especially if you grew up in a home with parents who didn't know how to deal with their own anger in healthy ways, much less help you deal with yours appropriately. Dad loses his temper and curses or throws things. Mom gives Dad the silent treatment, while slamming cupboard doors in the kitchen. Kids sit on edge, afraid of another explosion. Or maybe there isn't an explosion that day, but the children observe and experience the effects of constant hidden and unexpressed conflict that leaks out in sarcasm, withdrawal, passive-aggressive behavior, or slandering one another behind their back. Sometimes phony smiles mask a family going through the motions, unwilling to discuss and resolve conflicts.

Inevitably, children are affected by unhealthy family patterns and will express their discontent in some way: problem behavior, difficulties in school, depression, anxiety, or by becoming overly helpful to try to make the family what it should be. These kinds of problems are hard to connect with unresolved family issues; usually everyone focuses in on the problem child and any contributing problems in the family get overlooked. Children also express their anger more directly and obviously in complaints, raised voices, tantrums, crying, slammed doors, or demands. Unfortunately, rather than responding to such behavior by trying to understand what their children are upset about and teaching them to verbalize their anger in respectful ways, many parents either become defensive, telling the children they "try so hard," or the parents try to control their children's feelings and get into a power struggle about who the boss is and who will listen to whom.

If your parents didn't know how to deal with their anger by "speaking the truth in love"[9] or didn't attend to your feelings and help you to be angry yet not sin, then inevitably the sun went down on your anger[10] night after night after night —your anger was repressed into your unconscious—and today you are resentful, unless you've taken the time and energy since your childhood to do some weeding.

Rooting out poisonous weeds of resentment and forgiving those who have sinned against you is not something you can do in an hour, a day, or even a month. You can make a decision to commit yourself to do it, but actually doing it is an ongoing process. The more resentment that has accumulated in the storehouse of your unconscious, the longer it takes to work through.

The process of forgiveness involves owning up to and feeling the anger that naturally develops when you are wronged or think you have been wronged. You can't forgive without feeling angry over being sinned against. To "forgive" without feeling anger is to overlook sin or to minimize pain. Neither of these attitudes represents true forgiveness of sin.

Part of the healing process of forgiving is working through your pain. Underneath your anger over being sinned against are hurt feelings, perhaps of rejection, disappointment, abandonment, shame, or violation. You must deal with these feelings also because the offense cost you something and forgiveness means you've counted the cost of the offense and you are willing to release your offender from his or her debt to you.

Going through the forgiving process can be very unsettling and exhausting, yet it is beneficial. Through forgiving others you release the poisons of resentment from your body and soul. Whether the process helps to improve your relationship with the one who wronged you depends on how you and your offender deal with the issue of confrontation, which we will discuss next week.

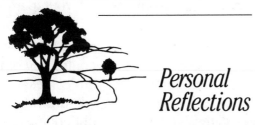

Personal Reflections

1. This week consider whether you have some unresolved resentment festering inside. The following is a list of symptoms that can be due to resentment. Check those that describe you.

☐ depression   ☐ need to be in control
☐ short temper   ☐ perfectionism
☐ critical of self   ☐ critical of others
☐ slander or back-biting   ☐ quick to give opinion
☐ passive-aggressiveness   ☐ ulcer
☐ low frustration   ☐ digestive troubles
   tolerance

2. Maybe bitterness is growing in your soul. If so, it's due to unforgiveness. Make a list of people you need to for-

give. For each person write the sins committed against you that you need to forgive.

1. _____

_____

2. _____

_____

3. _____

_____

3. How did your parents handle their anger when you were a child? Write an "M" for mother and a "F" for father beside any of the following responses that your parent(s) showed.

___ loss of temper   ___ silent treatment
___ fighting   ___ controlling others
___ slander or back-biting   ___ criticalness
___ quick to preach at you   ___ withdrawal
___ passive-aggressiveness   ___ underlying tension not solved
___ compulsive behavior   ___ sarcasm
___ spoke the truth in love   ___ resolved conflicts

4. Consider how you deal with your anger. Check the responses in question 3 above that apply to you. Note how your parents' ways of dealing with *their* anger has affected how you deal with yours. Also note how your parents' ways of dealing with *your* anger has affected how you deal with your anger.

5. Sometime this week meditate on Ecclesiastes 7:9, in which wise, old Solomon said, "Do not be quickly provoked in your spirit, for anger resides in the lap of fools." Interestingly enough, the person who loses his temper and the one who stuffs his anger inside and becomes resentful are often

the same person. Remember that "the man who fears God will avoid all extremes."[11] Picture your response to anger as a teeter-totter with the balance point consisting of speaking the truth in love and being angry without sinning. On the left extreme is the one who is obviously sinful in losing his temper. On the right extreme is the one who seems righteous by not appearing angry but actually is repressing his anger into resentment. Where do you sit on this teeter-totter? Perhaps you change positions on the teeter-totter, rarely staying on the balance point.

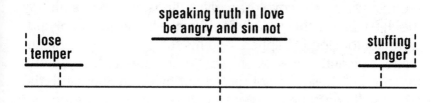

Making Peace
with Your Enemies

"You prepare a table before me
in the presence of my enemies."
Psalm 23:5*a*

In the high country of Table Mountain a sheep's enemies are many. Snakes, coyotes, wolves, lions, and bears all spy the defenseless sheep and would make them quick prey if it were not for Good Shepherd and his rod of protection. Meanwhile, poisonous weeds are subtle enemies hidden among the grass. If these are not rooted out by Good Shepherd, the sheep will consume the weeds and become sick or even die.

The hardest enemies to make peace with, though, are the other sheep! Two rams who are friends become enemies when both are courting the same ewe or when both are in competition for the same spot to graze on. Or sheep might become enemies when one leads another astray, one knocks another down with a head butt, or one uses mean sheep-talk on the other.

The sheep in Good Shepherd's flock on the tableland together enjoying their shepherd's provision, protection, and goodness. Then, following Jelly's lead, they shared that goodness with each other, forgiving one another for ways in which they had been offended.

Timi tried to carry this forgiving spirit to Pessamissi and Critter Doubter. Forgiveness also required her to confront them for the way in which they criticized her, magnified her fears, and mistreated her. She did so with an attitude of love. Timi didn't have to personally confront Pessamissi and Critter in order to forgive them, but confronting did help her to face her fears and to release her anger. The Doubters responded with angry defensiveness, claiming to have actually been helping Timi. Critter tried to shift his blame to Timi for confronting them when they were grieving Skep's death. Pessamissi doubted Timi's sincerity. Even though the Doubters would not make peace with Timi, Timi found peace for herself and freedom from that painful nerve of bitterness through forgiving.

The Doubters lived up to their name again. Previously they had declined Good Shepherd's many invitations to pass under the staff and join the fold because they wouldn't admit to their need for him; now they declined Timi's offer of forgiveness because they wouldn't admit that they had wronged her.

Who are your enemies? Who are the Pessamissis, Critters, and Skeps in your life who have hurt you? An enemy is anyone who has fought against your welfare without repenting and making peace with you. Your enemy may have abused you, betrayed you, been unfaithful to you, disappointed you, or hurt you in some other way. As with sheep, the hardest enemies for us to deal with aren't dangerous and strange animals in the woods, but friends or family whom we have trusted and been hurt by. It may be a critical brother-in-law, an abusive father, a controlling mother, an ungrateful son, a disrespectful daughter, or an unfaithful spouse. Sometimes our enemy is outside the household: a boundary-crossing neighbor, a betraying friend, a back-stabbing coworker, or a judgmental woman in the church.

Think about your relationships. How do you respond to people who have offended you? Do you stand up for yourself and confront them as Timi did? It's easier to just smile and act friendly with people even after they've hurt you. Or perhaps you gossip about or slander these offenders behind their backs. You may say, "Yes, I'll do that for you" and then turn around and don't do it in order to resist their control. That's acting in a passive-aggressive style. Or you may be fully passive, taking the doormat role by letting yourself be stepped on and mistreated again and again. Perhaps you make the opposite mistake and respond aggressively, losing your temper by saying words that cut like knives, throwing things, or getting physical with your offender. Or maybe you have other, more subtle ways, of seeking revenge.

It takes courage to confront a friend who has suddenly acted like an enemy and say to him or her with firmness, "I'm angry at you for criticizing me. I let your opinion matter to me, and you hurt me. I want to be understanding of whatever you were feeling or going through at the time, but regardless it's not right for you to talk to me that way and I cannot tolerate it."

It's difficult to articulate such responses on the spot when you've been wronged, unless you're quick-minded, in touch with your own feelings, and not enmeshed or lost in others' feelings. Especially people who are just learning to be assertive usually need to go back and confront the person later. That presents a new problem of anticipatory anxiety: the more you think about the confrontation the more anxious you're likely to get.

When you do confront someone who has offended you, be sure that you don't undermine the moment by offering your offender a backdoor out such as "I know I'm just being sensitive" or "It wasn't that big of a deal" or "I know you were just trying to help me." Minimizing the truth of how you were offended is a sign that you're not ready to confront; you're feeling too insecure about the relationship or you're not sure of the validity of your feelings.

Perhaps the hardest part about confronting someone is being prepared for any ways in which your offender may be defensive or avoid your feelings. You may need to use "the broken record technique"—keep repeating how you felt, not letting yourself get sidetracked by your offender's excuses, rationalizations, minimizations, evocations of pity from you, or turning the tables to play the victim. You probably will need to follow your initial statement with something like this:

"You seem defensive (or You're avoiding the issue). I'm not trying to attack you (or tell you that you're a bad person or blame you for all my problems). I just want you to understand how I felt hurt by you. If you will hear me out then I will also take the time to hear what you are feeling."

Jesus indicated that confrontation is an important part of forgiving: "If your brother sins against you, go and show him his fault, just between the two of you. If he listens to you, you have won your brother over. But if he will not listen, take one or two others along, so that 'every matter may be established by the testimony of two or three witnesses.' "[12] If you were abused by your offender or don't feel safe confronting him or her it may not be wise for you to personally confront your offender by yourself. You may need the help of your counselor, your pastor, or someone else you respect. Or you may want to confront by letter in order to make sure that you say what you want to say.

Just the mention of confronting someone like a parent causes many people to come up with all sorts of reasons why they shouldn't do that or don't need to. It's natural to want to protect someone you love or to want to avoid conflict with them. Yet if we can't be honest with someone about how we feel, the relationship certainly isn't intimate or healthy. Probably you are afraid.

To confront someone you love and need you have to be able to trust that this person will respond to your anger in a loving way that is also nondefensive. When you have no reason for such trust and it feels like your angry confrontation will destroy your connection with the other and cut you off from the caring you need, then you will naturally feel afraid. If this is the case, then the only way you can confront is to do so with the support of secure relationships with other shepherds or friends you can count on.

Although personally confronting your offender isn't a requirement of forgiveness, you will need to confront the issue of how you were sinned against and your feelings about that.

You confront the issue by acknowledging the reality of the way you were offended and then working through your feelings of hurt and anger. If you feel prepared and safe enough to personally confront your offender, then go ahead. The meeting will create the opportunity for an improved relationship with your offender.

Personal Reflections

1. What do you think: Is confronting someone who offends you consistent with being loving? Study Matthew 5:44, in which Jesus encourages us to love our enemies and pray for those who persecute us. Then read Leviticus 19:17-18, which clearly spells out the importance of confronting someone who offends you rather than seeking revenge or repressing your anger and bearing a grudge. Finally read Ephesians 4:15, 25-27. Here the apostle Paul explains the balance between loving and confronting. He teaches us to be truthful with others when they have angered us and to do so in loving and respectful ways.

2. Set aside some time this week to consider your own hesitations about following Timi's example of confronting your offenders. Check any of the following that describe your feelings.

☐ "I have no right to judge others, because I'm guilty too."
☐ "I don't like conflict and disagreement."
☐ "Others won't like it if I confront them."
☐ "To bring it up will just make things worse between us."

☐ "It feels wrong to be angry and to defend myself."
☐ "I'd just be blaming them for my problems."
☐ "I don't care that much about the relationship."

3. How do you typically respond when someone offends you or wrongs you in some way? Check those that apply.

☐ Ignore it   ☐ Be a doormat
☐ Feel very hurt   ☐ Initially think it's OK
☐ Try not to be so sensi-   ☐ Secretly slander your
    tive   offender
☐ Lose your temper   ☐ Fear being hurt again
☐ Speak the truth in love   ☐ Find subtle revenge
                                          later

4. Set aside some time this week to reflect. Write down the names of those who have wronged you and never made amends with you by sincerely apologizing, empathizing with how that felt for you, and working at being more loving. Briefly describe how each person wronged you.

1. _____

_____

2. _____

_____

5. How would your mother respond if you confronted her with the ways in which she hurt you as a child? (In order to identify specific parental sins you may want to review your Personal Reflections from Week 16, "Generational Patterns," in which you confessed the sins of your parents.) Put an "M" beside the following responses that you think she might have. Do the same for your father using an "F."

___ Feel unappreciated

___ Say, "But I tried so hard"

___ Change subject

___ Make light of your feelings

___ Become angry

___ Listen and then forget it

___ Work at changing their behaviors

___ Defend themselves

___ Give guilty apologies

___ Point out your sin

___ Point out their goodness

___ Cry and seek pity

___ Listen and understand

___ Seek to repair past damages

6. Later this week write a confrontation letter to one of your offenders. You may not want to mail this letter, but write it anyway. Even if your offender is dead or not in your life anymore this will be a valuable exercise for you in your forgiveness process. In your letter state the following:

1. You wronged me by _____

   _____

2. At that time I felt _____

   _____

3. Since then I have made some bad choices that repeated the pattern that you started. For instance

   _____

   _____

4. What I want (or don't want) from you now is

   _____

   _____

WEEK 39

The Lord's Table

"You prepare a table before me
in the presence of my enemies."
Psalm 23:5*a*

In preparing the table for his sheep, Good Shepherd devoted his time and his energy to them. He found Table Mountain and led the sheep there. He pulled out the poisonous
weeds. He found and cleared out the watering holes. He led
them from one pasture to another in the high country. He
restored them to their feet and forgave them when they fell.
He enabled them to make peace with their enemies and to
forgive. He protected them from predators.

Good Shepherd would give his life for his sheep. At
night he would lead his sheep into a sheepfold, bounded by
rock, brush, bramble, trees, canyon walls, or the side of a
steep ridge. At the opening of the fold he laid down his body.
He himself became the door. The sheep came into the fold
through him when they passed under his staff and were examined and treated. He closed the door by risking his life to
protect his sheep from cougars, coyotes, and other predators
that would attempt to attack the sheep in the fold. The sheep
who came to know and trust their shepherd felt secure and at
peace even in the presence of their enemies.

Though God is the Good Shepherd of Psalm 23, Jesus
Christ also is described as the shepherd in John 10. He laid
down his life for us so that we could have peace with God,
others, and ourselves. Jesus is the gate, and we can enter
into the sheepfold of eternal safety through putting faith in
His forgiving grace. When we put our souls into his hands,
we can trust that no predator will intrude into the fold and
snatch us out of his hands.[13] Enemies may hurt us or even kill

our bodies, but no one can harm that invisible and eternal part of us that we have entrusted to God and that He has been in the process of transforming into His image.

Genuine faith in God starts by believing in the truth of God's intervention in history in which He sent His Son Jesus Christ to become a man, live a sinless life even as He encountered all kinds of temptations, suffer many injustices, allow Himself to be crucified to pay the price that our sins deserved, and then raised Himself from the dead to conquer the powers of Satan, sin, and death. We receive Christ into our lives when we put faith in Him and what He has done for us by saying, "Yes, I am a sinner and I need God's forgiving grace."

Saving faith means to receive God's free gift of unconditional love. Because we are sinful and imperfect we cannot do anything to earn God's grace. God does all the work. He shows us that we need His grace. He draws us to Himself. He gives us Himself. He enables us to receive Him. He enables us by the power of His indwelling Spirit to grow to become more and more like Jesus in our character, so that we may have a life that is increasingly right, healthy, and fulfilling.

These are the truths Christians celebrate when they participate in Communion. Christians hold the bread and remember that Jesus is the "Bread of Life" who meets their every need when they feed on Him.[14] As they touch the bread they are reminded that God became a man. Jesus was named Immanuel, "God with us."[15] In Jerusalem and Judea, men and women touched and received healing from Christ 2,000 years ago. Eventually, though, many turned against Him, and He was nailed to a cross. In the Communion ceremony, the glass of wine reminds Christians that Jesus gave His life blood for men and women so that we could become new creatures.

His overwhelming goodness to us moves us to confess our sinfulness: our imperfections and our inability to earn this grace.

As much as the Lord's Table is a time for celebrating God's loving act in sending His Son, there are two painful and difficult aspects. First, receiving God's goodness requires admitting our need and our sinfulness. Second, when we truly receive His forgiveness we will work at sharing that forgiveness with those who have wronged us. It's difficult to admit our shortcomings, to confess them, to seek forgiveness from God and those we have injured, and then to make amends to those we've wronged. It's also hard to admit we have been wronged, to confront our offender, and to work at forgiving.

Despite the difficulty in seeking forgiveness for our sins and offering forgiveness to those who have sinned against us, it is the most spiritual thing we can do. There is no better way to worship God than to receive His grace for our sin and to share that with others. This is why Jesus said, "If you are offering your gift at the altar and there remember that your brother has something against you, leave your gift there in front of the altar. First go and be reconciled to your brother; then come and offer your gift."[16] Our brother has something against us if we have sinned against him or if he has sinned against us and we have not yet forgiven him.

Personal Reflections

1. Sometime this week read 1 Corinthians 11:17-34, in which the apostle Paul gives instructions regarding the practice of Communion. He instructs Christians to examine themselves so as to not partake of God's grace in an "unworthy way." Some people interpret that phrase to mean that we must do certain things to be deserving of taking Communion, like being a church member, confessing all of our sins, or

being more committed. These attitudes leave us feeling either guilty or prideful depending upon whether or not we think we measure up. Yet if we have to "do" anything to deserve to go to the Lord's Table, then it is no longer a table of grace and unconditional love. This week reflect on your Communion experiences. Have you ever beaten up yourself with guilt and condemnation at the Communion table? What do you feel guilty about?

2. Perhaps there are two ways of being unworthy at the Lord's Table: (1) to not admit to our sinfulness and our need for God's forgiveness, and (2) to try to do anything in order to earn or deserve God's grace. In the first case we are abusing God's grace by turning it into a license to sin, and we are denying our sinfulness. In the second case we are invalidating grace altogether by legalistically trying to prove ourselves to God. Pride often accompanies our actions.

When we truly receive God's mercy and unconditional valuing of our person, we breathe a sigh of relief because we don't have to prove ourselves. Because God doesn't condemn us we freely confess our sinfulness and desire more and more to do what is right and good for us and for others. If you participate in Communion at a local church, indicate which of the following attitudes best describe your attitude at the Lord's Table.

☐ I take Communion hastily, neglecting to examine myself and confess my sins.

☐ Before taking Communion I make commitments to do more of what I should.

☐ At the Lord's Table I examine myself, confess my sins, and then celebrate God's mercy and forgiveness.

NOTES

1. Galatians 5:23-24.
2. Hebrews 2:17; 4:15-16.
3. Isaiah 53:5.
4. This course of action is also recommended in Steps 4-9 of Alcoholics Anonymous' Twelve Steps.
5. Colossians 3:13; Ephesians 4:32.
6. Exodus 20:5-6; Leviticus 26:39-40.
7. Matthew 18:21-22.
8. Ephesians 4:25-27, _New American Standard Bible_.
9. Ephesians 4:15.
10. Ephesians 4:26.
11. Ecclesiastes 7:18_b_.
12. Matthew 18:15-16.
13. John 10:1-18, 27-30.
14. John 6:35.
15. Matthew 1:23.
16. Matthew 5:23-24.

*"Having had a spiritual awaken-
ing as the result of these steps,
we tried to carry this message to
others, and to practice these
principles in all our affairs."*

Paraphrase of Step 12, Alcoholics Anonymous

———————

*"You anoint my head with oil;
my cup overflows."*

Psalm 23:5b

STEP 10

Giving to Others

Summer in the high country of Table Mountain wore on, and the sun got hotter and hotter. Mornings and evenings were still cool, but the midday sun brought increasing discomfort to the sheep. Above the timberline, the sheep found no shade to hide from the sun's rays. An occasional breeze brought only temporary relief.

On one sultry day the sheep were grazing under the sun, eagerly looking forward to their mid afternoon splash. Suddenly a huge swarm of flies approached the flock. Like soldiers on an attack mission the swarm went straight for Wanda, surrounded her, and whirled around and around her like a tiny tornado. Some flies started to bite at her face; others buzzed in her ears and nose. With the unrelenting annoyance and agonizing irritation, Wanda felt she was going mad.

She began stomping her feet and shaking her head, trying to rid herself of the encircling flies.

"Baa-aa-aa-ah! Baa-aa-aa-ah!" she shrieked. Then she threw herself onto the ground and began rolling frantically in the dirt, still trying to free herself from the attacking flies.

During these few moments Doody had stood by watching Wanda being driven to absolute craziness by the flies. Now he could stand not one moment more of the sounds of the buzzing, whirling flies and Wanda's high pitched shrieks for help. He felt guilty watching her suffer. *She needs help!* he thought.

Doody rushed toward her and started kicking up dirt at the flies and screaming, "Shew-ew-ew-ah! Shew-ew-ew-ah!" The flies must have been angered by this disruption of their lunch because about half of the swarm turned on Doody and began to attack him.

Just then Good Shepherd reached Wanda and Doody. He started flailing his staff back and forth in the midst of the swarms of flies and chased them away from the flock. "Oh, thank you, Good Shepherd. I didn't think the flies would turn on me too!" Doody said.

"Yes, thank you, Good Shepherd," Wanda added. "And thank you for coming to my side, Doody." Doody showed one of his rare smiles, and both sheep snuggled up to the shepherd.

Good Shepherd pulled out his canister of homespun insect repellent oil and applied generous quantities to Wanda's head and face and then did the same for Doody and the others.

The sheep were once again at peace, though still hot. Fortunately, it was time to take a break from the afternoon sun to splash around in the stream and cool off. On the way to the stream two of the rams, Imp and Lone, took an interest in Wanda, who, to their eyes, was the prettiest ewe in the flock. At the same time they each strutted proudly and stoutly toward Wanda trying to win her favor. Suddenly, they looked at each other and realized they were in competition for the same ewe. Imp and Lone stared at each other for a few long seconds, but neither would back down. Then like two angry bulls they charged straight at each other and crashed heads! The thud from their collision echoed against the surrounding mountains.

Before Imp and Lone's mating battle got out of control, Good Shepherd separated them with his staff. They looked at each other with a simmering glare. Then they noticed Good Shepherd had pulled some grease from his backpack. He smeared the oil over their heads and shoulders. He was careful to apply extra amounts of the thick oil to the bruised and scraped places on their heads that especially needed the soothing and protection of his salve.

Once Good Shepherd was finished, though, Imp and Lone continued their fight for Wanda's heart as if nothing had changed. This time, however, when they butted heads they glanced harmlessly off each other, fell to the ground, and looked stupidly at each other. Feeling rather embarrassed and silly, they got up and joined the flock at the nearby stream.

Pessamissi and Critter Doubter had been standing near the stream watching Imp and Lone battle over Wanda. Pessamissi was also in the mood for mating, but she was tired of being criticized by Critter and wanted no part of him. As you might guess she was pessimistic about the possibilities of a romance working out for her. Nonetheless, her pessimism aside, she was desperate, and she knew that Imp also was in the mood. So when Imp reached the stream, she got up her courage and walked in front of him, strutting her stuff and showing herself off to him.

Imp wasn't interested in Pessamissi, but he felt sorry for her and knew he didn't have to compete for her. On an impulse he seized the moment and pranced over to Pessamissi and affectionately rubbed her head and led her away from the flock. Pessamissi thought this was all too good to be true! As she followed Imp she could be heard saying, "Are you sure you're interested in me, Imp? I'm afraid this won't work out. What about . . . "

Later in the week Good Shepherd noticed that Imp wasn't grazing much. He spent most of his time plopped in a disheveled and sullen heap on the ground. He looked miserable. Good Shepherd checked him over. In examining the wool around his head, he discovered that Imp was infected with the dreaded scab disease. Scab was a tiny parasite that feeds on sheep in warm weather, leaves them very sick and irritated, and could be deadly if not treated. Furthermore, it was highly contagious, spreading whenever an infected sheep rubs up against a noninfected sheep. Without attention the scab could wipe out the whole flock.

Good Shepherd wondered aloud, "How did Imp get scab? This is a bad case of it. I treated him and all my sheep with my oil earlier this summer and that should have protected him—oh, Pessamissi. Pessamissi gave it to him!"

Good Shepherd isolated Imp from the rest of the sheep and reapplied generous amounts of his homespun remedy for scab—olive oil mixed with sulphur and spices—to Imp's head and neck. When he checked the rest of the flock for scab he was relieved to see that none of the others were infected. As prevention he applied the oil to them also.

Gradually summer began to slip into autumn. The afternoons weren't nearly as hot anymore, and the evenings were becoming very cool. The leaves on the trees in the valleys below had been turning a beautiful mosaic of reds, oranges, and yellows. One morning Good Shepherd awoke surrounded by frost on the grass. This was his signal that autumn was here and it was time to head down the mountain back to the home ranch.

He softly sang a wake-up call to the flock, which began in a delighted whisper and gradually became louder until it ended in joyous song:

Yee-dee-ohh-dee-dee-ollie.
Yee-dee-ohh-dee-dee-ollie,
Arise, my little ones.
Let the light fall into your eyes;
Breathe in deep of the cold morning air;
Feel the frost that's here.
Yes, it's time! Yes, it's time!
Today we're going down the mountain.
Today we're going home.

Before leaving that day Good Shepherd gave the sheep some time to graze. After they had grazed awhile, he felt the wind picking up and noticed dark storm clouds approaching. Urgently, he shouted out the alarm: "Yee-dee-ohh-dee-dee-ollie! Hurry! We must go now!" He rounded up the sheep and headed toward the path that wound down the mountain. The sheep didn't know what was going on, but they knew it was an emergency. They were all so focused on moving down the mountain that no one even turned to glimpse once more the vanishing tableland.

As the sheep were racing down Table Mountain, the cold wind chilled their little bodies. Soon sleet was pummeling their coats, and they became soaked and shivering. Finally they reached the cave, the same cave they had slept in the night before they reached the high country. Everyone was glad to be out of the cold rain and sleet, but they continued to shiver. The sheep huddled together trying to get warm but they merely passed their wet chills back and forth. Whenever a sheep tried to shake sleet off his wool, the frozen droplets landed on other sheep and made them even colder.

Good Shepherd made a fire near the opening of the cave with some logs that he had stored in the fold. Then he pulled from his pocket his canteen of warm wine. He filled his cup to the brim and shared some with Wobble, who was quite chilled. Just a few slurps while sitting with Good Shepherd in front of the fire and Wobble started to feel warm inside. He then snuggled with Timi who was shivering and warmed her. Doody followed Wobble's example, taking a drink from Good Shepherd's cup and then snuggling with those around him to warm them up.

A Fly in the Ointment

"You anoint my head with oil;
my cup overflows."

Psalm 23:5*b*

Summertime in the high country was wonderful for the sheep until a fly got stuck in the ointment! For Wanda and Doody it wasn't just one fly but a whole swarm of swirling, buzzing, and biting flies. Nothing is more annoying and downright maddening than flies swarming around you!

The flies would have ruined the sheep's summer and been a constant distraction had it not been for Good Shepherd's oil. Flies don't like oil because they stick to it. And Good Shepherd had mixed into his oil sulphur and spices that repelled flies. Throughout the summer, Good Shepherd applied and reapplied this oil to his sheep's noses, ears, faces, and necks. This simple remedy brought about a miraculous transformation in sheep who were being pestered by flies. Once distracted, aggravated, and frenzied, the sheep became calm, free to go about their business, and happy again.

You don't have to be a sheep to know that few things in life are more distracting than flies. Flies swirling around your food while you're trying to eat. Flies buzzing around in your bedroom while you're trying to sleep. Flies biting at you in the yard while you're trying to work. Perhaps even more than the summer-only mosquitoes, flies help us understand the meaning of the word *pest.*

At least humans have hands to wave around and fly swatters to flap. Sheep are defenseless against flies. They are totally dependent upon their shepherd, which is why they love to say to him, "You anoint my head with oil."

John needed an anointing with oil. He was driven to distraction by all sorts of pests, big and little activities that nibbled at his energy, his relationships, and his spiritual health. These pests, though, acted so friendly and interesting that he didn't even know that he was distracted.

I couldn't keep up with John. He worked such long, hard hours as a salesman—each month he pushed himself to sell beyond his quota and get a bonus—that I felt lazy in comparison. He kept his yard and his car in such immaculate condition that I felt like a slob. On evenings and weekends he made multiple trips in the car running errands to get this or that or take one of his kids here or there, which left me wondering what I was forgetting to do. His social life made me feel like a loner. And his church involvement left me questioning my own level of commitment.

Feeling that I was missing something in life, I asked John how he did all this. I learned that he rose at 5:00 in the morning without an alarm, went to bed at 11:00 at night, drank four cups of coffee a day to keep him "cranking," and crammed every spare minute with one activity or another, because all of his time had to be productive.

"God gives us twenty-four hours in a day, and we need to do as much as we can with it," he told me. "You know the apostle Paul said, 'Redeem the time because the days are evil.'"

I got tired just listening to John. His life was full of activities. He never sat still. He didn't hear the birds chirp. He didn't see the flowers bloom. He didn't look deep into his wife's eyes. He didn't lie around at the beach with his family or laugh at his kids' silly behavior. He wasn't in touch with how he felt inside and what he really needed. He didn't examine his life except to try to figure out how he could fit in more things in less time. He couldn't say, "Enough." He lived for his adrenaline highs. He didn't listen to God.

I realized that John was distracted. Ironically, he did not really "redeem the time."[1] His life was full of good things, but he was missing out on the best things. He did all the urgent things but forgot about what was really important. He seemed to be living such a full life, but really he was empty inside.

John was full of anxiety and empty of peace. He did so much for people, but there was really so little of himself to give. I decided that I was glad that I slept too much, didn't work hard enough, wasn't as committed, and was generally more lazy and sloppy than he.

If you're like I am, then John's lifestyle could be very tempting to you. I should know better from past experiences —once I worked so hard that I burned out, overcrowding my life with "good" things until I had little free time, and failing to say no to people who wanted my help until my yes became meaningless. In spite of what I know from experience, it's easy to become distracted. I am surrounded by people who are living—or trying to live—a fast-paced, ladder-climbing, money-grabbing, fame-seeking, and pleasure-filling lifestyle. Their motives are disguised by a spouse, two kids, a house, a dog, friends, and church activities that seem to make it all worthwhile.

The apostle James had some strong words for distracted people who can't say, "Enough." (Believe it or not, the distracted life is not a product of our modern urban society. It existed in Bible times almost 2,000 years ago, out on dirt roads and farm houses.) He pointed out that distracted people are motivated by envy, selfish ambition, greed, and pride.[2] He called such people "adulterous" and "double-minded" because they were trying to live a selfish existence and still be Christians. Friends of a self-seeking world, they had actually become enemies of God, who hated this way of life.[3]

The apostle challenged them to resist the temptation to continue in their distracted lives by submitting themselves fully to God and coming near to Him. When distracted people slow down to evaluate their lives, they see that beneath the surface of what seems to be a good life are sinful motivations and an empty heart that misses both intimacy with others and genuine spirituality.

How can you slow down? According to Scripture, you must "purify your hearts" by humbly bringing issues of envy, selfish ambition, greed, or pride to God and receiving His cleansing mercy. We each need to grieve and mourn the loss of achieved or desired successes, recognitions, and pleasures.[4]

It's hard to slow down. There are benefits, though. You will be free to laugh and play and relax without feeling guilty. You will start to notice all sorts of things you never noticed before—leaves blowing in the wind, flowers at the side of the freeway, even a sparkle in somebody's eye. Once slowed down, you will find that it's easier to hear God's voice, and you will actually become more effective in your work. You will desire and enjoy helping others. Truly those who are quiet in soul come to know God.[5]

Personal Reflections

1. Perhaps distractions are buzzing around in your ears like flies. This week ask yourself, "Do I have trouble saying, 'Enough!'? Is my life overcrowded with good things that distract me from what is *best*? Do I live with a sense of urgency such that I miss what is *really important*? Do I have a restless, anxious spirit that always needs to be busy doing or thinking (even becoming obsessed) about something?"

2. Try the "yesterday exercise." Set aside ten minutes with pen and paper in hand. Write down *everything* you did, thought about, and felt inside yesterday. Whether mundane or extraordinary, embarrassing or flattering, write it all down

as fast as you can without editing or screening what you write. Then examine yesterday in light of this week's devotion.

3. Sometime this week take the time to purify your heart in God's cleansing grace. Write down four or five of the most time-consuming and energy-investing activities, relationships, and things in your daily life. (If you want to be accurate, ask your spouse or a friend who knows you well to help you with this.)

1. _____

_____

2. _____

_____

3. _____

_____

4. _____

_____

5. _____

_____

4. Motivations are complex and often disguised or hidden, but try to probe into your motives in each of the areas you identified above. Why are you invested in these activities? As you consider each area, ask yourself: "Am I partially motivated by any of the following?" Check any that apply.

☐ Envy (being discontent where you're at and wanting what others have)

☐ Selfish ambition (being driven to succeed and get ahead of others)

☐ Greed (never getting enough and wanting more and more)

☐ Pride (living life in your own strength without depending upon God or others)

5. With your daily schedule and its motivations in mind, make James 3:17 your personal prayer, praying for "the wisdom that comes from heaven." To reduce "distractions" from your schedule and to purify motives in your commitments you need godly wisdom, which is described as pure, full of quiet gentleness, peace-loving, courteous, allowing of discussion and willing to yield to others, full of mercy and good deeds, wholehearted, straightforward, and sincere.[6]

Head Butts

"You anoint my head with oil;
my cup overflows."

Psalm 23:5*b*

Summer is the mating season for sheep. Rams strut about and flex their muscles in front of the ewes, and the ewes prance around and smile shyly at the rams. Inevitably, two rams end up competing for the affections of the same ewe and get into a head butting fight over her. Although this makes the ewe feel desirable and special it can mean bruises, cuts, scratches, and wounded egos for the rams.

Imp, Lone, and Wanda found themselves in this kind of love triangle. Imp and Lone butted heads for the right to Wanda's affections and in the process they bruised each other. Before the fight got out of hand, Good Shepherd applied his oil to Imp's and Lone's heads. Their head butt became a head rub, and two sheep at odds were reconciled. The pain of their bruises and scratches was soothed by his healing oil.

It's those we love, and especially those we live with, whom we butt heads with. Often this conflict results from a "family triangle" in which two family members have some unmet needs or unresolved conflicts and instead of resolving them they involve another person (or activity) in their tensions in an effort to create some stability in the family.

A husband who doesn't feel valued by his wife is jealous of her attachment to their baby girl. A wife feels that her husband's career is more important to him than she is. A depressed wife doesn't feel her husband understands her and uses food to comfort herself and satisfy herself inside. A frustrated husband gets drunk to forget about his wife's nagging.

One lonely spouse has an affair. Another lonely spouse gets absorbed in church work.

Family members butt heads in other ways. Mother and Father can't resolve their disagreement, avoid each other, and later one or the other become angry at one of their children. Two sisters who often try to outdo each other end up fighting over the same guy. A daughter makes the family meals, dresses her younger brother, and helps him with his homework because mother is "too tired." Two busy parents neglect their child. A father molests his daughter in her bedroom at night, while the mother ignores the signs that her daughter is upset and something is wrong in their marriage.

Each of these examples of a family triangle results from unresolved personal or relational issues that affect others in the family. The key to a healthy family is a healthy marriage in which husband and wife love and value one another and resolve their relational conflicts. They encourage one another as each works through his and her own shortcomings, weaknesses, and defects of character. When parents have this kind of relationship with their spouse they are better able to care for their children and to help them to feel secure, loved, and valued.

If parents don't have healthy relationships in which their needs are being met, they will tend to relate with their children in ways that are neglectful, abusive, confusing, manipulating, or using them to meet their own needs. Furthermore, children learn by example, and in such a home they will lack a good role model for a working and loving relationship. When their parents are tense as individuals and as a couple, the children will feel insecure, uncomfortable, and tense in this kind of a home. Energy that they need for their own development and social relationships will instead be invested in trying to help their troubled or needy parents become whole.

The oil that turns head butts into head rubs is honest and loving communication. We need relationships in which there is reciprocal "speaking the truth in love." We need someone with whom we can discuss our needs and struggles and receive honest feedback and encouragement. When there is conflict we need to work through it.

Honesty in relationship is really the heart of recovery. Each of the steps to recovery that we have discussed is based on this principle. Humility, trust, accurate perception of God and self, confession of sin, delayed gratification, perseverance, boundaries, accountability, and forgiveness each requires the oil of honesty in relationship. Before we can carry the message and give to others, we must have a spiritual awakening as a result of these steps. Parents can give to their children only as they have been given to. We can love others only as we have been first loved by God through people we have respected and trusted.[7]

Personal Reflections

1. Read Genesis 2:24, which suggests that healthy relationship means that two people who are separate come together as one. Also read Philippians 2:1-4, where the apostle Paul teaches us that God seeks to develop intimacy (compassion, like-mindedness, oneness of spirit and purpose) with us so that we can do so with others. Paul says that intimacy requires that we put aside selfish ambition and vain conceit and we humbly consider others' interests as well as our own.

2. Think back to your childhood. Mark any of the following ways that your parents' unresolved issues or inability to get their needs met created any uncomfortable triangle involving you.

☐ One parent communicated to the other through me.
☐ My parents needed me to be their hero.
☐ My parents needed me to resolve their conflicts.
☐ A troubled parent needed my comfort or advice.
☐ I became the scapegoat and was blamed for family problems.
☐ I had to be super-responsible for an inadequate parent.
☐ A sexually frustrated parent related with me inappropriately
☐ My parents were so busy or out of touch that I got "lost."
☐ I had to be happy or humorous for a depressed parent.
☐ I had to minimize my needs or problems for a burdened parent.

3. Sometime this week picture yourself approaching the front door to your childhood home. What do you feel? What was a typical evening like at your house, and how did you feel? What was your favorite room or spot in your house? Who (if anyone) in your family would be with you in that place, and what would you feel?

4. What kind of oil was used in your home to deal with conflict? (Check all that apply.)

☐ Sweeping conflict under the carpet   ☐ Back-biting and slander
☐ Continual bickering   ☐ Aggressive fighting
☐ Angry outbursts   ☐ Blaming someone
☐ Forced apologies   ☐ Quick-fix prayers

☐ Walking on egg shells to avoid conflict
☐ Displacing anger onto other people and other
   things
☐ Punishment for hav-   ☐ Honest and loving
   ing conflict   communication

5. This week focus on one of your relationships. Work at speaking the truth in love and resolving conflicts. Ask your partner to do the same.

Giving Out of Emptiness

"You anoint my head with oil;
my cup overflows."

Psalm 23:5*b*

When the frost came, signaling that autumn had begun, the sheep needed to get off the mountain. If they stayed long into autumn they would freeze in the cold. Down below at the home ranch in the valley it would be warm through autumn and winter.

This year, however, the first fall sleet storm came so quickly that the sheep got caught in it. Good Shepherd hurried them to the shelter of the cave just below the tableland, but on the way many shivered in the frigid sleet.

Once in the cave the sheep didn't warm up right away. Even though they were out of the sleet, the cave was still cold and their circulation had slowed because they weren't running anymore. The cold sheep tried to warm each other, but they actually made each other colder. As they looked at each other they felt colder, seeing how chilly the others were. Whenever they tried to shake their wet, frozen wool dry they pelted one another with sleet. Only after Good Shepherd started the fire and passed around his cup of warm wine did most of the sheep warm up.

The chilled sheep couldn't give each other warmth that they did not have. As obvious as it sounds, many people haven't learned that lesson either. They try to give to others the warmth that they haven't yet experienced for themselves. Christians especially are prone to be quick in their giving, serving, and ministering because "good Christians help those in need." That idea is valid, as the Bible says we should "love one another," that it's "more blessed to give

288

than to receive," and as you "give . . . it shall be given unto you."[8] Giving to others is a healthy and good thing, yet it is difficult to give out of emptiness.

Jenny spent all of her thirty years giving out of emptiness. She is an adult child of an alcoholic father, and she became a Christian to find freedom from her childhood. In her home she got attention through her achievements and by being a good, responsible, and helpful girl. She didn't feel loved and valued except to the degree that she did what she was supposed to do. As a child she became like a responsible parent, having to help out her sisters and her parents with all of their problems. This made her feel important and needed in the family. This parentified child paid a heavy price, though: a lost childhood.

Jenny was very attracted to the good news that God loved her and had a special plan for her life. She didn't realize it at first, but when she became active in her Christian faith she brought the problems of her dysfunctional family with her. To her God was like another father who had standards that she must measure up to. Church was like another family of hurting people that needed her help.

At times Jenny would feel guilty and depressed when she didn't measure up or didn't help someone in need, but she quickly remedied that situation by doing things that made her feel significant and needed. There were also lonely times in which she felt that no one really knew her or understood her, but she was able to distract herself from those sad feelings by absorbing herself in helping other people with their problems and needs. When I told this woman that she needed to consider her own needs first she was outraged.

"I thought you were a Christian. You're telling me to be selfish. The reason I'm depressed is because I'm too focused on myself and not giving enough to others."

I encouraged Jenny to read 2 Corinthians 8:11-12, where the apostle Paul encouraged us to give to others but also warned us that our gifts are acceptable only when we give out of the fullness of what we have received and not out of the emptiness of what we still need. In order to be "full" we must first consider our own needs. I suggested to Jenny that maybe she was giving to others what she actually needed herself. She would see someone who was hurting and would try to help the person so that both the person and she would feel better.

Jenny didn't realize that she would help others in order to avoid feeling her own pain and to feel significant. She had a secretly selfish motive. She needed to give to others in order to feel good about herself, a typical element of being codependent. This made her "help" less helpful than it could have been and left her depressed.

Jenny's depression began to lift as she followed Jesus' advice and learned to ask for what she needed, seek for what she wanted, and knock on the doors of opportunity that were before her.[9] Once God, through people who love Him, warmed her cold soul, Jenny was able to warm others. Focusing on our needs in this way *is* "selfish," but in a direct and up-front way that is realistic, healthy, and respectful of others.

Personal Reflections

1. Are you like a chilled sheep trying to warm other chilled sheep? Or do you, like Wobble, get warmed and then try to warm other cold sheep? Do you try to give to others what you still need yourself? Or is your giving an overflow of the love, affirmation, and help that you have experienced from God and those you respect?

2. Meditate on the two greatest commandments: "Love the Lord your God with all your heart and with all your soul and with all your mind" and "Love your neighbor as yourself."[10] At first glance these commandments seem to say only that you're to give to God and give to others. Nothing is said about your needs. However, when we consider who God is, we understand He cares for our needs. Consider God—He is the one who loves us first. When we accept His love for us, we can love Him. We also can have a true love for others, for we know we are loved and our sins are forgiven. [11]

How are we to love our neighbor? As we love ourselves. In general you will tend to treat others in the way you treat yourself, and you will treat yourself as you have been treated by those you've trusted.

3. Are you codependent? This week consider your relationships with your parents, spouse, children, or close friends and answer the following ten questions with "yes" or "no."

1. Do you need to be liked by others to feel good about yourself? _____

2. When someone you love has a problem, do you feel responsible to help them feel better? _____

3. Does your self-esteem rise and fall with your effectiveness in helping others? _____

4. Do you put aside your interests and activities in order to share in others' interests and hobbies?

   _____

5. Do you feel that the behaviors of your parents, siblings, children, friends, or people you help are a reflection of you? _____

6. Are you more aware of others' feelings than your own? _____

7. Is what you say or do influenced by your fear of others' anger or disapproval? _____

291

8. Do you give to others in order to be liked?

_____

9. Do you value others' opinions more than your own? _____

10. Do you hint or manipulate to get what you want rather than asking directly? _____

4. Perhaps you had three or more yes responses, suggesting that you are dependent on others for fulfillment. The antidote for codependency is in following Jesus' advice in Matthew 7:7-8 to be direct and assertive with God and others whom you trust by asking for what you need, seeking for what you want, and knocking on doors of opportunity. This is a major change from being absorbed in other people's needs, feelings, or problems. Write down a few of your personal needs and consider asking your loved ones for what you need.

1. _____

_____

2. _____

_____

3. _____

_____

WEEK 43

Giving Out of Obligation

"You anoint my head with oil;
my cup overflows."

Psalm 23:5*b*

Doody couldn't stand to see Wanda with flies buzzing all around her, biting her, and driving her crazy. He felt guilty standing by and watching Wanda suffer so he tried to help. But Doody was no match for the flies. They just divided ranks and attacked him also. It was quite a comical sight, one sheep under attack by flies even as he screams, "Shew-ew-ew-ah! Shew-ew-ew-ah!" trying to save another sheep under attack as she cries, "Baa-aa-aa-ah! Baa-aa-aa-ah!" Fortunately for Wanda and Doody, Good Shepherd drove the flies away and then applied his fly-repelling oil to their heads, faces, necks, and bodies.

Imp was no less of a codependent sheep than Doody. He felt sorry for poor, pitiful Pessamissi who didn't have a ram to mate with, so he left the flock and went off with her. In giving of himself to Pessamissi and rubbing heads with her he caught her scab disease. He became very sick, but Good Shepherd had the antidote for scab, too. He applied oil mixed with sulphur and spices to Imp's infected areas, and Imp recovered.

Doody and Imp gave out of obligation. They did what they thought they should even to their own peril. Doody failed to consider that he too was defenseless against swarming flies and couldn't help Wanda. He tried to rescue her because he felt guilty watching her suffer, and he ended up being attacked by the flies. Imp neglected to consider what was best for him. He wasn't really interested in Pessamissi and knew better than to leave the safety of the flock and

Good Shepherd's watchful eye, but he felt sorry for Pessa-missi. As a result he was infected with scab.

It's a good thing to give to others if we're giving because we want to. To many people this is a foreign concept; they help others because they think they "should." Like Doody, they quickly feel obligated to give to those in need and feel guilty if they don't. This was the case with Jan, a dutiful Christian mother who gave and gave to her kids. No price was too great for Jan to pay in order to meet her kids' practical needs. She was obsessed with making them healthy meals, getting them prompt and good medical attention, helping them with their homework, buying them nice clothes, making the holidays special for them, and driving them to church activities. Her identity was wrapped up in doing these things for her children.

In fact, Jan was so busy working and doing things for her family that she didn't have time for herself, and she ignored her own deep needs. Ironically, by neglecting her own needs for affirmation and encouragement by others she could not meet the needs for affection and emotion in her own children. Only after she began to go to others, such as her husband and her friends or a support group, to meet her own emotional needs, could Jan freely give to her children out of a sincere desire. Before this she gave only out of obligation, because her own emotional needs were being neglected.

Jan was trying to do her duty and practice the Christian ethic of sowing generously, hoping that she would reap her reward later. The reward she was looking for was grateful children who would love her and be devoted to the family. While it's natural that she would want these things, she didn't realize that her care for her children had "strings attached" and would encourage them either to love her out of guilt or to distance themselves in anger. The apostle Paul teaches women like Jan how to give. Instead of giving out of emptiness and compulsion, Jan needed to learn how to become a "cheerful giver" by experiencing for herself the grace of God that abounds to her in her time of need.[12]

Other people give out of obligation in a different sense. Like Imp and his pity for poor Pessamissi, they give to those who need help because they feel sorry for them. And like Imp, who caught Pessamissi's scab disease, they do so to their own peril. Ashley, a young student at a Christian college, discovered that her friend Katie was bulimic and felt sorry for her. Ashley wanted to help Katie with her burden and so she tried to encourage her bulimic friend to hold her food down without throwing it up. In the process Ashley became so empathetic with Katie that she too became tempted.

Soon Ashley was also using food to manage her feelings. Food seemed to fill her emptiness without the risk of trusting people who would abandon her. Purging her food helped her control her weight, and it gave her the illusion of control over what she was taking into herself. She couldn't get rid of the part of her that needed and reached out for others' love only to feel rejected, but she could get rid of the food she took in.

Later when Ashley sought treatment she learned a valuable lesson in hindsight: rescuing people who are caught in a compulsive behavior because you feel sorry for them or because you think you should help them will get you into trouble. In the end, you probably won't even be helpful to the person in need.

The apostle Paul addresses this issue in the Bible; he encourages us to "restore" those who are "caught in a sin" by carrying their burdens. However, he also warns: "Watch yourself, or you also may be tempted."[13] You need to be in a strong enough position yourself so that you can give out of fullness and a capacity to give what is needed. But don't give out of a pride that causes you to give more than you're able or to ignore what you need. Instead, Paul teaches us to test our actions and where there is healthy pride or esteem to give what you have to others.

Furthermore, bearing someone's burden does not mean rescuing the person, or putting the other person's burden on your own shoulders and adding the weight of it to your own load. Instead, Paul writes, you help others by walking with them and steadying the load on their back with your free hand. This lightens their load and encourages them to learn to carry their own load.

Personal Reflections

1. Set aside some time this week to study the apostle Paul's teaching on giving in 2 Corinthians 9:6-11. He encourages us to be generous givers, promising that we will reap a generous harvest if we sow generous gifts. But he cautions us to not give out of the reluctance of unmet needs or the compulsion of obligation and guilt. Instead we should give cheerfully and freely. The only way to do this, he tells us, is to know the abounding grace of God, which supplies our needs and makes us rich.

2. This week think about your giving. What are some of the ways that you serve others? Who are the people or groups of people whom you're investing your time, energies, and gifts into? (This might include children, spouse, an elderly relative, friends, people in your support group or church, or a ministry.)

1. _____

_____

2. _____

_____

3. _____

_____

3. Maybe you are giving from unhealthy motivations, as Doody and Imp gave. Separately consider each person or group you're serving. Also consider the money you give to charities. How do you decide in your heart what caring or money to give? Which of the following tend to be part of your motivation?

☐ It's my duty.

☐ I feel guilty if I don't give.

☐ I give more than I have.

☐ I feel significant when I give.

☐ Giving distracts me from my pain.

☐ I want to share what I've received.

☐ I feel sorry for them.

☐ I owe them for all they gave.

☐ I identify with their needs.

☐ I identify with their problems.

☐ I give without considering my needs.

☐ I enjoy giving what I have.

4. Carrying the message of your recovery to others is an important step in your own recovery. But maybe you're not actively giving much of yourself to others. If so, why not?

☐ I'm burned out from giving and giving.

☐ I believe that I have nothing of worth to give.

☐ I feel too needy myself.

☐ I'm too depressed.

☐ The only way I know how to give is by being codependent.

5. Perhaps, for whatever reason, you believe that you have little of benefit to give to others. Read 1 Kings 17:7-16, which records the miracle of how a poor widow shared with Elijah what little oil and flour she had and God multiplied it back to her. This week share with someone something that you have to give, *even if it seems small.* Little things like a smile, a listening ear, or a word of encouragement can go a long way.

Giving Out of Fullness

"You anoint my head with oil;
my cup overflows."
Psalm 23:5*b*

Wobble was sh-sh-ive-rr-rr-ing cold in the damp and dark cave. His coat of wool was caked with frozen sleet. But instead of pressing himself against other frozen sheep or shaking the sleet off his wool and onto others, he went to Good Shepherd. Good Shepherd made a fire that melted the ice and dried his coat. And Good Shepherd shared his cup of warm wine with Wobble. Then the warmed Wobble snuggled up to Timi and warmed her. Soon all the sheep were following Wobble's example and walking toward's Good Shepherd's fire, drinking of his overflowing cup of warm wine, and sharing their new warmth by snuggling with others.

During that first autumn sleet storm Wobble and the others discovered the warmth of his full, soothing cup. "My cup overflows!" Good Shepherd declared. And a summer of aggravations—swarming and biting flies, head-butting battles, the threats of scab disease, and the pain of scraped and scratched skin—taught the sheep about the protecting and healing power of his soothing oil. "You anoint my head with oil!" The sheep were learning to rely on Good Shepherd for healing and comfort, and to share with one another.

Practicing the principles of recovery in all our relationships and activities awakens us spiritually and personally. It gives us a message to carry to others in need of recovery.[14] Being able to give to those in need from the overflow of what we have received from God and others is a great feeling. This very idea brought forth spontaneous praise to God from the apostle Paul: "Praise be to the God and Father of our Lord

Jesus Christ, the Father of compassion and the God of all comfort, who comforts us in all our troubles, so that we can comfort those in any trouble with the comfort we ourselves have received from God."[15]

Giving to those in need out of our fullness is truly fulfilling service. This is hard to understand, though, when you are in the beginning of your recovery. When you're in pain or in need it's difficult to think of other people's problems. It takes time for our Shepherd's healing oil to do its work on our painful wounds and our destructive compulsions. As we progress in our recovery by practicing the biblical principles of recovery one step at a time, bringing our needs into relationship, working through our issues, and receiving God's loving grace and guiding truth, gradually we will find that we are changing. We are in the process of being healed.

The beauty of the oil that heals our wounds is that it is truly an anointing oil as well. As we receive our own healing we are anointed and prepared to minister to others who are hurting.

Because of this principle, the best healers are wounded ones who have been healed and continue to receive healing for themselves. Good ministers have been ministered to by others. Good twelve-step sponsors have worked through the steps themselves and maintained sobriety from their compulsion. Good parents have received the good from their parents, forgiven the bad, and been "re-parented" as needed. Good friends have been befriended before.

In order to be helpful to someone, you don't need to have experienced the same trauma or addictive problem as the one you're helping. You only need to be sympathetic to it. You need to be open to your own similar pains. You need to admit to your own susceptibilities and temptations to do the same things. If you are not open to looking at certain issues or temptations of your own, then you will be impatient with others who feel that way (or you may not even recognize that they feel that way). Only by recognizing and expressing your own feelings and continually working through your issues can you find strength to support others.

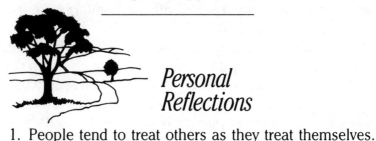

*Personal
Reflections*

1. People tend to treat others as they treat themselves. Are you treating your neighbor in loving ways? How are you treating yourself? Check any of the following self-talk statements that describe how you treat yourself (and others).

☐ "I shouldn't feel that way."
☐ "I need to stop feeling sorry for myself. Nobody wants to listen to these feelings."
☐ "I should get my act together and be more responsible."
☐ "If I would just try harder I could change that."
☐ "If I could only do _____, then everything would be OK."
☐ "That's too painful. I just can't deal with that."
☐ "I'm a horrible person. How could I have done that?"
☐ "I have to hurry up and work through this."
☐ "If I let myself feel this pain, I'll never get out of it."

2. This week consider Jesus' Great Commission to us: "Go into all the world and preach the good news."[16] In recovery language we would say, "Carry the message of your spiritual awakening to those who are hurting."[17] The apostle Paul is a great example for us in this. He traveled to many people, telling with them the good news of his own recovery story: he had met Jesus and was converted from the oppression of legalism to the freedom of knowing God's grace. When was the last time you shared your recovery story with someone?

3. Reflect on your journey of recovery. What issues have you been working through? How have you been anointed with God's healing oil? In what ways has your cup been filled to overflowing? In what ways have you received a spiritual awakening? Write out on a sheet of paper the story of your recovery as it has progressed so far.

4. Sometime this week follow Wobble's example of sharing your warmth with a cold sheep. Think of someone you know who doesn't know Jesus as his Good Shepherd and pray for that person. Pray that God would create an opportunity for you to tell this individual your personal story. Be careful not to be "preachy" or to speak out of reluctance or compulsion. Instead, simply tell the story of your recovery and how God has helped you work through your pains or compulsions.

NOTES

1. Paraphrase of Ephesians 4:16, King James Version.
2. James 3:14; 4:1-3, 6.
3. James 4:4, 8.
4. James 4:7-10.
5. James 4:8a; Psalm 46:10.
6. From James 3:17, _Living Bible._
7. See 1 John 4:7-21.
8. 1 John 4:7; Acts 20:35; Luke 6:38.
9. Matthew 7:7-8.
10. From Matthew 22:37-40, in which Jesus quotes Deuteronomy 6:5 and Leviticus 19:18.
11. Romans 5:8; 1 John 4:7-21.
12. 2 Corinthians 9:7-8.
13. Galatians 6:1-5.
14. See Step 12, Alcoholics Anonymous.
15. 2 Corinthians 1:3-4.
16. Mark 16:15.
17. Paraphrase of Step 12, Alcoholics Anonymous.

"Continued to take personal inventory and when we were wrong promptly admitted it."

Step 10, Alcoholic Anonymous' Twelve Steps

"Surely goodness and love will follow me all the days of my life."

Psalm 23:6a

Responsible Adulthood

The sun reappeared the day after the sleet storm. The sky was blue, the air crisp and cool. The smell of pine trees filled their noses, and the sheep heard the bird serenade—twirps and tweets and flapping wings. The squirrels added the pitter-patter of scurrying feet to the bird chorus. And now and again a wolf woofed!

Good Shepherd and his sheep were descending the mountain toward the home ranch and its warmer pastures. They were retracing the steps they had taken before. Their steps had been steps of discovery, change, and growth. Now, instead of following behind Good Shepherd, the sheep were in the lead. The sheep had learned from their journey; they knew the way home in their heart, and they knew they must stick together and stay with Good Shepherd. Even the once wandering Wanda was staying on the path. She was just in front of Good Shepherd, as she liked to stay close to him.

It had been a good summer for the sheep. They flourished under Good Shepherd's care and even left behind themselves productive and beautiful pastures in the high country. Good Shepherd's management and his rotation of grazing spots combined with the sheep's natural fertilization of the soil and their eating of invasive weeds and plants had actually improved the pasture. A poorly managed flock would have devastated the land.

Thinking back to the summer got Good Shepherd reminiscing about the journey. A proud smile came to his face. Pleasant memories with each of his sheep filled his mind—Timi's courageous confrontation and forgiveness of the Doubters for preying upon her fears in the valley—The healing of Jelly's angry, insecure jealousy of Wanda, which culminated in her asking for Wanda's forgiveness—Doody's newfound freedom to enjoy the moment and join the dancing celebration of the arrival at the tableland—Wobble's trimmed down body and new nimble-footedness, which created "Wobble's Tobble on the Table Top"—Lone's return to the flock after playing in the poisonous flowers with Wanda.

Ah, Wanda. What a wonder she has become! Good Shepherd thought. *Since being startled in the flowers by the rod she has stayed right at my side all the way up the mountain, in the high country, and even now on the journey down.*

He thought about Imp's taming of his impulsiveness with a patient wisdom when he heard Good Shepherd's voice and turned back from the broad path and onto the narrow path. Now Imp was becoming known for his initiative and was the lead sheep in the journey home.

Good Shepherd was proud of his sheep. What a happy contrast they were to the Doubters, who never did pass under the staff and join the flock because they lacked faith. Good Shepherd's sheep had learned so much in their journey. They had learned from their many mistakes, which they repeated again and again. Each time Wanda wandered, each time Lone withdrew from the flock, each time Jelly gave an angry head butt, each time Timi trembled, each time Imp got into trouble, each time Wobble wobbled—each time the sheep made a mistake Good Shepherd was there for them, patiently forgiving, compassionately restoring, lovingly affirming, and teaching a valuable lesson. Perhaps the sheep in Good Shepherd's flock were slow in changing, but they had changed. They were like new creatures.

"My sheep! My sheep! You're new! Each of you," Good Shepherd sang as he looked over each of his precious sheep.

> _Wanda, you've changed!_
> _I shall call you Wonder because you're always right at my side._
> _Lone, you're different too._
> _I shall call you Love because you love to be a part of the flock._
> _And Jelly, you've become a Gem._
> _Gone is the angry, insecure jealousy._
> _In its place is a peaceful contentment and a desire to get along._
> _Timi, you have grown up._
> _From now on I shall call you Currie because you have courage._
> _Imp, how you have changed!_
> _Go by the name of Inie because you lead the flock with initiative and you listen to my voice from behind._
> _Wobble, your tobble on the table top really was a hit!_
> _You shall be called Nimble._
> _Doody, you have slowed down and learned to dance and play._
> _From now on you're Dancer!_
>
> _My sheep! My sheep!_
> _You're new! Each of you._

A new chorus rose on Good Shepherd's happily singing lips.

Whenever I call your name,
Remember that you're not the same.
All of you! Your hearts are new.

The sheep all beamed in the glory of Good Shepherd's warm words. What a great day this was! They realized that they were indeed new. They had grown and changed in their journey. Their excitement carried them down the mountain that day and even in the days that followed. They felt light-footed and free. The trip down was a grand contrast to the struggle of climbing up. Fortunately Inie (the former Imp) made sure that all kept their feet on the ground lest they get too excited and too confident and impulsively fall forward on their faces!

Once down the mountain, they entered the Valley of the Shadow of Death. They all remembered the valley—the storm and the cougar especially. With Good Shepherd with them, however, they were no longer afraid, not even Currie.

Once in the valley they came upon a strange flock of sheep. This flock had been stuck in a rut all summer long, grazing over the same pasture again and again. This portion of the once-lush valley was like a dry, desert wasteland. And the sheep were wandering about aimlessly. Their shepherd was not to be found. Wonder especially felt sad for them. She remembered the lostness, loneliness, and hopelessness of wandering. She looked at Good Shepherd with the saddest eyes.

"Can we invite them to join us? If they stay at your side with me then they won't need to wander anymore." She truly was a Wonder to behold!

WEEK 45

Learning from Your Mistakes

"Surely goodness and love will
follow me all the days of my life."
Psalm 23:6*a*

Perhaps none of the sheep made more mistakes than
Inie. He had once run impulsively ahead of Good Shepherd
and drank the dirty water and got sick. He had run impatiently down the broad path to an unseen desert wasteland until
his ears heard Good Shepherd's voice behind him. At that
point he remembered the dirty water and how it made him
sick; he was starting to change. Up the mountain path he led
the way, still checking in with Good Shepherd to be sure he
was on the right track. However, during the summer mating
season then-Imp slipped back again and surrendered to his
impulsive urges and left the flock with Pessamissi. He caught
the scab disease, learning his lesson the hard way again.

Now as Inie was nearing the end of his journey, he had
two experiences forever pictured in his mind: seeing himself
plopped down beside the still waters too sick to drink, and
seeing himself lying in a heap, covered with scab, isolated
from the rest of the sheep, and too sick to eat at the grassy
table. Inie learned and was different. *Oh, how important that
I think things through before acting! I must listen for Good
Shepherd's guiding voice and check with him often.* Inie was
becoming a leader with initiative balanced by a humble reli-
ance upon Good Shepherd.

God the Good Shepherd would have us to grow into responsible adulthood also. Yet this is a step that is never completed, but one that we continue to take again and again.
That's because no matter how old, or wise, or mature we are

we still make mistakes. So with this step we continue to take personal inventory and when we are wrong we promptly admit it.[1] The mature are those who regularly take inventory of their mistakes and shortcomings and admit them to themselves, God, and others.

To be sure, we begin our journey of recovery, as well as our Christian life, "like newborn babies [who] crave pure spiritual milk." The goal is that as we have "tasted that the Lord is good" we would grow up in our salvation.[2] Unfortunately many people never get through even the first few steps of their spiritual recovery. The writer of Hebrews wrote to these people and encouraged them to be weaned and "go on to maturity." As many parents would attest, it can be a challenge to get their babies weaned from the breast and onto solids. Spiritually, we need to move from a diet of pure milk to solids, as "solid food is for the mature, who by constant use have trained themselves to distinguish good from evil."[3]

Another aspect of moving from infancy to maturity in your recovery is learning to speak the truth in love. Little children are easily influenced by what others say or manipulate them to do because they have no sense of themselves as separate. As infants, they don't know how to speak the truth of what they believe. Infants don't know how to love. Being honest and truthful with others and doing so in a loving and respectful way is a sign of maturity.[4] When you need or want something ask directly for it, yet with consideration for their needs too. When someone hurts you, tell him honestly and lovingly how you feel.

Growing from spiritual childhood to spiritual adulthood also involves developing the faith to see the sometimes unseen love of God.[5] Let's face it. God is invisible, and His love is not always easy to grasp in our hearts. We are largely dependent upon "ambassadors for God" in order to see God.[6] Inevitably because people we trust to show us God's love fail us, we will have some difficulties knowing God as He is. Like David, Job, and even Jesus in the Garden of Gethsemane and on the cross, we too will experience times when God's love seems to be hidden. This does not mean that our faith is immature. Quite the contrary. Mature Christians are those who face the reality of their struggles and express their troubled feelings to God while still clinging to the temporarily unseen love of God.

A faith that discerns between good and evil, lovingly speaks the truth of our needs and hurts to others, and strives to see the unseen love of God—that faith comes from God. Such faith enables you to lift your feet from one step to the next in your journey of recovery. With that kind of faith you can go through your problems instead of around them. Or as David said in Psalm 18:29, we can advance against a troop, run through a barricade, or scale a wall!

Even as you strengthen your weak knees and your lame legs[7] and plant your feet to stand firm in this faith, be careful lest you fall.[8] Remember Inie. He thought he had learned his lesson about impulsiveness at the fork in the path, yet he left the flock and caught scab disease. Like Inie, who was out in front with Good Shepherd following, we too need to come to a place of spiritual initiative and adult responsibility, but always exercising caution and checking in with God to see how we're doing.

Personal Reflections

1. This week consider the four aspects of responsible adult recovery that we need to practice continually. How are you doing in these areas? In each area rate yourself from 1 to 10, with 10 being "outstanding adult maturity."

_____ Admitting my mistakes

_____ Speaking the truth in love

____ Seeing the unseen love of God
____ Being careful to examine myself and check in
with God

2. As you progress in your journey of recovery there is a tendency to forget your past pains and struggles. We need to remember our story for two reasons. First, as Inie learned, remembering our susceptiblities and temptations lessens the likelihood of making the same mistakes again. Second, we need to tell our story to others. What pains or struggles has God brought you through?

_____

_____

3. Like Inie, you probably know the feeling of making progress in your recovery and then falling and slipping backwards. Then you rose to your feet and moved forward only to fall down again and slip backwards before getting up. Memorize and meditate on Proverbs 24:16: "For though a righteous man falls seven times, he rises again, but the wicked are brought down by calamity."

4. Consider your attitude about falling down. Are you patient with yourself even when you fall again and again? Do you feel guilty when you fall, even though the "righteous" fall? How quickly do you rise again when you fall? Do you tend to feel hopeless when you fall for the seventh time?

WEEK 46

What Is Your Name?

"Surely goodness and love will
follow me all the days of my life."
Psalm 23:6*a*

Valleys and mountain tops, barren desert and lush pasture, straying from the flock, and staying on the narrow path. Angry head butts and compassionate forgiveness. It's been a long journey for the sheep. They have encountered swarms of flies and quiet waters, storms of rain and sleet, and sunshine and blue skies. The wise ones learned to snuggle their chilly bodies in the shepherd's lap. Through it all—good times and bad, successes and failures—Good Shepherd remained with his sheep, loving them and teaching them.

Although the journey was slow, the sheep were growing and changing. Good Shepherd took great pride in his sheep. He delighted in their development, and he broke often into one of his spontaneous songs:

> *My sheep! My sheep!*
> *You're new! Each of you.*
> *Whenever I call your name,*
> *Remember that you're not the same.*
> *All of you! Your hearts are new.*

For all of us in our journeys of recovery and growth a point comes when if we look carefully we begin to see that we are indeed new. Lots of little steps suddenly seem big. The steps forward have outnumbered the steps backward. Our successes seem more prominent than our failures. We have turned a corner, and hope is in our hearts.

We reached out our hand in faith and found a hand to hold. We swallowed hard and trembled much, but we spoke the truth of our pain and our shortcomings and we found freedom.

The day you become aware of your newness is a grand moment. A change occurs in your self-concept; you have a new identity. The woman who was sexually abused by her father while a little girl no longer sees herself as a victim; she now knows she is a *survivor*. The man who lost years of his life and his family's life to alcohol no longer identifies himself as an alcoholic; through Alcoholics Anonymous he begins to see himself as a *recovering* alcoholic. The church-goer who has been plagued by guilt and self-reproach about her past begins through participating in a recovery group in her church to identify herself as a woman who is being *saved by grace*.

When Jesus Christ came to earth He fulfilled Isaiah's prophecy that the Messiah would "preach good news to the poor . . . bind up the brokenhearted, proclaim freedom for the captives . . . comfort all who mourn . . . bestow on them a crown of beauty instead of ashes, the oil of gladness instead of despair."[9] When with a broken heart of a painful past you mourn before God He will comfort you. When in humility you seek freedom from an addictive past He will release you. When you enter into the journey of recovery "you will be called by a new name."[10]

That is what happened to Jacob. His name meant "deceiver and cheat," and he lived up to his name, cheating his brother Esau out of his birthright and deceiving his aged father. Jacob's recovery journey began with his vision of angels ascending and descending a stairway. Jacob heard the Lord promise to be with him and watch over him wherever he went and to bless him and his descendants. Jacob believed God and went forward.

After many years of struggle, working for his father-in-law, in which Jacob experienced many family conflicts, hard times, and disappointments, he had begun a journey to make peace with Esau.[11] On the way, he now wrestled with God in the night, seeking for His blessing, and he overcame.[12] As a result, God renamed Jacob. Jacob became Israel and was known as "The Overcomer," even though he now walked with a limp, a reminder of his leg being wrenched in the struggle. The limp would always remind him of his shortcomings but also of the blessing of having overcome them.

When you receive God's grace in faith you become a "new creation"; God's Holy Spirit is in you, and you will never be the same.[13] You enter into a process in which God's Spirit works in your inner being, renewing you through difficulties and transforming you into God's likeness with increasing honor.[14] This "new self" is created in you by God and is righteous, holy, true, honest, and good. We are to "put on," or acknowledge, the new self by esteeming and nurturing this part of ourselves with God's love. The new self replaces our "old self," the person we identified ourselves as before inviting Christ into our recovery. The old self is corrupted by deceitful desires, dishonesty, pretenses, falseness, and pride.[15]

Unfortunately, many Christians struggle to see their new selves, their identity in Christ. They are afraid of being honest about their faults and shortcomings in order to bring them to the cross of Christ. They haven't grasped God's unconditional love for them. They haven't responded to His calling and purpose for their lives. They don't esteem the good things God has created and recreated in them. Freedom and peace come only when we understand that God's favor remains with us in spite of what we do. The new self within leads us to a fulfilling life in God.

Personal Reflections

1. Just as Good Shepherd gave each of his matured sheep a new name, so also God gives you a new identity as an overcomer in recovery. Do you know your new identity? Check the descriptions below that match how you identify yourself. (You may have some from each column.)

Prerecovery	In Recovery
☐ victim	☐ survivor
☐ struggler	☐ overcomer
☐ wounded	☐ being healed
☐ addicted	☐ recovering addict
☐ stuck	☐ moving forward
☐ alone	☐ beloved
☐ of little value	☐ highly esteemed
☐ in bondage	☐ being delivered
☐ resentful	☐ forgiving

2. Jesus said that we must lose our lives to find them, and He said that we must deny and hate ourselves.[16] Many Christians misunderstand these teachings to justify a low self-esteem. I think Jesus is saying that we must lose our old selves by denying and hating them in order to find our new selves. Jesus wouldn't want us to deny and hate the self that He nurtures and loves. Instead, He wants us to receive His affirmation of our emerging new selves. This week pray that God would help you to receive His nurturing affirmation and love for your new self.

3. Sometime this week re-read Reflections 1 and 2 above. Do you love and esteem the traits of a recovering

identity and of a new self lifestyle? Are you working through your issues of a prerecovery identity and an old self lifestyle?

4. The key to the sheep's discovery of their new selves was the encouragement they received from Good Shepherd. He affirmed, reinforced, and praised the sheep for their new emerging characters. He called each by a new name, reflecting their new character. That is what God did for Jacob too. This week think about your own personal history. In what ways have you felt encouraged by God and others for the new person you've been becoming? In what ways have you felt discouraged?

5. Do you lead with your limp as Jacob did? Just because we're new creatures in Christ doesn't mean that we aren't still tempted by fleshly desires to go back to our old lifestyle. Even as we progress in our recovery we're still susceptible to falling down. Leading with your limp means remembering your weaknesses and clinging to God's grace. Meditate on 2 Corinthians 12:7-10 in which God says that His grace is sufficient for Paul and that His power is revealed in Paul's weakness (his "thorn in the flesh"). Are you accepting of your weaknesses? Do you have them at the forefront of your mind?

You Know the
Way in Your Heart

> "Surely goodness and love will
> follow me all the days of my life."
> Psalm 23:6*a*

David speaks for the sheep when he sings out, "Surely goodness and love will follow me all the days of my life." Goodness and love followed the sheep in the form of Good Shepherd. By his very nature the shepherd is good and loving, and he follows them wherever they go. There is no place where they could go that his love could not find them.

He followed Wonder when she wandered into the dark cave and when she frolicked in the poisonous flowers. He found Love all alone just before the coyote did. He saw Gem's insecurity and need for love when in jealousy she was head butting Wonder. He found Currie in the dark night of the Valley of the Shadow of Death where she was in a crying, trembling heap. He retrieved Inie from the impulsiveness that led him to the pothole of dirty water and from the broad path. He found Nimble before the vultures did, when she had wobbled and fell and couldn't get up.

Good Shepherd found the good in his sheep when all seemed bad. They became new sheep. They have learned much in their journey and are growing into responsible adulthood. Their hearts have been made new. So now Good Shepherd invites them to take the lead as they retrace their steps down the path of righteousness that winds down the mountain back toward the home ranch. Good Shepherd follows his sheep. They know the way in their heart. They have gone this way before. So now Good Shepherd watches over them from close behind. He guides them as needed with his voice, which they know well.

This is the heart of recovery: *God's goodness and love will follow you all the days of your life.* Wherever you've gone, whatever you've done, whatever has happened to you —He follows until He finds you. When He does find you, His quiet words to you remain: "This is the way, walk in it."[17]

Most of us have trouble comprehending a seeking, finding, freeing, and forgiving love like this. All of our lives we've had to be good, do what's right, please others, achieve, find our own answers, and be helpful in order to be loved. But God says it's not entirely up to us to find His love. He finds us and we respond. We fall on our backs, look up, and He's there. We're in pain, we cry out, and He hears.

In the beginning of our journey of recovery Good Shepherd is very directive. We follow Him. (If we stray He follows us and finds us.) He *makes* us lie down in green pastures of grace. He *leads* us beside the still waters of His love. He restores us back to our feet when we fall. He *leads* us down paths of righteousness. In the middle of our journey when we come to the Valley of the Shadow of Death our faith is tested and stretched because He isn't out in front of us pointing the way anymore. In fact, it feels like He has abandoned us, but He is actually at our side, with us.

Then as we near the end of our journey, He follows behind us because we know the way home in our hearts and we have grown from spiritual infancy into adulthood.

"How can this be so?" you ask. "How can it be right for us to be in the lead and for God to follow? How could we listen to our hearts? Aren't they evil?" Indeed it's scary to be out in front. We're more comfortable in a dependent position in which He has the responsibility to tell us directly and clearly what to do and we simply obey. Yet as we grow up in God and mature we find that we hear His Spirit more clearly and He can direct us less directly. He's still there with us, however, sometimes whispering from behind and other times quietly waiting for us to use the knowledge and experiences He's given us to make our decisions.

Our hearts are our compasses for the journey. With our hearts in tune with the Holy Spirit, we read, interpret, and apply to our daily lives the Word of God. With our hearts we join hands with fellow sojourners in recovery. We listen to the counsel, comfort, and encouragement of the indwelling Holy Spirit, who is always present, all-knowing, all-powerful, and perfectly loving.

David knew the importance of our hearts, and he expressed that when he said, "I will praise the Lord who counsels me; even at night my heart instructs me."[18] He drew a parallel between the counsel of the Lord and the instructions of his heart. The meaning of this is that it is through our hearts that we hear the counsels of God.

You should always double check your heart-compass with verifying signposts. Consult the map of Scripture and the advice of expert guides; the trail markers of unfolding events are also helpful. But don't bury your heart-compass deep in your pocket and forget about it or you will never learn how to read it. Your emotions are important. Take heart in what you do.

Personal Reflections

1. What do you think? Is it wise and Christian to learn to follow your heart—your feelings and motivations—to discern God's will? Do our hearts act like engines that direct us to good or bad? Read the following Scriptures: Jeremiah 17:9-10, which points out the potential for evil and deception from our hearts; and Mark 7:20-23, in which Jesus lists a number of evils that can come from the heart. Then read Eze-

kiel's prophecies that God will give us new hearts that will want to follow God's laws in Ezekiel 11:19; 18:31; and 36:26. Solomon notes that the desires of the righteous end in good (Proverbs 11:23.) Finally, read about the nine heart-characteristics called the fruit of the Spirit in Galatians 5:22-23.

2. When was the last time you listened to the counsels of your heart? This week consider your deepest longings, dreams, and desires that flow from the wellspring of your heart. As you mature in the Lord, your heart will increasingly be aligned with God's heart. Remember, God cares about the longings of your heart and likes to satisfy your desires as you delight in His presence.[19] Write down three of your deepest desires or dreams.

1. _____

_____

2. _____

_____

3. _____

_____

3. One day this week focus on your image and experience of God. To what extent do you experience Him as a God whose goodness and love follows you and finds you? Perhaps you tend to think that it's all up to you to seek and find God and that even then He might be hiding from you or be angry at you. Have you ever felt as if God distanced Himself from you because of your sin? What places of trauma, addiction, or sin has God found you in? What places do you need Him to find you in?

4. Set aside some time this week to meditate on Revelation 3:20. Picture one of your struggles from question 3 above as being like a room that you're in. The door is closed.

Jesus comes to the door and calls to you. Then He patiently waits for you; from outside the door He listens and empathizes with you. Then picture yourself slowly opening the door to let Him in.

WEEK 48

Do You Leave Goodness Behind?

"Surely goodness and love will
follow me all the days of my life."
Psalm 23:6a

Sheep actually help the grass they graze on. After they have grazed awhile they instinctively lie down on the higher areas of ground where they drop their feces (a perfectly balanced manure). Then when it rains the waters will wash the manure into the ground and carry it down to the lower areas in the field so that the whole field will be fertilized. Sheep also help pastures by eating weeds and other invasive plants that otherwise would restrict the growth of the grass.

Good Shepherd's habit was to move his sheep to another pasture after they had grazed awhile so that no one pasture would become overgrazed. With pride he would look back on the pasture where his sheep had grazed and see that it was vibrant green. The sheep had fertilized it and weeded it. Under the care of Good Shepherd the sheep actually improved the pastures they grazed on. Goodness had followed them. And goodness would continue to follow them all the days of their lives because each of them had grown. Their new names reflected the goodness of their changed characters.

As it is with sheep so it is with us. The test of our growth and progress is in what we leave behind us. As you walk your journey in life step by step, what follows you? What impact do you have on other people's lives? When people look at your character and your lifestyle what do they see?

Some people seem to create conflict, whereas others resolve conflicts and bring peace. Some people are quick to inspire fear and to worry about what might go wrong; others bring a calm assurance that keeps things going smoothly. Some people will flatter you and tell you what you want to hear; others will speak the truth to you to help you grow. Then there are people who always find something to complain about; in contrast, others will deal with what is bad while still appreciating what is good.

Some people make others uncomfortable, others put people at ease. Some leave people frowning, others leave them smiling. Some rarely lift a finger to help, others are quick to do kind things without being asked. Of course, there are people you just don't trust and people you know you can count on to keep their word.

It seems "bad" people and "good" people inhabit our world and that their quality depends upon their character and lifestyle. That's exactly what Jesus said. "Every good tree bears good fruit, but a bad tree bears bad fruit. . . . By their fruit you will recognize them."[20] Jesus later explained that the fruit is not necessarily miracles, great deeds, or noted accomplishments.[21] It is a transformed life, a change in the inner person."But the fruit of the Spirit is love, joy, peace, patience, kindness, goodness, faithfulness, gentleness, and self-control."[22] This fruit isn't observable on stage in front of the crowds. Instead, it's seen backstage in your relationships with friends and family and in the ordinary, daily events of your life.

When I was a child my father grew grapevines in our backyard. One year he let them grow without pruning and they weren't very fruitful. That fall he decided to prune them back heavily, so much that I thought he had killed the vines. Much to my surprise at the end of the next summer we had a bountiful harvest of healthy, tasty grapes. This was a valuable object lesson for me, which illustrated Jesus' parable of the vine and branches.[23] Like a grapevine, our personal lives need to be pruned with discipline if we are to grow and bear fruit.

Pruning is a good metaphor for recovery. The vine that is cut back in the fall "recovers" in the spring with new growth and an abundance of good fruit. So also our lives are pruned by hardship and suffering. Such hardship may be due to our sins, others' sins against us, difficult circumstances, or some combination of these. Yet such hardship is an opportunity to spring forth into a recovery process that—though painful and difficult—can yield new growth and good fruit in our lives.

The key to successful recovery from pruning is to remain in relationship with the Good Shepherd and His Son, Jesus Christ. As pruned branches, we need to stay connected to the vine in order to receive the flow of nutrients from the vine that enables us to grow and become fruitful. How do we stay connected to Christ? By obeying His command that we love one another. We receive Christ's love through those Christians who love us. Others receive Christ's love when we love them. Each branch of the grapevine is connected to the others through being connected to the vine itself. In order to progress in our recovery and to be fruitful we really do need each other's love.

Personal Reflections

1. This week ask yourself, "Does goodness follow me? How well are the nine fruits of the Spirit [shown below] growing in my life?" Consider this in the context of your relationships with your spouse, your best friend, a family member, or those you wish to help. Ask someone who knows you well to help you answer this question.

- love
- joy
- peace
- patience
- kindness
- goodness
- faithfulness
- gentleness
- self-control

2. Take a few minutes one day this week to re-read the paragraph on pages 323-24 in which I give some examples of different types of people. Consider each example of good and bad fruit and ask yourself, "When people look at my character and my lifestyle what do they see?"

3. Sometime this week read Jesus' parable of the soils in Matthew 13:3-9 and 18-23. The farmer's seed lands on four kinds of soil, which represent four different people's responses to God's grace: (1) seeds on the path are eaten by birds and represents those who don't understand the message of God's grace and never really get into recovery; (2) seeds on the rocky ground with shallow soil sprout quickly and die and represent those who respond to the good news by quickly entering into recovery but don't dig their roots deep enough and so fail to last long; (3) seeds on the thorny ground grow but are choked and unable to bear fruit and represent those who fail to work through the steps to recovery and don't bear much fruit because they are distracted and deceived by worldly values and worries; and (4) seeds sown on the good soil produce a large crop and represent those who receive God's grace and progress in their recovery and growth.

Which soil best describes your recovery process?

---

4. Are you being pruned? Perhaps you have been undergoing something difficult recently. How have you responded to this difficulty? Have you allowed dead or unfruitful parts of your branch to be cut off? Pray that God would use this difficulty to help you become more fruitful.

5. Recall Wonder's response to the wandering sheep in the valley. She knew well the feeling of wandering around aimlessly and felt compassion for them. She invited them to

join Good Shepherd's flock. Do you know any wandering sheep who are spiritually or emotionally "lost"? This week look for a lost sheep who needs recovery. Pray for that person and try to help him or her in whatever way you can.

NOTES

1. Step 10, Alcoholics Anonymous' Twelve Steps.
2. 1 Peter 2:2-3.
3. Hebrews 5:14; 6:1. Read Hebrews 5:11–6:1 for the context.
4. Ephesians 4:14-15.
5. 1 Corinthians 13:8-12.
6. 2 Corinthians 5:20; 1 Corinthians 12:27.
7. Hebrews 12:12.
8. 1 Corinthians 16:13.
9. Isaiah 61:1-3.
10. Isaiah 62:2.
11. Genesis 29:15–30:43.
12. Genesis 32:22-32.
13. 2 Corinthians 5:17.
14. 2 Corinthians 3:18; 4:16-18.
15. Ephesians 4:24; Colossians 3:9-10.
16. Luke 9:23-24; John 12:24-25.
17. Isaiah 30:21.
18. Psalm 16:7.
19. Psalm 37:4.
20. Matthew 7:17, 20.
21. Matthew 7:21-23.
22. Galatians 5:22-23.
23. John 15:1-17.

"Sought through prayer and meditation to improve our conscious contact with God as we understood Him, praying only for knowledge of His will for us and the power to carry that out."

Step 11, Alcoholics Anonymous' Twelve Steps

———————————

"And I will dwell in the house of the Lord forever."

Psalm23:6b

STEP 12

Faith

The fall season was slipping away; soon it would be winter. Good Shepherd and his sheep had been continuing their journey on the path that headed toward home. Inie was still in front, skipping along as he led the others home.

Turning a corner, where there was a pile of tumbleweeds, Inie looked straight ahead and exclaimed, "Hooray! We're home! We're home!" He galloped toward the home ranch. Soon he saw the familiar reddish-brown barn that would keep him warm on cold winter nights. Surrounding the green pasture was the white-washed picket fence. And off to the side the stream-fed clear blue waters seemed to whisper their welcome.

Little Currie was right behind Inie, a new position for her. Currie's little legs blurred as she dashed for home. Her eyes became big as saucers and were darting back and forth as she looked for her neighbor playmate. Currie wanted to tell her friend Blue Bell about all of her adventures. She began panting as she paced back and forth along the fence that divided the two pastures.

"There in the corner!" Currie raced over to where Blue Bell would be. *It's good to be home again!* she thought as she ran. She stopped herself in midstride as a new truth dawned. *I never left home! Home for me isn't only here at the ranch's green pastures and still waters. It's also on the path and even in the valley and up the ridgeline path and on the tablelands and down the ridgeline path. Home is being with Good Shepherd and the other sheep. He cares for me and keeps me safe and secure as long as I stick by his side.*

Happy to know this new truth, Currie drew closer to the neighbor's pasture and Blue Bell. When she finally got a good look at Blue Bell she was so shocked she almost fainted. What happened to her roly-poly, happy-go-lucky little friend?

"Is this really you, Blue Bell?" But the little blue bell on her collar confirmed that it was.

Blue Bell looked like a bag of bones. She was gaunt and sickly looking. The ground she lay on was covered with her urine and feces. The "pasture" around her was a dirt field with patches of brown grass here and there. Her empty stare seemed to rest on the lush green pasture that Currie was standing on.

After long moments of dead silence, Blue Bell's gaze finally met Currie's eyes. When she saw Currie's eyes filling with tears, Blue Bell parted her cracked lips and opened her dry, parched mouth. "Timi, I—."

"Blue Bell, my name is Currie now," Currie interrupted. "Good Shepherd changed my name because I've overcome my timidness and I am now known for my courage. I have so much to tell you, but first I want to hear about you. You look quite sad."

"I wish I could have gone with you, Timi, I mean Currie." Tears formed below Blue Bell's eyes and began to run down the dry skin on her face. "It's been horrible here. The summer kept getting hotter and hotter. And it just wouldn't rain. Then our owner left us to fend for ourselves and didn't return until a couple of weeks ago. We have been wandering back and forth from one fence to the other scrounging for stray weeds and nudging our noses into patches of matted-down brown grass. And all the while we were just inches from your pasture on the other side of the fence." Fortunately for Blue Bell and her friends, Good Shepherd's irrigation system helped the grass survive the drought, even though he wasn't there to tend to it.

Currie reached her head through a slit in the fence and dropped a mouthful of green grass in front of Blue Bell and then whispered in her ear, "Maybe this spring you can slip under the fence and join us. I'm sure Good Shepherd would love to have you."

"My journey was a scary one," Currie said, and she began to explain the events of the past summer far from the ranch. "The hardest part was in the Valley of the Shadow of Death. There was a huge rainstorm one night, and I got stuck in it. And in the midst of it the Doubters mocked me and criticized me and told me I'd die. And there was this dancing shadow that they said was a hungry bear. I was so scared. I wanted to just get out of there! But then Good Shepherd found me, and he reassured me. I felt OK the rest of the time in the valley and enjoyed playing in the flowers and in the stream.

"Later we were climbing up the ridgeline path, and I slipped off to the side and slid down a ravine. I almost rolled all the way into the canyon! But I got caught in a pricker bush. It saved my life, but it scratched me all up. Good Shepherd's staff delivered me out of that jam, and his oil comforted my wounds. I sure learned a lesson about watching my steps!"

As Currie continued the story, she realized how Good Shepherd had brought strength and courage to her life. "As we finished our climb up to the high country I was feeling stronger, and once we got there I was thrilled. I had made it! We danced and played, and it was so beautiful and the grass was very tasty. And the water—oh, how sweet! In fact, I was feeling so good that I gathered my courage and confronted the Doubters for how they had hurt me. They wouldn't accept my offer of forgiveness, but Good Shepherd was so proud of me. That's why he gave me my new name."

Currie, the former Timi, gave another mouthful of green grass to Blue Bell and said, "What do you think, Blue Bell? Wouldn't you like to come next year?"

Blue Bell nodded and then looked off to the side beyond Currie. Her eyes sparkled for the first time since Currie had been back at the home ranch.

Currie looked over her shoulder, and there behind her was Good Shepherd, smiling and nodding in approval.

Making Conscious Contact

"And I will dwell in the
house of the Lord forever."
Psalm 23:6*b*

On her journey Currie learned to stay in contact with Good Shepherd even if he wasn't right next to her. This was a hard lesson for her to learn. Initially, she was scared when she could not see the shepherd. In the valley during the storm she thought Good Shepherd had forgotten about her. He hadn't, and after he rescued Currie she grew in her trust in him.

Later when she fell into the pricker bushes, she called out to Good Shepherd. She knew he would hear her cries. And when she confronted the Doubter family she knew that Good Shepherd was with her. Then at the end of their journey, as they were returning to the home ranch, Currie was right behind Inie, at the front of the flock. She knew that Good Shepherd was still with her. Currie learned that she could keep Good Shepherd in her mind all the time, wherever she went, even if he wasn't right there in her sight.

Learning to maintain conscious contact with God, even in the midst of difficulty, is what faith is all about, and it is an essential step in the journey of recovery. A recovering drug addict named Daryl found this to be true. For the previous six years, beginning in college and then as he launched his radio career as a disk jockey and an on-site news reporter, Daryl had used cocaine to get him "up" and to maintain "peak performance." Whenever he felt self-doubt or a lack of motivation he sniffed some cocaine and was ready to go.

Leaving cocaine was tough for Daryl. He replaced cocaine with attendance at Cocaine Anonymous meetings, phone calls to his sponsor, writing in his prayer journal, and memorizing Scripture verses. Over time he learned to utilize these disciplines whenever he was tempted to abuse cocaine. He made conscious contact with God through expressing his feelings of shame and discouragement to others as unto God and by writing about those feelings in his prayer journal.

In contrast to Daryl was a very religious man named Stephen. From outward appearances Stephen was a devoted Christian; he read his Bible every day and was very active in his church. As I got to know Stephen I discovered that he was very distant from his feelings. Like Daryl he too struggled with feelings of self-doubt and depression. But instead of expressing these feelings to others and to God, he would push them back down and quote to himself Scriptures like "I can do all things through [Christ] who gives me strength" and "Rejoice in the Lord always."[1]

Stephen was using the Bible as a lid of repression to cover up his unwanted feelings. He was trying to use God like a fireman to put out his fires and rescue him from trouble. He wasn't in contact with his real self, and he wasn't in contact with the real God. His faith was insincere and dishonest. It lacked the courage to deal with pain and struggle. He used his faith to avoid uncomfortable feelings.

On the other hand, Daryl's faith was alive. He was learning to make contact with God in the midst of his difficulties. He did this by bringing his troubling feelings into relationship with others. Not only did he seek help in times of temptation and struggle, but he had regular times to be with his support group and to practice other disciplines such as prayer, journaling, and Bible study.

It is through regularly making conscious contact with God in spiritual disciplines that you learn to habitually and continually practice the presence of God that lets you "dwell in the house of the Lord forever." Of course, this side of heaven you cannot achieve complete and unbroken contact with God. But, as you strive to improve your conscious communication between the real you and the real God you will progress in your recovery and growth.

The apostle Paul refers to this contact with God as "walking in the Spirit."[2] This means to "be joyful always; pray continually; give thanks in all circumstances for this is God's will for you in Christ Jesus."[3] This kind of a faith walk is one of resting in God's love for you. Yet, we are to make "every effort to enter that rest"—the "Sabbath rest" of resting in God's grace to you in Christ.[4] In a sense we are to work at resting.

Working at resting is a paradox. How do you strive to maintain contact with a God of grace without doing so legalistically? It's a matter of embracing the goodness and love of God that follows you all the days of your life, of continually responding with the faith that dwells in the house of the Lord. It means having an attitude that says, "Yes, I want to rest in what God has done for me. I need to know God's grace and truth here and now." Yet, realistically this takes discipline and commitment that can quickly turn from a faith-response of "I want to" into a legalistic initiation of "I should."

Personal Reflections

1. This week, as often as you can, try to make conscious contact with God. Set aside some time each day to practice a spiritual discipline such as prayer, Scripture meditation, writing psalms to God, praise, quiet reflection, or ministry to others. As you do the discipline reflect on God's love for you.

2. Dwelling in the house of the Lord, or practicing God's presence, means maintaining continual contact with God. Try to extend the encounters you have with God in your spiritual disciplines into your everyday life. Try to be aware of God's presence with you—He is always with you—as you sleep, shower, dress, eat, interact with others, walk outside, drive in your car, do your work, or relax at home in an easy chair.

3. Sometime this week meditate on Romans 12:1-2. Note that Paul says that worship is a lifestyle lived "in view of God's mercy." He alludes to the Old Testament sacrificial system, which Christ fulfilled once and for all by becoming the perfect sacrifice for our sin. We become "living sacrifices" when we respond to God's grace in Christ by putting our lives upon His altar, renewing our minds to know and follow God's will for us.

Picture yourself putting your hurts, your temptations, your frustrations, your questions, your relationships, your work, and your dreams for the future all upon the altar of God. Then offer yourself to God. Ask God to cleanse you and all these expressions of you with the blood of Christ.

4. Is your faith more like Daryl's (the ex-cocaine addict) or Stephen's (the man with the toxic religion)? Do you regularly express your troubled feelings to God, or do you use your faith to try to convince yourself that you shouldn't feel depressed, anxious, angry, guilty? In times of difficulty is your prayer to God that He teach you and encourage you *through* your difficulty or that He rescue you *out of* trouble?

Dwelling in the House of the Lord

"And I will dwell in the house of the Lord forever."
Psalm 23:6*b*

In one grand moment, Currie realized that home was being with Good Shepherd wherever he was; home was not just the home ranch. She felt at home playing with Blue Bell along the fence or lying down in the green pasture under a shade tree with her shepherd. By letting Good Shepherd's extended staff be like his hand to hold, Currie faced her fears of leaving the home ranch and learned to discover a sense of home at each step in her journey.

Currie found herself at home on the path of righteousness that led from the home ranch to the Valley of the Shadow of Death. Even in the valley itself, where Currie encountered many fears, she learned that her shepherd was with her. Then in the tableland, where she was surrounded by enemies like poisonous weeds, flies, scab disease, cougars, coyotes, and snakes, she learned to trust in the comfort of her shepherd's rod of protection and his staff of guidance. Currie made herself at home in other ways too, forgiving the Doubters, passing under the staff at night, feeling the comfort of Shepherd's oil on her wounds, and dancing and singing to "Wobble's Tobble on the Table Top."

Currie and the other sheep were at home on each step of their journey because Good Shepherd was always with them—caring for their needs, guiding them to the right path, and protecting them from their enemies. In stark contrast, Blue Bell did not feel at home even though she stayed at her home ranch all year long. Her owner was not a shepherd. He abandoned her in the hot summer months and neglected her needs. Many days Blue Bell stood at the fence gazing over at Good Shepherd's pasture longing for a home that was really a home.

Do you have a sense of home? When you're with family or friends do you feel warm, secure, loved, and comfortable letting your guard down to just be yourself? Many people I know have struggled to feel at home on their life's journeys. A middle-aged man named Jeff told me that each day after work he heads straight home rather than stopping to do errands on the way because he longs for the feeling of being at home. Yet, Jeff sadly commented to me, "There's a scared and lost little boy in me, and I just don't feel safe expressing those parts of me with my wife and my children around. I guess I don't share my real feelings with anyone because I don't want to feel needy."

Jeff did not have a sense of being at home in this world. He never has. He grew up in a home in which his parents argued frequently. He recalled that as a child he would try to shut out the arguing and complaining by retreating to his bedroom and putting his pillow over his ears. But the fears and insecurities inside wouldn't go away. His parents never seemed to resolve their conflicts. And no one seemed to notice how scared he felt.

Looking at me with a calm but calloused face, Jeff concluded, "One day I decided I wasn't going to be scared anymore. From then on I just acted strong, like things didn't bother me. But now I realize that I do have needs inside."

With my help, Jeff began to open, even discover, his feelings. As we came to understand his previously hidden fears and insecurities he didn't feel as lost anymore. Together we felt sad that in his life he had missed out on a sense of being at home.

We all need a home: a relationship in which we feel secure and affirmed for who we really are. The shepherd boy David knew how a scared and wandering sheep needed a shepherd's care and a sheepfold's security. In fact, he cried for such security himself throughout the psalms. "Keep me safe, O God, for in you I take refuge."[5] Once, when under attack by the armies of King Saul—in spite of his loyal devotion and service to the king—David's faith sang out, "I love you, O Lord, my strength. The Lord is my rock, my fortress and my deliverer; my God is my rock in whom I take refuge."[6] Later in his life, when his heart was distressed by his sinfulness, he found God's forgiveness and responded thankfully, "You are my hiding place; you will protect me from trouble and surround me with songs of deliverance."[7]

In his relationship with God, David found a home. It's good to remember though, that David's security in God was encouraged through human friendships. Jonathan, David's best friend, comforted and protected David when Jonathan's father, the king, unjustly attacked him.[8] And Nathan the prophet listened to David's confession of his sins of adultery and murder.[9] The best way to find refuge in God is to start by finding trustworthy and godly people who can share God's comfort with us.

Personal Reflections

1. This week consider the twelve steps of your Psalm 23 journey. Which of the steps is (are) the hardest for you to feel at home with?

- [ ] 1. Admitting that you need God to be the shepherd of your life
- [ ] 2. Resting in God's care for you in the green pastures
- [ ] 3. Drinking in God's love to see yourself as He does

☐ 4. Acknowledging that you've fallen down and sinned

☐ 5. Saying no to the easy path and yes to the right path

☐ 6. Persevering in the valley and trusting that God will work out for your good all the difficulties you encounter

☐ 7. Trusting in the rod of discipline and protection

☐ 8. Passing under the staff of accountability

☐ 9. Forgiving the enemies who surround you in the tableland

☐ 10. Allowing the oil that comforts your wounds to anoint you for ministry to others (in which you can give out of an overflowing cup)

☐ 11. Listening to your new heart so that goodness follows you

☐ 12. Being at home with the Lord on your life's journey

2. Read Psalm 31 sometime this week. In verses 1-5 David describes taking refuge in the Lord to be protected from being "put to shame." David knows that he could be caught in many traps, and so he asks for God to lead him. The way David takes refuge in the Lord is to surrender his spirit into the hands of the "God of truth." He does this in verses 9-18 where he expresses his feelings of sadness, shame, fear, and anger. Then in verses 19-24 his faith in the goodness of God sings out loud. In this and many other psalms David demonstrates the kind of faith that is the heart of recovery.

3. This week write your own psalm to God. Use Psalm 31 as a model for how to take refuge in God by recording in a journal your feelings and expressing your belief in God's goodness.

4. Do you have a shepherd who helps you to find a refuge? As David said in Psalm 31, a refuge is a safe place in which you will not be "put to shame." When you're with a person who is a refuge you can express your feelings, your needs, and your personality; and instead of feeling embarrassed you feel embraced. Do you rely on God as this kind of a refuge? Do you have friends or family who are a refuge for you?

Passing the Baton

"And I will dwell in the
house of the Lord forever."
Psalm 23:6*b*

The sheep were slow-footed and prone to fall, but they were able to continue because they were in a relay race. Throughout the journey different sheep were the focus of attention as they learned their lessons and ran their race. Their journey, recorded in this book, has been a relay—one sheep would run for a while and then pass on the baton to another sheep. The sheep observed one another's races and together they struggled, fought, learned, grew, and cheered each other onward.

Now the sheep are back at the home ranch; yet the race is not over. Next spring they will once more run the path through the valley and up to the mountain plateau. Some new runners will join the race, such as Blue Bell and the new lambs that are born during winter. Who knows, maybe even one of the Doubters will become a believer and carry a baton.

I know how it feels to join in and run a long race: twenty-six long miles in each of four marathons. In my first marathon I was so eager that I sprinted out at the sound of the starting gun. My adrenaline was up, and I was so excited that I felt like I was running on clouds. About three or four miles out I checked my stopwatch, and I realized that I was way, way ahead of the pace I had set in my mind before the race. I thought nothing of it and continued dashing ahead.

As the miles wore on, my pace steadily dropped. Running mile after mile, up and down hills, and squinting in a sun that got hotter and hotter were all draining me. Drops of sweat ran down my forehead and stung my eyes. At about mile thirteen painful blisters began to form on my feet. My legs got heavier and heavier. My energy level dropped more and more. It became more difficult to breathe in the oxygen I needed. Runners were passing me right and left with increasing frequency and I got more and more discouraged.

At about mile twenty I hit "the wall," a place of keen physical and emotional pain, and I thought I could not lift my legs and run another step. Then I did what I swore I would not do, and I started walking and running, walking and running. The periods of walking grew longer.

Somehow I finished. I collapsed at the finish line and spent the next couple of days drinking fluids and walking gingerly on my tender feet. My legs were so sore that I avoided every stairway I saw.

I learned a few things from that first marathon. In my next race I trained better in the weeks and months prior. Before the race I loaded on carbohydrates to peak my energy. I wore better shoes. I also wore my race shirt to remind myself of the finish line. I invited my dad to watch, and he cheered me on every four or five miles. And, most important, I paced myself from start to finish. I ran so steadily and was so relaxed that the steady pounding of my feet and the consistency of my breathing put me into a trance. Before I knew it I had finished. I didn't break any speed records, but I ran the whole way and I enjoyed the race. Afterward I walked away easily, even climbing up and down stairs without wincing in pain.

Many times in my life when I have had to endure hard times I've thought back on my marathon experiences. What I learned is that if you train, set your sights on the goal, rely on an encourager to cheer you on, and pace yourself—one step at a time, mile by mile—then you can finish your race. This includes the race of emotional recovery and spiritual growth, which is like a relay race in which each of us runs our race and then passes on the baton to someone else.

As you run the race that is marked out for you, you need to throw off the extra burdens that slow you down and you need to look out for the sins that so easily trip you up. You run the best race you can by fixing your sights on Jesus who ran the perfect race. He isn't your only example and fan, though. Those who have run the race of faith before you, such as Abraham, Moses, David, Paul, and maybe a parent, a sponsor, or a friend, have passed the baton on to you and now stand among many witnesses to cheer you on.[10]

Personal Reflections

1. This week consider the analogy that your journey of recovery and growth is like a relay race. Read 1 Corinthians 9:24-25 in which Paul uses this analogy. He encourages us to run the best race we can by training hard, looking forward to our eternal reward, and being self-controlled.

How are you training so that you can progress in your recovery and growth? Which of the following have you invested yourself in during the past month?

☐ Praying   ☐ Studying the Bible
☐ Reading self-help ☐ Attending a church
 books   support group
☐ Attending a twelve ☐ Receiving a sponsor's
 step group   support
☐ Receiving a friend's ☐ Being in therapy
 encouragement
☐ Being discipled or counseled by a minister

2. What kind of prize or crown will be your reward? What do you want to receive as the reward to your recovery?

☐ Abstinence ☐ Better relationships
☐ Improved self-esteem ☐ Intimacy with God
☐ A soul at peace ☐ To enjoy my life
☐ Emotional stability ☐ Accomplishing my
goals

3. How are you doing so far in your journey in the area of self-control? How well do you discipline yourself in doing what is good for you and helpful to your recovery? Which of the following things are you doing for yourself?

☐ Saying no to compulsions and self-destructive behaviors
☐ Staying in touch with my feelings
☐ Relying on the accountability and feedback of others
☐ Practicing spiritual disciplines
☐ Asking for what I need

4. Who are the heroes of your faith? Who in the great cloud of witnesses is encouraging you in your recovery and growth? How have these people helped you?

The End of Recovery

"And I will dwell in the
house of the Lord forever."
Psalm 23:6*b*

The sheep's journey started the previous winter when they were grazing in the green pastures and drinking from the still waters at the home ranch. In the spring Good Shepherd led his sheep down the path of righteousness through the Valley of the Shadow of Death. In the summer they enjoyed the cool temperatures, lush grass, and beautiful views of the mountain tablelands. In the fall they headed back down the path for the home ranch. Now that the sheep were back at the home ranch their journey wasn't over. They were beginning it all over again.

The new year ahead would bring them through another cycle of the four seasons. They were entering the winter season of resting at home and receiving blessings from Good Shepherd. But that period would pass quickly, and once again it would be time to put those blessings to use and spring into the season of new beginnings by stepping out onto the path. The growth of spring requires storms and so there will be difficulties to endure on the path that goes through the valley. Like the previous year, summer would be a season of making peace with various enemies in order to enjoy the high country. And autumn's cold would once again drive the sheep back down the mountain and challenge them to test their new growth and find their way home with Good Shepherd following.

Our journey of recovery is also one in which we go through seasons of blessings, new beginnings and new difficulties, making peace with enemies, and practicing our new

344

abilities. Each season of recovery has its steps of growth. These are steps that we must take again and again, season after season, year after year. No one is able to complete the steps to recovery in this life. Even as we grow and change and become new, we will still fall down again and need help getting back up.

Like the rest of God's creation we have been subjected to the frustration of being incomplete. We long to be perfected and glorified. We long to have complete access to our heavenly Father.[11] The promise of heaven is the very presence of the Good Shepherd. That shall be a wonderful day, yet we know we have not yet obtained it. So we press on to take hold of this heavenly prize of entering into the glorified state with Jesus.[12]

Pressing on means persevering through difficulties. This is the journey of faith: rising after we fall even though we will fall again,[13] forgiving again even though we will be sinned against again,[14] trusting God even though He leads us through many difficulties,[15] and believing in an unseen God's love even though we may not feel loved.[16] In our faith journey we can continue onward even though we have not yet received all that has been promised, and we can hope for good in the midst of evil even though all things have not yet been worked out for our good.[17]

Hebrews 11 describes a Hall of Faith: men and women who persevered through difficulties. They sinned, were sinned against, experienced horrible persecutions and hardships, lived as aliens in a strange world, and did not receive in their lifetime all that was promised them. They persevered because they "saw him who is invisible."[18] This is the definition of faith: "Now faith is being sure of what we hope for and certain of what we do not see."[19]

If in this life we received all that we hoped for and didn't experience difficulties then we would not need faith. But the reality is that life is often painful, unfair, confusing, discouraging, and lonely. And being a Christian doesn't make life easier. In fact, throughout the Bible we are reminded that we will suffer. The only way to persevere in your recovery is to hold onto the promise: "He who began a good work in you will carry it on to completion until the day of Christ Jesus."[20]

And what a day we have to look forward to! A day without sunsets, without pain or recovery—a day in which we are face to face with our Creator, the Good Shepherd. On that day we will hear Him say, "Come, you now may enter into the fullness of My love, joy, and peace. I have so much to show and give to you."[21]

Personal Reflections

1. Read Ecclesiastes 3:1-11 where Solomon says, "There is a time for everything, and a season for every activity under heaven." God's promise to us is to make all the seasons of our lives beautiful in their time. Consider the following twenty-eight seasons in the context of your recovery. Note that each season Solomon mentions—whether it's one of joyously taking something in or sadly letting go of something—has a purpose. Depending upon your personality and where you are in your recovery process, some seasons will be more difficult than others for you to enjoy. For each season prayerfully ask yourself, "What needs to be birthed in me? What needs to die in me? What do I need to plant in me? What do I need to uproot in me?"

Taking In	Letting Go
____ Birthing	____ Dying
____ Planting	____ Uprooting
____ Healing	____ Killing
____ Building	____ Tearing down
____ Laughing	____ Weeping

___ Dancing	___ Mourning
___ Gathering boundary stones	___ Scattering boundary stones
___ Embracing	___ Refraining
___ Searching	___ Giving up
___ Keeping	___ Throwing away
___ Mending	___ Tearing apart
___ Silently listening	___ Speaking
___ Loving	___ Hating
___ Making peace	___ Making war

2. Later this week reconsider the twenty-eight seasons of life that Solomon has identified. Check those seasons that you tend to avoid or struggle with. Pray that God would help you to discover the beauty these seasons can have in your life.

3. Meditate on the glory of "And I will dwell in the house of the Lord forever." We don't know just what heaven will be like, but we do know that our recovery will be complete. Imagine all of your deepest emotional needs being met, your temptations removed, your issues resolved, your relationships healthy, and your God right there with you. Thank God in prayer for what He will do.

4. Pressing on through the difficulties of recovery is unbearable unless you develop the faith that sees the unseen. Memorize Philippians 1:6: "Being confident of this, that he who began a good work in you will carry it on to completion until the day of Christ Jesus." Make this verse the hope of your recovery.

5. As a closing reflection on this journey you have taken with our Good Shepherd consider the story of Enoch's life. Enoch was the great, great, great, great-grandson of Adam. He represented the seventh generation of man. For the last

300 years of his 365-year life he walked the steps of life hand in hand with God.[22] Then he prophesied that at the end of time the Lord would come down from heaven with thousands upon thousands of His holy ones to judge the ungodly.[23] And in the end "he was commended as one who pleased God."[24]

Enoch's faith became perfect. He achieved complete and unbroken conscious contact with God and then came into His presence. Enoch completed his recovery. It took him 365 years, but he finished all the steps.

Enoch is the example of a faith that endures. He is also a reminder that unless God gives you 365 years to live you won't reach complete maturity until you get to heaven. But in this life you can know the lasting inner peace that comes from walking with the Good Shepherd.

NOTES

1. Philippians 4:4, 13.
2. Galatians 5:16.
3. 1 Thessalonians 5:16-18.
4. Hebrews 4:11 (see verses 1-11 for the context).
5. Psalm 16:1.
6. Psalm 18:1-2.
7. Psalm 32:7.
8. 1 Samuel 18:1-4, 19-20; 23:16-18.
9. 2 Samuel 12 13.
10. Hebrews 12:1-3.
11. Romans 8:18-23.
12. Philippians 3:10-12.
13. Proverbs 24:16.
14. Matthew 18:21-22.
15. Job 13:15.
16. 1 Corinthians 13:4-12.
17. Hebrews 11:13; Romans 8:28.
18. Hebrews 11:27b.

19. Hebrews 11:1.
20. Philippians 1:6.
21. 1 Corinthians 13:12; 1 John 3:2.
22. Genesis 5:18.
23. Jude 14-15.
24. Hebrews 11:5.

Moody Press, a ministry of the Moody Bible Institute,
is designed for education, evangelization, and edification.
If we may assist you in knowing more about Christ
and the Christian life, please write us without obligation:
Moody Press, c/o MLM, Chicago, Illinois 60610.